C000320009

Christopher Hilton has covered motor racing since
1976. He has written extensively on other sports and
reported on four Olympic Games. He has had four
novels published, also *Conquest of Formula 1*, *Ayrton Senna*
(a Corgi paperback), and *Alain Prost*. Christopher Hilton
lives in Hertfordshire.

Nigel Mansell

Christopher Hilton

CORGI BOOKS

NIGEL MANSELL
A CORGI BOOK 0 552 13343 4

Originally published in Great Britain by
William Kimber & Co. Ltd.

PRINTING HISTORY
William Kimber edition published 1987
Corgi edition with additional material published 1988
Corgi edition reprinted 1989
Corgi updated edition published 1992

Copyright © Christopher Hilton, 1987, 1988, 1992

This book is set in 10/11 pt Baskerville by
Colset Private Limited, Singapore.

Corgi Books are published by Transworld Publishers Ltd.,
61–63 Uxbridge Road, Ealing, London W5 5SA, in
Australia by Transworld Publishers (Australia) Pty. Ltd.,
15–23 Helles Avenue, Moorebank, NSW 2170, and in
New Zealand by Transworld Publishers (NZ) Ltd.,
3 William Pickering Drive, Albany, Auckland.

Made and printed in Great Britain by
Cox & Wyman Ltd., Reading, Berks.

Contents

Illustrations in Colour

The smile on the face of the lion.

Jean-Marie Balestre, then President of the goverment body, doing what he generally did, talking. Mansell does what others generally did, listen.

Mansell wasn't the lion at Ferrari – no, he was *il leone*.

The sweep on Monaco in 1990 where Mansell ran a strong second until the engine failed.

Ferrari folk chewing over the nitty-gritty. Alain Prost makes a point, Steve Nichols the designer ponders it.

Mexico '90 and Ferrari folk celebrating the team's first win-double since 1988. Prost has just won the race, Mansell 25.351 seconds behind him.

Any pit stop is a precious handful of fraught and fleeting seconds. This one in 1990 went right . . .

Race four, 1991 and the great title challenge begins. Thus far Mansell's Williams Renault hadn't finished a race. Now at Monaco he takes second place.

Mansell majestic at Monza, Autumn 1991. Prost looks bemused, Senna does what people generally did (again), listens to Balestre.

The man of '91: power, poise, concentration, judgement.

(The above pictures courtesy of Jaf Sherif, IPA; CSS, DPPI (Paris) and Renault)

The moment the dream died. Turn One, Suzuka, Japan, lap ten, 20 October 1991. The brake pedal went soft and Mansell went off. *(Pascal Rondeau/Allsport)*

Some watched from afar, some watched from closer but there

was nothing any of them could do expect wonder what might have been. (*Pascal Rondeau/Allsport*)

Fraught and fleeting seconds at Estoril produced the unbelievable: this wheel churned away from the car as Mansell accelerated from his pit stop. The dream had begun to die. (*Carlos Mastos/Zoom*)

Illustrations in Monochrome

Acknowledgements

I am indebted to the *Daily Express* and *Daily Star* for the use of their files. I have leant heavily on the excellent *Autosport* magazine which has covered Mansell's career from the beginning; and latterly to the Grand Prix reports of Nigel Roebuck which are so accurate, perceptive and informative. The sumptuous *Autocourse* annual has been invaluable. The description of Gerhard Berger's accident at Imola is taken from *Grenzbereich* by Berger, published by Orach, Vienna. The Keke Rosberg quotation is taken from *Keke, An Autobiography* by Rosberg and Keith Botsford (Stanley Paul). Thanks, also, to the *Sunday Telegraph* for the quotation on page 78. For their time and help I am grateful to Dave Price, Peter Warr, Eddie Jordan, Tony Jardine, Martin Hines, Ann Bradshaw, Jackie Stewart, Barry Griffin, Maurice Hamilton, Peter Windsor, Niki Lauda, David Owen of Williams and particularly Martyn Pass.

Three Octobers

He pressed the brake pedal and it felt soft. An instant later the corner which had been unfolding before him like some slumbering serpent – it was exactly that shape – reared in a wild rush of images: the car travelling fast, fast, fast over to the left, juddering as it crossed the curved white kerbing, then twisting back towards the track which was now so far away, the car sideways and gouging dust from the darkened reaches of sandy-shale as it buried itself deeper and deeper into the arc of the run-off area. Within the dust storm a piece of the car was wrenched off and flung away, then another. Under its own impetus the car turned completely around and moved backwards towards the tyre-wall at the far end of the run-off area, the speed ebbing from it until it came to rest.

Turn One, lap 10, the Japanese Grand Prix at Suzuka, 20 October 1991. Nigel Mansell clambered out and scampered across the track and, helmet in hand, began the long walk back. Another World Championship over – over as two before it had been and each of them joined by a strange thread, almost a malevolent thread.

There had been the long, panting, flat-out straight at Adelaide when a rear tyre exploded and that rush of images was terrifying as well as wild. Lap 63, the Australian Grand Prix, 26 October 1986.

There had been Suzuka before, a tight snake right–rush–left sequence of corners and another kerb, another rotation, another tyre-wall. That one he hit so hard he scattered it in a bomb burst and the car was airborne and corkscrewing, landing so hard that his spine took the full force. It was not even the Japanese Grand Prix, 30 October 1987; it was only qualifying for it.

Now this. A brake pedal which went soft. All across 1991 he had hunted Ayrton Senna, previously seen as impregnable in his Honda Marlboro McLaren. He had decisively out-driven Senna and he had become the man. Very typically he had not surrendered himself to outrageous misfortune. Three events might already have broken the spirit and the will of a lesser person. In Canada on the

11

last lap and virtually within sight of the finish his gearbox failed. His lead was so great that he could have walked to the line before Nelson Piquet, second, reached it. At Spa he was in the lead and controlling the race when the electrics failed. In Portugal the frankly unbelievable engulfed him. He was leading comfortably again but the pit stop went terribly, terribly wrong and as he left the pit the right-rear wheel was not secure. It came off.

This had not happened to any Formula One driver for a generation.

Canada–Belgium–Portugal and 30 points perished. *If* he had had them he would have arrived at Tokyo Airport with 99, Senna only 80. To prevent Mansell finding complete fulfilment at last, Senna would have had to win both the Japanese and Australian races without Mansell's getting another single point. But Mansell didn't have the 30 points. He needed to win the Japanese and Australian races, and Senna finish virtually nowhere both times. And then the brake pedal went soft.

Three October days, three distinct culminations linked by the thread that each time he was flung off the circuit into a crash and no other car was involved at all. This itself was an oddity, an irony – damn nearly bizarre in a motor-racing context. No other driver forced it to happened; no dicing and jousting produced it; no desperate duelling created it. Fate itself, perhaps, and that was all.

The first was the worst. He'd been closer to the Championship than at any time in his life and when the tyre exploded he could have lost his life. You can pluck a host of other moments from his career because it is rich in them on a monumental scale – all the way from meagre to magnificent, all the way from penury and obscurity to Lotus to Williams to Ferrari to Williams again – but one place offers itself as the natural starting point: the first of the three Octobers, the day he might really have done it, the day he was a mere 18 laps from it.

The cars are moving in stately, ordered progress round the streets of Adelaide on the parade lap and in a moment or two they will form up on the grid and 20,000 horsepower will be shrieking, and as the red light blinks to green the 20,000 horsepower will be unleashed . . .

1 Agony in Adelaide

Nigel Mansell had come through Singapore, where he changed aeroplanes to be in Adelaide quicker. He had a very important appointment with Greg Norman, the Open Champion, at a place called the Kooyonga Club. A pro-celebrity golf tournament. Nigel Mansell loves golf and it did seem easily the best way to start the weekend of his life. Oh, there'd be photographers there and reporters and hands to be shaken and polite words to be spoken and generally a bit of a fuss, but the whole of 1986 had been that anyway. A bit of a fuss.

Between March and this October, Mansell had driven his Williams Honda in fifteen races and won 72 points. Britain had produced six world motor racing champions and now, in this final race, Mansell could become the seventh. He needed only finish third to do it. Of the two men who could stop him – Piquet and Alain Prost (Marlboro McLaren) – either had to take the race and Mansell *not* finish third.

After a whole season of turbulence, sadness, shocking bad fortune and shocking good fortune it had come to this. Third place would make him . . . well, immortal in any acceptable sense.

But now it was Tuesday, 22 October and he was at the Kooyonga Club and he engaged in some banter with Norman and, if rumour be true, he outdrove him twice. A newspaper carried a photograph of Mansell that day: his hair short and in place, his moustache short and in place, wearing a short-sleeved shirt, his strong forearms striking the ball out of a bunker, flinging sand as it went.

It was good to relax, necessary to relax (and necessary for Norman to be complimentary because Mansell is a good golfer who doesn't care so much for losing).

The race was on the Sunday: near enough.

Fortunately, perhaps, this was by no means the first time that the championship had been decided on the final race and so it would never acquire the dimensions of a freak event. It had happened in

13

1982, 1983 and 1984 and only Prost himself had broken the sequence in 1985 when he'd won it at Brands Hatch, with South Africa and this same Australian Grand Prix still to go. If that was a testimony to how evenly balanced teams and drivers were, it also meant that just about everybody had been through it before. Piquet had in 1983, Prost in 1984; Piquet's team had with Keke Rosberg in 1982, Prost's team with himself and Niki Lauda in 1984. They all knew the form for a shoot-out.

But Nigel Mansell hadn't been through it before. Many, even among those who wished him well, had had moments of doubt in the early days about whether he'd ever get this far. Even a year ago, the idea of his going into a shoot-out for the championship would have wrung wry smiles from the disbelievers. He had proved them all wrong. Here he was at Kooyonga, here he really was and the talk was of championships. He had brought his wife Rosanne with him and she would say she'd be glad when it was all over. If you need a good woman to cope, here she is.

Most of Britain shared her sentiment that they'd be glad when it was over. Nigel Mansell from Birmingham had shown the world. Now all he had to do was win the world. Not exactly the same thing.

He spent two quiet days minding his own business – well, nearly. On the Wednesday he spoke to 300 Adelaide businessmen and got a standing ovation. On the Thursday he played golf again in the morning and went to the track to film a commercial for Mobil, one of his earliest sponsors and still one of his greatest supporters.

And now it was time to begin qualifying for the race.

Friday, 24 October

It was a time for thinking, wondering, calculating; a time for the psychology of it, three utterly separate men and a single prize which could not be shared. Prost, who knows exactly what he is talking about, said gently and deliberately that he was happy it would be straightforward for him: win or bust. He felt Piquet would feel the same: win or bust. He felt it might be more complicated for Mansell, because if you try and drive a percentage race a lot of calculations can go wrong.

Mansell understood that, too. He himself fully intended to win the race, no nonsense, and let the lesser permutations take care of themselves. It was the only way to approach it.

But the psychology would inescapably begin in qualifying – two hour-long sessions, one on Friday, one on Saturday, with the

14

fastest lap getting pole position. If Mansell had pole, Piquet and Prost would have to get past him – or be bust. Pole was the place to be. Pole could command the race. Pole could slow the pace, quicken the pace, dictate to all the rest. Command.

Every qualifying session is a time-trial and a test of tactics. Each driver has two sets of special tyres for fast laps. When do you use them? You go out with your last set ten minutes before the end, do a fast one, you find somebody else has waited a little longer and beaten your time and you've no tyres left to make a counter-gesture.

On the Friday Mansell need not have worried. He put in a thunderous lap of 1 minute 19.255 seconds with Prost and Piquet nestled in behind – we are talking about fractions of a second over a course 2.348 miles long, remember, but important fractions. Fractions that put you high into the symmetry of a grid.

Prost 1 minute 19.785.

Piquet 1 minute 20.088.

About half way through the session rain fell so there could be no late counter-gestures against Mansell's time. Cars always go slower in the wet, even these cars. He was a pole – until the Saturday session, anyway. He need not have worried then, either. Mansell picked his moment just over ten minutes into the session and thumped in 1:18.403. That was rendered unassailable when another car belched oil all over the track. The front of the grid was essentially settled.

MANSELL

                    PIQUET

SENNA

                    PROST

Sunday, 26 October

The Goodyear tyre people, who are no fools, had examined the situation and the qualifying, and said to the teams using their tyres: 'Make your usual stops for new ones, the way you have all season.' Among others that was McLaren, that was Williams. The teams, who are also no fools, thought, 'We'll wait and see.'

The two columns of cars came slowly round the right-hand corner, past the multi-coloured backdrop of advertising hoardings, came to rest, waited. Mansell – shrewd, don't let anybody kid you he's not – had noticed some dirt on the track in front of his grid position, and when the cars had gone off on the parade lap which had brought them so slowly back to the start of the race, he had accelerated hard for an instant, laying rubber from his tyres down into the dirt for grip. Now, when the settling was complete, Mansell had his car pointed precisely into the twin scars of black rubber he had laid.

Red light, all at once.

The shrieking.

Green light, all at once.

The unleashing.

Under the sheer force of acceleration Mansell's car twitched – a current might have been coursing through it – just a twitch, corrected instantly, by a touch of the hand on the wheel. To his left Ayrton Senna (John Player Special Lotus) was trying to get past him on the outside and he twitched, too, more heavily. In the very centre of the track Piquet got away in a straight line: third. Coming up hard on Piquet, Keke Rosberg (Marlboro McLaren): fourth. At Rosberg's elbow, Prost: fifth. Behind them, the wild, wild rush of a cavalry charge gaining a momentum of its own, everyone in it jostling for an advantage. One car was bumped and hemmed, it lurched, it went on, into the cavalry charge.

The chicane, left and then right, seemed to be rushing at them. When they were through it the whole track broadened like an aerodrome runway on the short lunge towards a sharp right-hand corner. The cars spread out. Senna went right to have the inside line, Mansell was outside him and at his rear wheel, Piquet tucked in behind Mansell, Rosberg coming up hard outside Mansell.

Senna took the corner. Piquet, using Mansell's slipstream, went right, too, and was past him. Rosberg still coming hard under a momentum all his own, followed Mansell through.

Now the short lunge called East Terrace to a sharp left-hander. No change. Now the short lunge to a sharp right-hander. Half way between the corners Rosberg went past Mansell – on the outside.

Senna, Piquet, Rosberg, Mansell, Prost.

A left-right kink and a right-hander, all rushing at them, rushing at them. Prost swarmed at Mansell, probing, searching, then backing off a car's length, waiting. On the straight Piquet slip-streamed Senna, turned his Williams out and to the left, went past Senna on sheer power. Showers of sparks cascaded from the under-tray of the Williams as it bottomed out. Its speed on the straight was 215 miles an hour.

They crossed the line and that was lap one: Piquet, Senna,

Rosberg, Mansell, Prost. It had lasted 1 minute 33 seconds and three men had led it . . .

Piquet pulled clear, Rosberg instinctively attacked Senna, Prost still waited behind Mansell. Eighty-one laps to go. In the rushing at each corner there was time to run fast and yet wait.

Rosberg danced right and pushed Senna back to third. Rosberg, in the last, exultant race of his career – race number 114 – fully intended to win or, if it came to it, help Prost become world champion. They were McLaren team-mates. Lap two: Piquet, gap, Rosberg, gap, Senna, Mansell, Prost.

Lap three and Rosberg was catching Piquet. Mansell was absolutely behind Senna, Prost was absolutely behind Mansell and these three moved in a fluid, fixed concert, observing the spacing of sensible speed at a 150 miles an hour. On the pit lane straight Mansell accelerated and went right past Senna. A delicious moment. He was third. It would give him the championship if he could run another 79 laps there.

Lap five: Piquet, Rosberg, gap, Mansell, Senna, Prost – and under one second between Piquet and Rosberg. The blink of an eye, less.

Lap seven: Rosberg took Piquet at the chicane. It was a rare moment – not for Rosberg alone, who'd seen all this before – but for the frightened, huddled masses in shadowy living rooms in Britain counting on their fingers at 3.20 in the morning. If Rosberg won the race, it would give Mansell the chanpionship – even if Mansell didn't finish.

Prost came through past Senna and went for Mansell. Rosberg, flying alone, pulled sharply away from Piquet.

Lap ten: everything changed. Prost took Mansell and pulled decisively away from him. In the shifting early currents of a race you feel for shape, direction, a kind of settling. It was not yet, not quite yet . . .

Prost – so sure of touch, so certain in his control – began his pursuit of Piquet. It would last until lap twenty-two. By then Piquet would have gone past René Arnoux (Ligier) on the straight, lapping him, and Prost would be able to see Piquet. First he, too, would have to overtake Arnoux – this same Arnoux who had once partnered him at Renault, this same Arnoux who didn't like Prost any more than Prost liked him. Prost closed on Arnoux. How would Arnoux respond? They followed each other through one corner, then another, then a third, nose to tail. That third corner was a right-hander. As they rounded it Arnoux pulled aside so that

17

Prost could go comfortably by. As he did, Prost saw Piquet perhaps a hundred yards ahead beginning to turn into the next corner, another right-hander.

Soon enough Piquet was trapped behind two back-markers and Prost was coming hard at him.

This would be a significant moment. Once Prost was through, only Rosberg lay ahead. All McLaren need do would be to hoist a signal board telling Rosberg to slow down, give Prost the lead. And the race. And if Mansell stayed fourth that would make Prost World Champion.

Rosberg's lead was twelve seconds.

Mansell was nineteen seconds behind him and five seconds behind the Piquet–Prost struggle.

On lap twenty-three Piquet seemed to pull away from Prost – but only a little, perhaps the length of three cars. Going into a right-hander, Piquet made a mistake and spun completely round so that he was facing Prost. Prost saw a gap and was clearly through it. Piquet put his foot down and rotated the car through 360 degrees in a small run-off area. As he did a back marker went by . . . then Mansell. Even as Piquet came back onto the track with a flourish of wheel-spin, everything had changed.

Mansell was third. It would give him the championship.

Now it settled. Mansell didn't catch Prost. Piquet didn't catch Mansell. None of them were catching Rosberg.

On lap thirty-two Prost dived for the pits. His right front tyre was punctured. As it deflated he'd had an alarming moment on the straight. Mechanics struggled to get a jack underneath the car. The tyre change took 17.13 seconds. By then Mansell and Piquet had gone through.

Goodyear examined the tyre and concluded it was an ordinary puncture which might have been caused when Prost clipped a back-marker a couple of laps before. It was definitely an ordinary puncture. They examined the other three tyres which had just been changed and concluded that they were not worn; they could have gone to the end of the race. Goodyear immediately passed this (seemingly priceless) information to Williams. Mansell and Piquet could press on without losing time with tyre stops or risking tyre stops which might go wrong.

Prost was now twenty seconds behind them. Everything pointed to Mansell. Rosberg was in front, masterly, uncatchable. Good. Mansell was in second place. If it stayed like that he was champion – easily.

After thirty-five laps Mansell was twenty-five seconds behind Rosberg and Piquet seven seconds behind him. Prost, coming hard again, was twelve seconds behind Piquet. On lap thirty-eight Piquet put in the fastest lap – 1 minute 22.065. On lap forty, while Mansell was momentarily ensnared between two back-markers, Piquet broke that – 1 minute 21.901. Inevitably Piquet was up behind Mansell, and still Mansell had back-markers in front of him. Once they were gone, Piquet darted to the right but Mansell blocked that. Coming out of a right-hander onto the straight Piquet went half onto the kerbing and the car flicked – but he got it back under control and struck at Mansell. Piquet feinted right and as Mansell seemed to block that, dived left and was through. Mansell had let him.

Mansell was unconcerned. He was third, Rosberg was still leading. It was lap forty-three, just past half-distance. Piquet moved off in a desperate attempt to get to Rosberg, but Rosberg was more than half a minute away. And even if Piquet did catch him, Mansell was third.

But Prost was still coming hard and he had those new tyres. He broke the lap record. He was a mere twelve seconds behind Mansell: *mere* because he was coming so hard. Mansell clung to Piquet. On lap forty-seven, when Mansell glanced in his wing-mirrors, he could see Prost in the distance. The gap: nine seconds. On lap forty-nine Piquet set the fastest lap – 1 minute 21.722. But Prost was clearly visible now, wheeling and turning with that awesome control under pressure. On lap fifty-three Prost set the fastest lap – 1 minute 21.526. He broke it again on lap fifty-four. Now he was up with Mansell.

Mansell had to hold Prost at bay; he couldn't afford to let him through.

Piquet, Mansell and Prost were running together in a concert of movement. Piquet, seeing Prost on Mansell, accelerated away. That was lap sixty. Mansell had the edge in straight line speed so that however close Prost thrust his McLaren in the corners, he was having to wait, wait, wait.

It was lap sixty-three.

Rosberg was ending his career in rare style. Good old Keke. Then, without warning, he heard a 'brrrr' from behind him. He thought – a reflex calculation at these speeds – that the engine had failed. He didn't know that tread from his right rear tyre had worn loose and was slap-slap-slapping against the bodywork. He cruised to a halt at the edge of the track. He parked the McLaren, got out, shook his head. Rosberg walked away, out of Grand Prix racing.

Unnoticed, Prost had slipped past Mansell.

Barry Griffin of Goodyear, watching on a television monitor, had seen Rosberg's tyre go and knew instantly that it could happen to Mansell and Piquet. He started running towards the Williams pit to tell them to bring both drivers in for new tyres. He could not know that he would only have 92 seconds to make it. Not long enough, not long enough . . .

Mansell was third and it would make him world champion. He had done everything right, he had made no mistake and his tyres were fine. It didn't matter that Prost was closing hard on Piquet. It was lap sixty-four. Only eighteen left, only 42 miles left. Johansson in the Ferrari was a whole lap behind Mansell. It was an enormous safety margin.

They came out of the right-hander into the long Brabham Straight. Prost had just overtaken Phillipe Alliot's Ligier and was now clear of it. On the straight, Alliot dutifully hugged the left, leaving the whole of the rest of the track open for Mansell to go through. He did and, accelerating up towards 200 miles an hour, was now in line behind Prost. Alliot tucked in behind Mansell to get a 'tow' from the Williams down the straight.

It happened instantly.

The contrast between this orderly procession of three cars and the images of chaos was so sudden, so sharply drawn that the eye could not absorb it all at once.

Mansell's left rear tyre exploded. Strips of rubber flailed the surface of the track, flapping madly. The suspension of the car ground against the surface of the track. That flung back a cascade of sparks, molten orange, molten yellow in a column, twelve feet high. It was like a shell burst. These sparks scattered in a falling shower, spreading, now, a molten carpet across the track.

Prost was gone. Alliot was five feet to Mansell's right and abreast of him. Alliot's impetus would carry him clear.

Mansell's tyre had disintegrated so far that strands of it lapped like the tentacles of some wounded octopus, thrashing and thrashing in agony.

Mansell hit the brakes. The three tyres he had left threw back smoke as the brakes locked them to the surface of the track. But the Williams was now leaning at a crazy angle and as he braked the whole car went madly left-right in a series of convulsions.

Nigel Mansell was fighting for his life.

He was doing at least 150 miles an hour.

The whole rear end of the car danced away from him left-right left-right. He fought the steering wheel. His head was pitched left-right left-right and still he fought. The suspension was churning white sparks which fled from the car.

At the end of the straight was a right-hand corner and, if you didn't make that, a run-off area directly ahead.

He aimed for the run-off and as he reached towards it the car pulled wildly to the right. He fought that. He got the car back somehow. Still his head was being pitched left-right. He did reach the run-off area. The car did – under its own terrible impetus – swivel right again. Deep into the run-off area it struck a concrete wall, the front right wheel absorbing the impact. His head was pitched back a last time. It was all over.

It had been an astonishing piece of driving to control the car, and it had lasted fifteen seconds – a lifetime.

'At that speed, self-preservation is all you have in mind. I had to correct the car again and again.' He knew it and said it: I am lucky to be alive.

Piquet, leading, got immediate signals: You get yourself in here fast for new tyres. He did. It was necessary to do it, right to do it and Piquet was thankful it was done. It cost him the championship but, like Mansell, he knew and said: I'm alive and I'm happy.

Prost kept on, smooth and easy, and won the championship for himself, Piquet finished four seconds behind him after a long charge. It might as well have been four hours.

An image of Mansell comes back: in the pits, face heavy with sweat, the eyes mournful, watching, impotent, cast down, as Piquet and Prost went round and the championship was gone.

Prost said: 'I am sorry, honestly, for Nigel.'

Rosanne had contained all the strain until now. All at once she could contain it no longer. Mansell stood beside her. Slowly they moved away, a clutch of reporters following. Every one of those reporters knew the questions they wanted to ask. None could find the moment. So they followed. At last one of the reporters asked quietly if they could speak. Yes.

Mansell said: 'It has been a long, hard season and you think of all the things you've gone without – companionship, friendships, your children. Rosanne and I have got to get together and get to know each other again. It makes it all rather hard to swallow. It will take time to get over it but I will, although at the moment next year seems a long way away.'

The tyre – or rather what was left of it – was taken to Goodyear's base at Akron, Ohio for examination. The mystery deepened. When the tread was analysed it suggested that wear had not caused the explosion. Nor does a puncture seem likely. Tyres don't explode when they puncture, they deflate. It seems likely that what happened to one tyre on lap sixty-four of the Australian Grand Prix on a crisp, chill late afternoon in October 1986 will remain forever wreathed in mystery. It had already become woven into motor racing folklore.

The fifteen seconds were so spectacular that they will live on long after the championship has become just another championship, to be recorded in chronological order with the thirty-six which had gone before it.

When he'd had a little time to find perspective, Nigel Mansell said what he was always going to say: 'I'll be back.'

2   This is What I'm Going to Do

The dark green Lotus was reaching up towards 160 miles an hour
as it flowed along the back straight this seventy-fifth and last time.
It turned into the final right-hand corner and the cheering had
already begun. Aintree, 21 July 1962. The British Grand Prix was
being run on a circuit built within the Grand National course and
the cheering came from stands more accustomed to the grunting
and snorting of tired horses. As the Lotus flowed out of the right-
hander into the finishing straight the crowd could see it now: number 20, long and sleek and low, almost dwarfed by the height of its
tyres, lovely in the simplicity of its shape – unadorned save for the
small, famous Lotus badge at the tip of the bonnet and the two small
words Team Lotus on its flank. As it was on the finishing straight,
the crowd could see, there peeking from the narrow cockpit, a heavy
helmet and goggles, and hands on outstretched arms holding the
wheel perfectly steady. Jim Clark, one of the greatest of all drivers,
crossed the line 49 seconds ahead of everybody else.

Somewhere lost in that crowd, a seven-year-old and his father
watched – fascinated.

It was a time for fascination and an era of fascination. Clark in
the Lotus . . . Graham Hill in the BRM . . . Bruce McLaren in the
Cooper . . . Jack Brabham in the Brabham . . . John Surtees in the
Lola. Even the names were potent. And here they all were, Surtees
following Clark home, then McLaren, then Hill, then Brabham.

When Nigel Mansell got home to Upton-on-Severn, a quiet
place in Worcestershire, that same evening he told his nanny very
seriously that he was going to be a racing driver and he was going to
drive for Lotus. Seven-year-olds do say these things. Great fires are
kindled in young imaginations by the first touch of days like these.
When Donald Bradman scored 309 in a day at Leeds in 1930, a
fourteen-year-old was lost somewhere in the crowd, watching –
fascinated. And that was Len Hutton, 364, the Oval, 1938. You
can multiply the examples countless times. Mansell's conversation

with his nanny would be typical, and unremarkable, among generations of kids who saw their first football match, saw, perhaps, George Best weave magical paths between static defenders or Denis Law bicycle kick goals facing the wrong way; saw, perhaps, Barry John cut through a shifting wolf-pack of Rugby players streaming across a field at him and score quite untouched under the posts; saw, perhaps, Muhammad Ali shuffle and sting, shuffle and sting, shuffle and smile as some of the most fearsome men in the world tried to hit him and couldn't.

And the generations of kids say: *That's what I'm going to do*. Only one in the many hundreds will actually do it. The currents pull too strongly the other way. The rest? They'll play hard at school, maybe keep on a bit after school but by then they'll have addressed themselves to getting and keeping a job, there will be a girlfriend, marriage and all too soon they'll be middle-aged and taking their own kids to watch Coe or Cram or Ovett, and when the kids get home that same evening they'll say: *That's what I'm going to do* . . .

Mansell was different. He meant it. This is worth dwelling on, however briefly. From this moment on it would run like a theme through his life. He would mean what he said and say what he meant and whatever dangerous and outrageous things happened to him, whatever hardships he would endure – and they would be many – he held to the conviction he had had when he was seven.

There was pedigree for it, and this is not always the case. He was born in Birmingham on 8 August 1954, one of four children – brother Mike, sisters Gail and Sandra; his father Eric had raced karts in the Midlands and his grandfather had watched kart racing. Eric Mansell was an aerospace engineer, a wise parent, and would do nothing to discourage his son.

But now, in the early 1960s, the family were living at Upton. Rural it was, and that was lucky. Years later Mansell would remember it with typical clarity. He had a friend on a farm who 'had an old Austin 7, a real banger which would never have been allowed near a road. And he had acres of land. We would drive this old wreck round the farm, through the fields. The grass was so high and we were so small we could never see where we were going. We just put our foot down and went! We never bothered about brakes. We stopped by crashing into stone walls.'

Crashing. It is a word we will return to because it, also, will run like a theme through Mansell's life.

The problem about speed, and it is a problem, is that once certain people, who are not like you and me, have tasted it they must have more. Progressively, life becomes inadequate, even meaningless, without it. When you are twelve there is only one place to get more speed and that is in a go-kart. And there was a go-kart, an old one, for sale in a garage in Hall Green, Birmingham. Mansell persisted until he and his father went to have a look. It would cost £25 and was powered by a lawnmower engine. Eric Mansell gazed at it and Nigel Mansell gazed at it. 'I was allowed to drive it round the forecourt and I smashed it into a petrol pump. My father was forced to buy it because I had bent it.'

There's that word crashing – well, smashing, anyway – again already.

The go-kart was not, of course, intended to break lap records at Silverstone, it was only a way of feeding the compulsion for speed; but at the bottom of the garden or round the allotments. You could reasonably have concluded that it was a phase and Mansell would grow out of it and that the go-kart would find its place in the shed to be rediscovered, perhaps, many years later, by chance in a moment of purest nostalgia for forgotten dreams of long ago. No. Mansell grew *in to* it. And one fine day someone whispered fateful words to young, impressionable ears. *You can actually race those things, you know.* The lovely innocence of it. Go along and *race*.

Shennington is – or was – a disused airbase in the Midlands. It had become a permanent home for karts, and a very typical home at that: just over half a mile of concrete track, plenty of bumps, plenty of corners, plenty of those tight, twisting chicanes. In 1968 Nigel and Eric Mansell took their kart there. A grid of around twenty-five others lined up and they all set off in the typical wild flurry of movement. 'It wasn't until we entered that first race that we realised we were never going to be able to race our particular kart. For every lap I did the others did two. So Dad bought a more powerful engine. It cost £34.'

Ah, but this is the decisive moment. This is when it begins to get serious, when you've tasted it and you loved that wild flurry of movement, and the compulsion is leading towards more sophistication – however humble – and, just as significant, you didn't *like* other kids going past you.

'In the next race I ran into a wall. The marshal came up and I said: "It's all right, the chain has fallen off." He looked down at the kart and said: "Forget it, son, your engine's fallen off." '

Martin Hines is a karting expert, arguably *the* karting expert. 'Nigel started off in junior 100ccs and in those days they were capable of something like 60 miles an hour. When you consider that those karts just had five-inch drum brakes stopping them and the tyres were more like wood than rubber, it was horrendous even doing 60 miles an hour.'

But this is the whole point. It is, initially, the horrendous aspect which appeals so strongly, especially to teenagers who believe they are immortal, anyway. It is also real racing and it feeds the compulsion unmercifully. If you glance at a grid in any Grand Prix today, amongst all those rich and famous people a good two-thirds of them will have started exactly like this. 'Generally speaking,' Hines says, 'it is the cheapest form of motor sport.' Hines remembers those days. 'Nigel was always a nice, pleasant, reasonably placid sort of bloke. Father and son seemed to be out of the same mould, they got on very well together and they took their racing very seriously.'

Eric Mansell spent £50 on a new kart . . .

Nigel took the lead in a race and, 'I just couldn't believe it. I was so excited I fell off. I had the race won. My father went berserk. But it taught me two important lessons. The first was that if you ever want to win, you must remember that if you lose your head you lose the race. And it taught me Dad was as hooked as I was.' Dad himself says: 'As a little lad racing go-karts he used to explode and get into all sorts of tantrums, but finally I got it through to him that the only result of all that was his concentration went and his driving was shot to pieces. He started to realise that it is the bloke who stays cool and calm who scores over the guy who gets excited and all heated up.'

It was a lesson Mansell would never forget. His first win came at Turnhill, Shropshire in 1969 and it was to be the first of many in karts.

Hines again: 'He progressed into the 200 cc Villiers class – that was the old two-stroke Villiers motor cycle engine, also used in invalid carriages. They probably had a top speed of 80 miles an hour but more significantly it's one of the oldest classes of *gearbox* karting anywhere in the world. His first race with it at Burton Wood in the Midlands he went out amongst a very large grid and won, which was amazing, first time out with a gearbox. That showed his aptitude immediately.'

Aptitude? He had plenty of that: seven times Midland champion between 1969 and 1976, Welsh champion 1970, 1971, Short Circuit British champion 1973, Northern champion 1972. These are long forgotten races in long forgotten places but they fed the compulsion. And if you are beating them all – winning, winning, winning – the compulsion grows. At sixteen he told his father he wanted to be a professional driver. Eric Mansell was, as I have said, a wise man. He absolutely insisted that his son serve an apprenticeship as an engineer with Lucas. 'I didn't think so at the time,' Nigel has said, 'but it was one of the best things which has happened to me. Now I understand the technical side of my job.' The job, of course, would be getting the fastest cars in the world round faster than anybody else. It would take a decade to get there.

As part of his studying, he was at Solihull Technical College. It was 1970. One day coming away from the college he glimpsed 'the shortest mini-skirt you've ever seen' and pulled his car smartly up. 'Want a lift?'

The girl was studying home economics and helping her mother run a grocery shop in the Kings Heath suburb of Birmingham. 'She came over to the window and said, ''I know you, don't I?'' It turned out she thought I was somebody else. But being no fool I said, ''Of course you do.'' She got in and I wouldn't let her get out until she agreed to see me again.'

She was called Rosanne.

The first date was utterly romantic. He took her to watch a kart race at Shennington. 'It was a freezing cold day,' she remembers. 'I never realised that go-karts could go so fast. It was incredible, a bit worrying but also exciting.'

Soon enough Rosanne would understand how worrying it could be. Mansell crashed at Morecambe in 1974 and, as Hines says, 'He had concussion, breaks and bruises. He was in hospital for quite a few days and on the serious list. It took him months to recover.'

Rosanne would have to accept that the man she loved fully intended to spend his life racing and this would be an inescapable part of it. She would say, 'We are both as single-minded as each other.' She would never become like the exotic creatures – and creations – who decorate race meetings and adorn the pit lane. She would remain without pretensions and, whatever the circumstances, an entirely normal mother when the time came. Mansell caught that when he said, 'She's my best friend as well as my wife, and I know I'm that to her.' She would say, 'I would never ask him not to race.'

In the mid-seventies, it is necessary to give the other dimension to his life. He worked at Lucas Aerospace as a laboratory technician developing instruments. He became a production manager working on tests beds and fuels, including a multi-roll combat aircraft and the RB 211 jet engine. He moved to Girling where he was a senior sales engineer in the tractor division. He had a degree in engineering.

27

In other words, he was always going to be far, far from the sort of sportsman who thinks only through the medium of football boots.

All he really wanted was to drive professionally. 'I talked it over with my father and he said he couldn't possibly support me, but I knew I could make it if only I had the chance.'

Make it. Ah, that. *I knew I could make it.* Ah, that. Across the next seven or eight years he and Rosanne would be the only two people who truly believed he would ever make it. Wherever you probe, whoever you ask – with only one exception – they all sing the same chorus: He didn't seem to have any great ability but what he did have was this superhuman, all-pervading determination. You only had to meet him for a minute to see that, you couldn't miss it, he wouldn't let you. And people who have known determined youngsters join the chorus: Never seen anything like it . . .

He was still in karts in 1976 but was beginning to find them 'boring' and he had had his first race in a 'real' car that year.

He used the savings to buy a Formula Ford and took it to Mallory Park. 'We put,' Rosanne says, 'all our savings into that second-hand car.' She accepted that she would have to keep on working to pay the bills, as an economist at the West Midlands Gas Board at £24 a week. Those savings had been built up by Mansell doing three jobs: his engineering, making picture frames and selling pictures.

Autosport, the magazine which carries extremely comprehensive coverage, had one precious paragraph that year of 1976 – perhaps the first paragraph bringing Mansell to a national audience. It was another race at Mallory. During his heat, 'Mansell, in only his fourth race, impressed by taking a close fourth place in an elderly Hawke DL 11.' In the final, 'On the last lap Barry Pigot just pipped Mansell for fifth.' In 1977, it was time to become the professional. The karting days were over.

Formula Ford is a frightening place. It is a championship spread over a season and it bristles with young drivers who may or may not understand what 1600 cc engines in single-seater racing cars can do. The cars buzz round like a swarm of hornets, the crashes are frequent and spectacular. It is also the sure way serious drivers begin to prove themselves. Karts are all very well – they're like a swarm of *smaller* hornets – but they can be an end in themselves. Formula Ford is the first clearly recognisable step on the journey towards Formula One. It is never going to be easy.

In June 1977 – it was a practice session on a Sunday – Mansell was going into Paddock Hill Bend, Brands Hatch wheel-to-wheel with another car. At every corner, and this one more than most, there is a 'racing line' which is the best and most direct route through. There is room for only one car on this line and so it is contested zealously. This now happened. The cars touched wheels and Mansell was pitched into a horrifying series of cartwheels down the slope beyond Paddock Hill Bend.

Marshals ran to the car and expertly removed Mansell – so expertly that Eric would later pay public tribute to how they saved his son 'more suffering.' Mansell's neck was badly hurt. In hospital doctors told him: 'I would never race again and that if I got up without permission I would be paralysed for life.' The idea was that he would lie on wooden boards for six months until his neck had healed. 'I was as near to packing up as you can get.' He reasoned that if he couldn't race again, what was he doing lying here? After five days of it he did get up, discharged himself and went home. (A specialist subsequently asked him, 'Do you want to be alive or not?' And six years later, the man in the other car came up to Mansell at a Formula One meeting and asked him, 'Remember me?' Nigel Mansell was not amused.)

He was racing again within five weeks, in the surgical collar he would wear for the rest of the season. And he was racing well. He'd begun with a Javelin car, and changed to an Irish-made Crossle. He would win twenty-seven of his forty races.

By autumn the Brush Fusegear Formula Ford championship beckoned and I unashamedly rely on *Autosport* again for these precious fragments.

Silverstone, late August: he won his heat and was second in the final after a 'fine tussle' with Pigot. Mallory in September: he took the lead in a 'brilliant manoeuvre at the esse bends. Mansell drove round the outside of Trevor van Rooyen (a South African) on the 13th of 15 laps and took the flag by .08 of a second'. Donington in September: van Rooyen and Mansell broke away, van Rooyen leading. Mansell got him at the chicane on lap two. Van Rooyen got him back at the chicane on lap five. Mansell got him back on lap six, van Rooyen got him back on lap eight. Two to go. Van Rooyen 'desperately' pulled alongside but went on to the grass at the chicane because Mansell wouldn't give way. (The racing line again.) They were together on the last lap along the straight, van Rooyen nosed ahead, cut across too quickly and clipped Mansell's car. Mansell regained control but both cars were now wrong for the chicane – Mansell actually sideways. While he corrected that, van Rooyen spun in the chicane, and Mansell nipped by and won it. Snetterton in September: he was invited to test-drive a Lola, the first Formula Three car he'd handled and the next stage up. He was quicker than the regular test driver. But that was only a diversion. The Formula Ford championship was still to be settled.

Silverstone in September: he took pole from van Rooyen and beat Derek Warwick's lap record. (Warwick, from Hampshire, was, if one could pursue an analogy with schooldays, in a class above Mansell, having reached Formula Three, but their subsequent Formula One careers would run concurrently and they would become friends.) Mansell made a mistake and was third into Copse Corner and almost crashed into the swarm of hornets all around him. At the chicane he 'nudged' van Rooyen in a strong move to get in front. On the third lap three cars came under the Daily Express Bridge towards the chicane and Mansell took the lead with a 'demon out-braking move.'

He won at Oulton Park and came to Silverstone again in October for the championship decider, van Rooyen leading him by six points. Mansell needed pole position, victory and the fastest lap. 'It will,' van Rooyen said tersely, 'be a fierce old do.' It was. Mansell qualified 0.5 seconds quicker and had the points for pole. But he was lying third after the first lap, moved up to second, surged round the *outside* of van Rooyen at Woodcote to lead. Now he needed fastest lap. 'I was driving like a maniac to do it.' He did it. He was champion.

Many are the dreams which lie broken. Nigel Mansell was twenty-three. He could reasonably assume that he was going in the right direction – quickly. Many are the young men who think this, especially if they have won championships. But they are still at a stage where money is absolutely crucial and money was precisely what Nigel Mansell didn't have. He needed to move to Formula Three in 1978. In retrospect it was all very clear. They'd sell their flat.

The flat, in Alton near Solihull, had two bedrooms and a view of Alton Mere. 'I really liked that flat,' Rosanne said. 'I hated selling it but it was the right thing to do.' After paying off the mortgage, the Mansells had £6,000. With this he was going to buy his way into Formula Three.

It was never going to be enough.

Pit Stop

Enough? Whatever is enough? You see the difference. Motor racing is the only sport where you need money to play. In all the others you can make the implements: a wicket from a jacket laid on the ground, a bat from any old piece of wood, a ball from any old ball; a football pitch can be magically created from any old piece of ground, two jackets for goalposts and any number can play from one-on-one to twenty-on-twenty. And then there's athletics. If you can run, you can run anywhere. But this is to miss one of the big points: you can do all of these things as often as you wish for as long as you wish. It used to be a common sight, wasteland, parkland, grassland, street corner and the ebb and flow of games or, for the solitary kid with the terrible compulsion, playing alone. You hold your old piece of wood, you cast a ragged tennis ball against a wall, hit it when it comes back and you're playing your own Test Match and it lasts as long as you want. You don't even need a lamp-post for a wicket but it helps because you never have to appeal against the light if you want to go on alone, when sad, sad darkness falls.

But with cars – you have to have a car to play. Even a lawn-mower go-kart costs money, and this money may be – is – far beyond the reach of far too many families who have discovered that the Depression didn't end in the 1930s. To play you need the car and a circuit, marshals, mechanics, first aid units and it all costs. You simply cannot say that it is in any sense democratic. It is not. It is exclusive and talent will not necessarily save you. If you have no access to a car you have no chance to prove you have talent. If the compulsion is truly strong enough, you've a better chance, of course.

Enough? Whatever is enough? The question keeps coming back. Here is part of the answer. Gerry Corbett works for Silverstone Racing School: 'The fairly usual route in is to go through a school like ours. It's a short-cut. Total cost of a complete course: about £600. Then they spend perhaps a year racing in *closed* events. Total cost: another £1,000. Then at some stage they have to break loose and do things on their own. That means Formula Ford 1600. Nowadays, because of the professionalism, it will probably cost £35,000 to £40,000. You'd buy a pre-1974 car for about £5,000 and learn, you'd be a family team, the second year you'd go into a professional team' – which is where you hit the £35,000. 'In 1977 that would have been £8,000 to £10,000.'

Corbett adds: 'The whole point about a racing school is that youngsters don't have to become committed until they've sampled it. All racing schools have an introductory lesson, a sampler, if you like. Our sampler is £45.'

The unwritten history of motor sport, the one which will never be written because it can never be written, must be strewn with seven-year-olds who saw Fangio-Moss-Clark-Hill-Stewart-Hunt but, when the time came, needed £45 and didn't have it. The racing school cannot in any sane sense lower their prices. There are countries which regard motor racing as prestige and plough money in as some kind of investment. Alain Prost, so the story goes, spent the equivalent of £75 of his own money before French sponsors began paying. In Italy motor racing is obsessive and good publicity, and impoverished British Formula One teams have been known to reach for a young Italian to put in their second car to pay their bills.

Here there's Racing for Britain, a voluntary group which raises and distributes money to make the thing more democratic. They can only help so many. And the problem remains: time. Every instant you can wheedle in a car is precious, every instant measured, accounted for. You cannot go on every night until sad, sad darkness falls, learning, experimenting, perfecting. And the law of diminishing returns holds true: the less money you have the less time you can buy in a car. Mansell would sell everything he had for just five races in 1978.

Some argue that because motor racing is undemocratic it has the appeal of exclusivity; others argue that it's all very well kids playing football but there are a strictly limited number of cars available, it is expensive and dangerous to run them, and if you don't feel the compulsion strongly enough to overcome all the obstacles, why should you get in one rather than somebody else? In other words, as Charles Darwin discovered, the Origin of Species proves the survival of the fittest. It involves determination, and that's a word we have used before about Nigel Mansell.

But you still have to stake out money. Family money, sponsors' money – which you won't get, not you, an unproven youngster –

32

or, as in the case of Mansell, his own money and what else he could borrow. Corbett: 'I met him when he came along for his first lesson. Mallory Park. Dare I say that he was one face in thousands? There was nothing outstanding about his ability. He was seventeen. It involved learning how to change gear in a non-synchromesh Formula Ford car. It was learning new techniques, becoming co-ordinated with the car. It lasted about two hours. He decided that he was so keen on moving up the ladder that he wouldn't do it through a racing school. He would do it independently. He double-mortgaged everything.'

So we have it, and it is neatly in place. A Brummie, brusque, spade-is-a-spade sort of bloke, too impatient for the driving school before that season in Formula Ford, now through that season, eyeing Formula Three. At least the face among thousands had become the face among a few dozen. Formula Three is much more rarified than Formula Ford, and less people can play. But five races? The boy himself had no chance.

3   The Long, Hard Road

Rosanne stayed away from the garage of the rented flat in Hall Green. It had been converted into a gymnasium so that her husband could keep fit and, as a way of encouraging himself, he had arranged a sequence of enlarged photographs of the crash at Brands Hatch along one wall, the Formula Ford skidding and somersaulting. 'I'd rather not see them,' she said, as any woman would, 'I don't go into the gym now.'

Racing drivers are dispassionate about accidents because it is necessary to be so and often you'll see a driver have a bad moment, unbuckle his seat-belts to get out of the wreckage, run back to the pits to get in the spare car. Mansell was like that by 1978 and regarded the photographs as both a reminder of 'the facts of life' and a potent incentive to be fit – the better to survive any future accidents. He concluded that it was easier 'to push more weights and train harder' when he was looking at the photographs.

He had the five races. He'd paid for them and they would be in a Formula Three works March. It was an awesome gamble at an awful time. 'Friends took us out for the occasional meal,' Rosanne said, while Mansell remembered it as vividly as any crash: 'We had nothing. No home, no money. I had no job. It was easily the worst year of our lives. Hell.' He was sustained because Rosanne was with him absolutely. They postponed any thoughts of children. She would continue to pay the bills.

Formula Ford is not a place where you linger longer than you need. All motor racing is about going forward and upward and you ascend a well-established scale. You begin in karts, you master single-seaters in Formula Ford, you get yourself smartly into Formula Three which, paradoxically perhaps, enables you to by-pass Formula Two – now Formula 3000 – straight to Formula One in a single bound. Why? Formula Ford is sophisticated but Formula Three more so and crucially, although you only have a bit more power you can alter the way the car is set up aerodynamically. This

34

opens up all manner of possibilities. The transition might only take you three or four days superficially but the real difference is great: bigger budgets, more testing, more refinements, more scope.

And then Formula One? A current Grand Prix driver explained that: 'In Formula Three you start to get noticed, you get your name in the papers and if you have outstanding talent the Formula One teams want to get their hands on you then – nice and early. There's nothing wrong with Formula Two, nothing at all, it's just that Formula One teams don't want to wait that long. In case another Formula One team gets its hands on you.' And then there's the other factor. When you're young and hungry they don't have to pay you so much and in some cases *you* pay *them*.

So Mansell went to Formula Three. Five races was, I repeat, an awesome risk because it offered so little time to show whatever talent he had. A whole season, that would have been the platform, time to master a new car then go for it. But five races . . .

At least he wasn't entirely new to it. During 1977 he had competed a few times in Formula Three when he wasn't actually driving in Formula Ford, one race in a Puma, the others in a Lola. He'd had a fourth at Silverstone, a fifth at Thruxton. It would have been the perfect preparation for a whole season in 1978. But five races . . .

Formula Three that year contained drivers who would in due time become wreathed in splendour. Nelson Piquet, world champion, 1981, 1983. Prost, world champion, 1985, 1986. Stefan Johansson, capable of making a Ferrari go fast.

Mansell took the March to Silverstone in the month of March. Peter Windsor, an Australian journalist, was to become a confidant and adviser: 'A man I knew well, John Thornburn, used to ring me up quite a lot and he had given Keke Rosberg (world champion, 1982) his chance in England. One day he rang and said, ''I'm doing all I can to try and help this guy Nigel Mansell. He's an ace. I tell you, he's the quickest thing since Keke.'' I met Mansell at the beginning of 1978 at Silverstone and he was on pole. Piquet was second quickest, Warwick third. I was so impressed with his confidence. He shook my hand – a firm handshake – looked me straight in the eye and talked about golf, tennis, running, driving.

'I thought: This is not the average Brit who is whining and complaining that he doesn't have any money. He'd put every cent he'd got into this Formula Three car he was driving. It was a wet race (he came second) and his visor misted up or something but he really drove well. It was very clear even then that he had the finesse and sensitivity in the wet to make him very special. He only did a few more races, set fastest lap in one, and then the money ran out.' In fact it went like this: Thruxton seventh, Brands seventh, Oulton seventh, Donington fourth.

His five races moved *Autosport* to say that he had shown 'great flair in his all too rare outings.' There were scant consolations. In June he won the British Drivers' Award – for younger drivers, of course – and that gave him a chance in a Europa Formula Two race at Donington. People were noticing him – and then he was gone. He didn't qualify for the Donington race. That was June.

Windsor again: 'The rest of that year he spent running ten miles a day, punching a punch-bag, keeping fit. And during the days he also wrote letters to potential sponsors and he was putting every brain cell he had into getting back into racing. Those were bad times. No drive, no recognition for the pole he'd got at Silverstone, nothing at all.'

And that was 1978.

An old friend had an office-cleaning business in Cirencester and Mansell ended up working there three days a week on the administration side or cleaning windows himself.

Then came a bit of old-fashioned good fortune. Unipart were to sponsor a Formula One team in 1979.

They would have March cars with Dolomite engines and the team would be run by Dave Price. 'I was, I supposed, in a unique position. There wasn't many people in Formula Three who could employ two drivers, give them cars and *pay* them. They had to do a roadshow, you know, go round and meet dealers in the evenings, but they got paid extra for that. So I drew up a short list. I spoke to all the people on the list (except Mansell) and in the end I had already made up my mind.'

Price remembered one of Mansell's races in the Lola. It is on such things that careers can turn. 'I had never spoken to him. He came down to Twickenham, where we were based then, and we had a chat. He impressed me as being so strong and so determined. He was on his uppers, a bit, sold his house, everything. But his determination . . . we gave him the drive.'

Windsor says: 'They had only one good engine and that of course went to the number one driver (Brett Riley). It meant Nigel had to run his car with less rear wing (poor engine = less power = less possibility of pushing a car along with big rear wings = less downforce = less grip). So he just had to control the car on corners with no downforce to help him.'

Price does not agree. 'I know Nigel thinks he didn't get the best engine but none of them were any good! I don't think there *was* a good Dolomite engine . . .'

Demonstrably, Riley was quicker in 'qualifying, practice, whatever. It wasn't a big difference but it was always a bit of difference.'

At the Daily Express International Trophy meeting at Silverstone in March, Mansell took part in the Formula Three race and, on a wet day, stormed off into the lead. On lap six of twenty rain fell again and three laps later a certain Andrea de Cesaris, a young Italian, got through and finished four seconds ahead. Mansell followed him doggedly home. But de Cesaris had, without Mansell knowing it, missed the chicane on lap two and since this had such consequences it needs clarification.

The chicane, approached at high speed under the Daily Express Bridge 200 yards away, is (or was, it's gone now) an artificial S-bend put there to slow the cars. Its boundary lines are kerbs and cones. Often you see two or three cars jostling as they near it but there's only room for one of them to thread through the S at a time. Others collide or lose control and instead of getting in to the S keep straight on, miss it altogether and go through the cones. You get disqualified if you do and this now happened to de Cesaris. Mansell had won.

'I don't,' he said, 'believe it!'

It was a rare moment. 'Because the engine was so uncompetitive he was usually dicing for fifth or sixth place in races but you could really tell that talent was there,' Windsor says.

The British Grand Prix was at Silverstone, too, in July. It is far more than one motor race, it is a gathering. There is a programme of races with the Grand Prix the centrepiece. Formula Three was part of the programme and a wonderful chance for youngsters to show Formula One what they could do. The great men of Formula One might well be watching: Ken Tyrrell, Frank Williams, Ferrari, McLaren, Colin Chapman of Lotus . . .

'Chapman, like all good managers, didn't run the whole team himself, he had a lot of good people to help – a bit like Reagan runs the Presidency,' Windsor remembers. 'Peter Collins was the team manager at the time and I introduced him to Nigel. Peter said to Chapman: "Look, Mansell's good, he's an Englishman and you've got to watch him." At the Grand Prix Nigel met Chapman (legend has it that Mansell said "You need me!") and then we stood by the chicane – Chapman, Peter Collins and myself – watching the Formula Three race.' Mansell had qualified thirteenth, a place in front, incidentally, of Prost.

The chicane: its perils had been amply demonstrated in March by de Cesaris – for the purposes of this narrative – although those perils were evident at just about every race meeting, always had been since the chicane had been built in 1977. The chicane: making many and varied demands. You must brake from maximum speed at just the right point, you must be aware of others doing the same thing at your elbow – over the cones and out, remember – and you must be able to handle your car with great precision. It's so tight that you flick right-left and you're through.

The chicane sucks you in, spits you out.

Chapman did watch Mansell. Chapman said, 'He's running sixth.'

' "Yes," we said, staring down Chapman's throat, "but look at the way he's taking the car through the chicane. He's got no power at all but look how quick he is, look at the way he brakes." '

Chapman pondered that a moment. '*Yes,*' he said.

In retrospect, no roll of drums could have been more significant than this one simple word.

Mansell finished sixth. A month later the Formula Three people trooped off to Austria as a support race for the Austrian Grand Prix. Mansell was yet to acquire the sophisticated habits of travel. Price says: 'In the hotel he'd look at the food and say "I don't like that and I don't like that." Every night I had to get him steak and hot milk. You ever tried getting steak and hot milk in an Austrian hotel? It was funny, *really.*'

In this season of 1979 Mansell would finish second twice, at Thruxton and Donington – the latter in September where he was beaten by someone who would reach Formula One and make no impact at all, an Ulsterman, Kenny Acheson. Many are called, few chosen.

It is worth stressing how difficult Formula Three was in *any* car. Drivers came from far-flung places to compete – Brazil, New Zealand, Sweden, Japan, Spain, even Colombia – and they hadn't travelled those distances without the deepest determination of their own. They all sensed that they were close to Formula One. All they had to do was demonstrate it in public. That was why they had travelled so far.

Later in September they went to Oulton Park, Cheshire for another round of the championship. Mansell was sixth quickest in qualifying but, on a lovely autumnal day, an early crash stopped the race and it wasn't re-started until twenty minutes later. De Cesaris made a bad start and promptly nudged Johansson aside to take seventh place. He lay behind Mansell and Irishman Eddie Jordan.

On lap two de Cesaris gave Mansell the Johansson lunge but Mansell wasn't having any of that and de Cesaris found himself almost off the track. De Cesaris was not, let us say, a driver to be discouraged. Two laps later he lunged again . . .

Eddie Jordan: 'We were all queuing up to get through the hairpin. Suddenly Mansell's car went end over end over end. I couldn't believe it.' De Cesaris had struck Mansell side-on and pitched him into this barrel-roll across a run-off area. The car came to rest upside down on grass and marshals spent several minutes struggling to free Mansell. He was taken to Chester Hospital with severe bruising and a broken vertebrae but released later the same afternoon.

'I'm stiff and sore but otherwise OK,' he said. He asked to thank the chap who 'held the drip all the way to hospital'. His memory of what had happened was clear (they aren't always): 'I looked in the mirrors coming down the hill and saw de Cesaris was a little closer but I was right behind Eddie and I never thought he would try and come past. The next thing I knew I was rolling over.' Echoing Jordan, he added: 'I couldn't believe it.'

Jordan already knew Mansell was capable of 'mind over matter' – 'he has the strongest view of his own ability' – and it was just as well. Two days later he was sitting at home taking three pain-killers a day when the telephone rang. Mansell could only pick up the receiver awkwardly because of the pain. It was Chapman. Are you free, Chapman mused, to do some testing with us?

The world of Formula One had spread itself in front of him.

Mansell said: '*Yes*.' In retrospect, no roll of drums could have been more significant than that, either.

Chapman: 'I didn't think you'd be able to make it. We heard you had a bad crash.'

'Not me. Must be somebody else with a similar name . . .'

The testing would be at the Paul Ricard circuit in the South of France but before that Mansell went, as a spectator, to another meeting at Silverstone and sought out de Cesaris. There was plain speaking but, as someone noted, 'No blows were exchanged.' That, too, was just as well. Nigel Mansell is a very strong man.

The Oulton incident had been so severe that, as he flew down to Ricard, he had prescribed himself six pain-killers a day. Double the dosage. You cannot, you simply cannot, pass up the chance actually to get into a Formula One car. Many hundreds dedicate their lives to the moment and never find it. Nor get near finding it. Let me be more precise: they never once get in a Formula One car, *even to sit*.

Testing has a two-fold dimension. Teams hire circuits to experiment with engines, wings, tyres, anything, everything, and, occasionally, to have a look at young drivers. It might seem rather casual and informal, three or four teams, perhaps, in an empty circuit on some forgotten weekday using the time as they wish. You may see a car doing a full Grand Prix distance, others doing single laps as they try something, then drifting lazily into the pits to tell how it worked – or if it worked. It is on these days that drivers who seem publicly to dislike each other can be found chatting amicably in other teams' motor homes – places they regard as hostile terrain during actual meetings – and have been drawn there because the rumour is that the kettle's on . . .

The young man contemplating his first moment in a Formula One car does not know – or care – about such things. He is beset by many pressing problems. Will he be able to control the car? Mansell's Williams, vintage 1986, did 0-120 and back to 0 in under six seconds.

Under braking, 5 G is compressing you. And if you think the acceleration is going to blow your mind, consider this: it brakes faster than it accelerates. We are no longer outlining the jolly cavalry charging of Formula Ford nor the inherent possibilities of Formula Three, nor the capabilities of any known sports car. This is *it*.

The young man standing beside the beast-like missile can't help reflecting, even if he knows little or nothing about its ultimate performance, that it cost a lot of money to make and it's all too easy to get it into a spin, skim it off a circuit, damage it. He's seen that often enough on television, watched experienced drivers do it in the races. What chance has he? And, more particularly, what second chance has he if he damages it the first?

Any team which knows what it's doing – and most do – tell this young man standing there holding his crash helmet rather sheepishly and eyeing the missile: *take your time, don't get out there and try to prove your great truths to us all at once.*

And – as if to emphasise that you are not alone in your moment – Lotus had five drivers present this late October day in 1979: Elio de Angelis, Italian, already in Formula One who had driven fourteen races during the season for Shadow Ford; Eddie Cheever, an American with strong Italian connections; a small, neat Dutchman, Jan Lammers; Stephen South, a Briton who was at that time bathed in publicity and regarded as The Coming Man. Mansell's presence, someone noted, was 'surprising'.

Untypically, the weather, which in high summer can burn the skin off your forehead, was windy and showery. The session was to be conducted on the 2.02 mile test circuit, not the full Grand Prix track. But that didn't matter. It was physically close enough to the real thing, using the same pits, playing out against the same backdrop – the bleached, wooden hills of Provence. The Mediterranean wasn't at all far away. You'd seen the names on the signposts on your way up to the circuit: Bandol, la Ciotat, Cassis, all conjuring exotic summers and topless beaches.

It certainly wasn't Birmingham.

And at last, at last Nigel Mansell did clamber up and into a Formula One car for the first time in his life. Immediately the gearbox wasn't right and he had to get out again! Then it rained . . .

Late that same day the real chance came. He negotiated 35 laps safely enough and his best time, one minute 13.91 seconds, was considered eminently respectable. 'Once I was firmly strapped in I was OK, but when I accelerated hard the power took my breath away in every sense. I couldn't blank out the pain completely but I really enjoyed driving that car. It convinced me more than ever that this is what I wanted to do.'

That first taste is sweet and sour. As you bring *their* car back into the pits *they* are not waiting with a twenty-page legally binding international contract to make you rich beyond avarice. No. And then there's the problem of what to say to them. *They*, after all, have been running this team for many years and have had their world champions. Even the mechanics, who've seen a few like you come and go, leaving no trace, are highly skilled people, tuned to every nuance of every nut and bolt on the missile. Dare you risk saying that the car wasn't set up right, that you should have had a different compound tyre? If you've any common sense – or any sense at all – you don't exactly do that. You say: 'I've waited all my life for this and it was worth the wait. Thank you.' And if you find a kindly face among so many strangers examining you – Bob Dance, chief mechanic, known as The Vicar because of his thirst for tea, would do nicely at Lotus – you wait until you can ask it discreetly. *Did I do all right?*

Formula One drivers are more impatient than most people, and embryonic Formula One drivers more impatient than that. The first touch of the Formula One car feeds the compulsion much, much more strongly than that first touch of being at Aintree watching them could ever do. That first real touch . . . that first moment when you are out there alone, master of it, and it, like all machines,

41

obeys you – that can give you a glow to warm you all the winter while you wait for the telephone to ring again.

(Formula One business is habitually done by telephone. The mail certainly won't deliver letters, even with first-class stamps, before tomorrow morning. Very few action men in Formula One doubt that tomorrow is a long and dangerous way away.)

Mansell waited: Chapman had not been at the session – even a man as mobile as Chapman couldn't be everywhere all the time. How could Mansell know how he'd done, or if Chapman had heard how he'd *really* done? (Windsor, of course, was taking care of that discreetly.)

In due time Mansell would receive a call and then a testing contract. This did not mean that Lotus thought he was so technically competent after 35 laps that he could scrutinise their cars at 200 miles an hour and tell them where they'd gone wrong. It did mean he could drive the cars on some sort of regular basis – de Angelis got the drive itself – and as anyone will tell you, miles on the track are important, the more the better. Get comfortable with the world flooding by much faster. Learn to change down from sixth to fifth at that 200 miles an hour. Learn circuits, learn braking points, remember them. Get friendly with the beast. Preferably, wrestle and tame it in all weathers until you can exploit its staggering potential to the full and you and the beast and the grey unfolding track blend into the sublime. The drivers all learn to bitch later on and when they do this is not sublime, but that's another story . . .

Pit Stop

This laboured and belaboured lust for Formula One may seem obvious. After all, you're a racing driver and what could be more natural than wanting to be among the best? One must assume that this applies equally to chartered accountants, double glazing disciples on your doorstep at dead of night, journalists, Marxist-Leninist running dogs and all points in between. They all want to be the best. The comparison doesn't survive further scrutiny. The best chartered accountant in the world is *not* followed by a couple of hundred reporters to his office, television millions do *not* wait breathless as he lifts his pen to sign pieces of paper, his office is *not* – we must assume – decorated by the best feminine talent a country can rustle up wearing garments not unadjacent to pocket handkerchiefs and precious little else. (This is also sadly true of journalists.)

Formula One is this and more. It generates enough money to make a chartered accountant's palms moist. Lauda is reported to have said no to six million dollars for a season, that's £4,000,000, that's £76,000 a week. Think about it. £76,000 a week. Not that you expect to get that, although Formula One is the place you've always been going towards. Because you race, you want to go faster. The place to do that best is the ultimate place, above which nothing stands: Formula One.

The cars are produced virtually regardless of expense with technology so sophisticated that they examine moon shots and get over to NASA to see which bits would adapt to make cars go faster. Kevlar, used for bodywork, is an obvious example. Goodyear, the tyre people, use Formula One as a test bed for Jumbo jet tyres which take all that pressure at the instant of touching down. Formula One, their man Barry Griffin says, is the only place where the pressures are comparable. Think about it.

And of course Formula One is complete unto itself. It has its own tribal customs, its own calms and storms. It is glamorous, if that word has any real currency left in it, and if you drive well it is deeply fulfilling on the most personal and private level. Here are the best, hottest, most expensive cars and you've got one of them. Only thirty other people on earth have.

Because it is so complete it envelops young drivers and they travel the world within it, so that all the people – mechanics, technicians, drivers, journalists, officials, fellow travellers – you say cheerio to at Ricard will be exactly the same people you say hello to in Detroit, Michigan or wherever a couple of weeks later. It is so enveloping that some, when they retire, feel oddly in exile and linger awkwardly at races because they have found nowhere else comparable to go. The reason is simple. There *is* nowhere comparable.

The interesting aspect is that the wild and wonderful teenager in his Mini Cooper flinging it round the chicane at Thruxton on a wet Sunday afternoon already knows this and is going towards it as fast as he can. Of the thousands en route at any given moment, and we are talking about everybody from kart racers in Brazil all the way to our Mini Cooper, a bare handful make it. There are too many obstacles along the way.

The handful? They are the thirty, virtually all regulars in Formula One. You might get two or three newcomers per year as vacancies occur, not more. And even then the newcomers haven't really made it because they'll be in the smaller teams with slower cars and all the journalists will be talking to drivers in the other pits, and the television cameras will lose you because you're at the back of the grid and producers follow the front-runners – unless you have a crash, or until you get lapped, and then tribal custom demands that you get out of the way to let Prost or Piquet through and your televised moment is gone, quickly and in a most humiliating way. And you'll have to bring your own birds. The local ones have an instinct. They'll be in the other pits, too.

But you're nearer. You cultivate the moguls who run the big teams and you cultivate them carefully. You don't misbehave on the track – experienced drivers shout at you for baulking them and this is part very serious abuse, part initiation. You try to demonstrate that you're making the slow car go faster than the moguls thought it might. And then you ring the moguls often – but not too often – and pop round to their motor-homes during quiet moments at meetings and explain how invitingly available you are, *sir*. And then – maybe – you get into a car which can win races. Of the thousands who set out on their journey, about a dozen men get this far. Of the dozen, perhaps three, perhaps four will become world champion. Whatever else it is, it's a numbers game and the odds are always heavily against you, right to the end.

4 The Lotus Eaters

The afternoon of 17 August 1980 was warm and dry. It might not
have been. You get thunderstorms, and overnight one had played
out its echoing, thunderous melody. But now the gently undulating
hillocks and pastures in the footsteps of the Styrian mountains were
already covered with 50,000 people – the young men drinking, as
is their custom, big frothy beers, the families spreading their
picnics, the children playing their endless games on the grass.

Below them, half way along the straight, twenty-four cars stood
motionless, each facing towards the sharp rise to the first corner, a
chicane called Hella Licht's. A most innocent name. It means only
Hella's light.

The Osterreichring. Exactly 54 laps of 3.692 miles and after
Silverstone the fastest Formula One track of all. Few gathered for
the Austrian Grand Prix – because of the contours of the land they
all seem to be sitting in tiers round an amphitheatre – would know
very much about the car at the very back, although it was obviously
a Lotus. Teams invariably only run two cars and there were certainly two Lotuses further up the grid, Elio de Angelis on the fifth
row, Mario Andretti on the ninth. What on earth was this other one
doing?

Mansell had signed the testing contract and it also included three
races. This was the first of them. Hence three cars. (De Angelis and
Andretti were, of course, the regular and contracted drivers.)
However constricting three races might seem, it was a chance,
a very real chance to show that he was worth more than three
races . . .

You don't win your first race. Only two men, Giuseppe Farina
and Giancarlo Baghetti, have ever done that. What you do is drive
to stay out of trouble, drive to finish, and your placing doesn't
matter a damn, really. You drive to demonstrate that you can drive
and the more laps you drive the more people will believe you can
drive. And nowhere do you make a fool of yourself. That's the

45

discipline, that's the expectation. And don't worry so much. The people who know will soon know whether you've got it or not.

Few scanning the motionless cars knew that there before them a great and bitter misfortune was being played out. Mansell waited on the grid. Round him mechanics topped up fuel in the tank. After a few moments Mansell felt a burning. Some of the fuel had 'found its way down to the back of my seat. I had reached the point, the very minute, I had worked towards all my life – and there I was getting my backside burned.' He was asked very seriously if he wanted to step out of the car and walk away, forget the race. He gave the only possible reply: No, no, no. So the mechanics poured water onto the petrol to douse it as best they could.

Then the mechanics left the grid and all the cars were alone. The light went green and the 24 surged up the hill, streamed through the Hella Licht's and followed the contours of the corners which are known, appropriately, as kurves.

After a few laps the water had evaporated leaving only the petrol. 'It had soaked into my overalls.' Mansell wasn't on the way to any particular glory – a dangerous word, anyway – but to first and second-degree burns. When petrol fumes can't escape they set off a chemical reaction against flesh. He kept on until, mercifully, the engine broke down on lap 41. By then the petrol had made his harmstrings shrink and he would need a week of physiotherapy before he could straighten his legs. Rosanne says, 'I remember the night he came back. As we drove from London Airport his legs started to seize up. He was poorly.'

Welcome to Formula One.

Mansell being Mansell, he was at the Dutch Grand Prix at Zandvoort for the next race two weeks later and put the car on the eighth row of the grid. This was good. But, in the race, the brakes went on lap sixteen, went all at once as he approached a corner. He went off but was unhurt.

Truly, welcome to Formula One.

Two weeks after *that* he was at Imola for the Italian Grand Prix but his car didn't survive the initial practice session on the Friday. He was bedding in new brakes and obediently moved over to let another car go by, spun on the loose edge of the track and hammered into a barrier.

On the Saturday Mansell was given a spare car with, as someone said, 'strict instructions to keep it on the road.' He did, but brake problems prevented him from qualifying for the race. He was first reserve and for several tantalising hours might well have got in because Jody Scheckter (Ferrari) was injured – he'd spun off, given his car a good old thump and jarred his neck. So Mansell took part in the traditional warm-up session on the morning of the race and was, amazingly, right up there with the quickest drivers. But Scheckter decided to race – Formula One drivers generally do – and Mansell had to watch.

Mansell's three races, or rather two, might seem disasters. He hadn't finished at all, although that was hardly his fault. He'd damaged a car but cars do get damaged. It certainly wasn't his fault that at Imola, after he'd gone off the track and left the car where it had come to rest, someone else – Manfred Winkelhock (Arrows) – went off at precisely the same place and into the Lotus, rendering it beyond immediate repair. Cynics could argue that if Mansell hadn't gone off in the first place his Lotus wouldn't have been there to be hit. But he was young, he was learning it all and you have to make some allowances. In fact, he had not been a disaster.

In Formula One people speak of 'learning curves' and everybody starts at the bottom of their own particular curve. Odd. In an occupation which is fast and also frenetic – there is a significant difference – you must have patience.

It might take an age to actually win a race and in Mansell's case that age would last five full years. (Some never make it at all. A certain Jean-Pierre Jarier drove 136 races and didn't finish higher than third.) The question astute people in the pit lane want answered is not necessarily how quickly you can move up your curve but how high the curve will go and, ultimately, if it will go all the way to the world championship.

Very few were as astute as Anthony Colin Bruce Chapman. Small, restless, bristling with that certain forbidding presence of the entirely self-made man, he had started as a 19-year-old engineering student at London University when he had built an Austin 7. (That he and Mansell should both have begun in the same sort of car and both be engineers was entirely coincidence.) The body of Chapman's Austin 7 was made of plywood. Soon enough he would borrow money from his fiancée, later his wife, Hazel – legend has it at £25 – and build more cars in a lock-up garage behind her home in Muswell Hill, north London. He was always restless.

By 1958 Lotus were in Formula One and beginning their own learning curve. By 1980, while young Mansell was struggling in the third car, Chapman had had a colossal, awe-inspiring five world champions: Clark (1963, 1965), Graham Hill (1968), Jochen Rindt (1970), Emerson Fittipaldi (1972) and Mario Andretti (1978). By

1980, Lotus had won a colossal, awe-inspiring 71 races. And after sojourns with other sponsors, their black and gold livery – they were now with John Player – had become as familiar as the rich-red of Ferrari itself. Perhaps more so.

Chapman, like two other major team owners, Ken Tyrrell and Frank Williams, was essentially an Englishman and no amount of travel, no amount of constant dealing with people from overseas of all shapes, sizes and species in all situations was going to alter that. Of course he wanted more world champions. Of course he would prefer them to be British; and Mansell was from Birmingham, the heartland.

For 1981, Andretti moved to Alfa Romeo. Some drivers do move around a bit and between 1968 and 1982, when he finished, Andretti would drive for Lotus, March, Ferrari, Parnelli, Lotus, Alfa Romeo, Williams and Ferrari in that order. What became important, as it so often does, was the vacancy he left behind him for 1981. Mansell was hired as the number two driver behind Elio de Angelis, now firmly established with the team. It was something Mansell would always remember and treasure, this 'faith' in him by Chapman; it was something he would speak about publicly with a certain, careful, deepening emotion. If you have ever been very alone with your convictions, and you've sold everything for them, and done jobs – sometimes almost menial – for them, and you find someone who shares them and he's had five world champions, you'll understand.

In 1981 Mansell would drive in 13 of the 15 races and, in sum, it would all be as turbulent as the vignette of 1980 had been. Mansell would say at the very start of the season: 'I've dreamed about it for so long that all I can do is think about driving . . . and maybe one day being able to afford a house with an indoor swimming pool. (Of this, more later.) It's not the tremendous speeds which turn me on but being able to control something that fast.'

The *Daily Express* reported that it would cost Lotus £1,250,000 for Mansell to race in 1981. Five years before he'd still been in karting . . .

The season began with an accident at Long Beach, California, a street circuit where accidents do happen. He was one of six drivers to discover this – among them Lammers, who'd tested that first day at Ricard with Mansell and was now with the German team ATS. In Brazil he was eleventh, in Argentina he didn't finish (engine) and so he came to the unlovely and unloved Zolder circuit in Belgium, a place where, as one cynic put it, 'The best thing is the

48

quality of the chips from the van in the paddock.'

It was a chaotic race, even as chaotic races go. Two mechanics were run over and the drivers stopped in a protest after two laps. The race was re-started for the original seventy laps and then rain, an occupational hazard and a common commodity in this part of Belgium, fell heavily enough to stop the race again, this time terminally, on lap fifty-four. By then Mansell was in third place, 43.69 seconds behind the winner, Carlos Reutemann (Williams). They were the first Grand Prix points of his life.

Mansell, normally wary of undue intoxication, said, 'It is the breakthrough. Hopefully, though, it's just the start.'

At another level he left Zolder 'upset' by what had happened to the two mechanics.

He had won good points. How good? No Englishman had finished in the first three since James Hunt in 1979. Better still, though he got nothing in the next race at Monaco he was fourth fastest in qualifying during the first session for the grid. And in the race after that he finished sixth. It was confirmation that he was capable of scoring points regularly and that's rare, that is, so early on. 'I'm a down-to-earth sort of guy,' he would say, 'and that's how I'm going to stay.'

Chapman accepted that comparisons with Jim Clark were admissible: 'It is no use denying it, the similarities are there. Even at this stage I instinctively know I've got a boy who is going to go all the way to the top. I can already feel he and I are developing the kind of relationship Jimmy and I shared.' Chapman added, as he would, that some 'rough edges' remained to be smoothed in Mansell's driving.

Chapman, of course, understood the mechanisms of publicity and must have known that any mention of Clark would be a highly emotive comparison to draw. (Clark, killed in a Formula Two race in 1968, had only ever driven for Lotus in Formula One. He was absolutely brilliant, won 25 races and was still mourned as a mythological figure.) What is certain is that Mansell believed in Mansell and Chapman believed in Mansell. It was enough.

By July they were both at the British Grand Prix at Silverstone. This, his first there, seemed to have come at precisely the right time.

Silverstone, deep in the pleasant and forgiving countryside of Northamptonshire, is not so far from Birmingham. It always attracts a vast crowd – one of the largest of any Grand Prix in the world – and they come, inevitably, with special affection for any British driver and that makes, equally inevitably, special demands

49

on that driver. If every one of the sixteen Grands Prix is a stage, this one – for anyone remotely British – is centre stage. You get a throng calling out 'Hello Nigel' although you've never seen a lot of them before. You get the BBC doing profiles of you, journalists following you around. The British Grand Prix is very big news in British newspapers, and you're British . . .

Chapman, meanwhile, had conjured one of his great masterstrokes, a 'twin-chassis' car. One chassis was the bodywork, side pods, wings, radiators. Moving *within* that was another chassis holding the cockpit, front and rear suspensions, gearbox and engine. De Angelis had used it already but amidst much typical howling of protest from other teams it was ruled illegal. For Silverstone, Britain's Royal Automobile Club – who hold the title to the race – said a modified version would be acceptable. So Mansell went to Silverstone to drive it. On the first day of the meeting Ferrari, Talbot, Ligier and Alfa Romeo howled in protest again and the stewards spent most of the day debating it. They excluded the car. Chapman, angry, said: 'We keep coming up against subversive methods from FISA.'*

Ironically, while the stewards were locked in their debate, Mansell was struggling with the car on the track. He was only eighteenth fastest. The car had been converted to a 'twin-chassis' immediately before the meeting and would now, between this Thursday qualifying session for the grid and the final Friday qualifying session, have to be converted back. It was achieved somehow, but the car simply couldn't be competitive. From the original it had been converted and reconverted within three days. Mansell failed to make the grid.

'I can't find words to express my utter misery, humiliation and blazing anger at the bloody fiasco of the past few days,' he said. 'There is no question that I have been the innocent victim of all the Lotus–FISA power politics.' At the end of that final session, when he realised that he hadn't made it, 'I just had to run away from everybody for at least twenty minutes to sit completely on my own in silence.'

Ironically the race was won by another Briton, John Watson, who demonstrated what Mansell had missed. As Watson's McLaren was halfway round his last lap out at Stowe Corner, the cheering could be heard in the pit lane a mile away . . .

* Federation Internationale du Sport Automobile, the governing body based in Paris.

Ah, the learning curve. It makes great demands. For the next five races – Germany, Austria, Holland, Italy, Canada – he scored no points but he rounded the season off with a fourth place at Las Vegas. In 1981, his total of eight points made him fourteenth in the championship. De Angelis had fourteen points and was eighth.

For 1982, Chapman had hired a new team manager, Peter Warr. Educated at Malvern College, he spent his National Service in the Royal Horse Artillery and something of that would stay with him: the upright posture, a slightly brisk way of dealing with people. He had always been drawn to motor racing. He raced himself in the 1960s in lesser formulae – raced, in fact, Lotus cars. He had joined the company in 1958, working in the racing car sales section. He would leave and re-join Lotus twice. Now, in 1982, it was his second coming.

Tall, nearly angular, Warr reminisces with great clarity, covering the time from when Mansell joined in 1980: 'Colin was very keen to have a British driver in the team and Nigel was very actively promoted. He started out absolutely right as the guy in the third car getting the occasional race and building some experience. He was paid according to his status. Then he came good quite by chance at Zolder and as a result he felt he was an overnight star. I'm not quite sure how it happened, but he managed to persuade Colin that he should have a major revision in his pay structure, which in my opinion was the wrong thing to do. It gave him the financial cache of being an established Grand Prix star when patently he wasn't.'

(Financial note: Grand Prix drivers are like other human beings in at least this one sense – they don't like to tell you how much they earn. But it is certain that Mansell's negotiation with Chapman produced a lot of money. How much? Enough to keep you and me happy from one Christmas to the next.)

'Part of the arrangement which flowed out of those discussions was that he should have equal status in the team with Elio de Angelis.'

Now this, surely, was reasonable. In a world where you get what you can get, Mansell was only doing that. The whole subject of a number one and a number two driver is delicate because it involves, at some point, a man's pride. As I've said before, these are competitive beings and they all want to be the best. The official title Number Two doesn't sit easily with that, although you'll have to carry it during your apprenticeship. The problem is that you and your team may not agree on the exact moment when your apprenticeship is over. (Warr himself would solve the problem in a most

51

spectacular and astonishing way in years to come by hiring a driver called Ayrton Senna and allowing *him* to choose his Number Two so that Number Two wouldn't get in *his* way.)

But now, in 1982, Mansell and de Angelis would have equal status, as they say. In terms of background alone, Elio de Angelis was impossibly remote from Mansell. His father was extremely rich and owned a construction company near Rome. It simply doesn't matter that the Italian lira is weak at any given moment. *This* many lira aren't weak. His father had a Class One offshore powerboat and that gave his son that first, decisive touch with speed. (Comparison: Mansell and the lawnmower go-kart, costing £25.) De Angelis was an accomplished pianist, had a West German model for a girlfriend and a pad in Monaco.

He was extremely good-looking with that perma-tan you get living constantly in hot places. He could be charming, he could be moody. But in a racing car you could forget all that. He was fast and he had an unsuspected quality for his background: He kept on as doggedly as Mansell did to finish races, even if he was a lap behind the leaders.

Warr: 'When I arrived at Team Lotus Nigel got off on the wrong foot because the first thing he did was to tell me which mechanics he was going to have working on his car. I had to explain to him that that wasn't the way Team Lotus was run any more. But Colin gave me very strict instructions that he was to have absolutely equal treatment with Elio – so much so that we were in an era where there was one batch of Cosworth engines and one batch of John Judd engines and I even took Nigel to Judd's factory and afterwards I said: "OK, Nigel, you've seen what he's got to offer, which do you want?"

'So we were involving him in some of the decision making, but he was still at that time in a frame of mind – and I think it was because of the way he had come up through motor racing – that the world was against him. So he was always looking everywhere for why he wasn't getting the best treatment, or where he was not getting what Elio was, instead of concentrating on his own thing. With the result that he got a reputation both inside and outside the team as an excuse finder. That, I think, inhibited his development.'

Warr and Mansell had an uneasy relationship, just as Mansell and de Angelis did. Warr does admit that, 'At that time Team Lotus were also struggling.' It is no great admission – everybody could see it – but it is central and crucial to what was happening. A struggling team rarely generates contented people, and if it does

52

they're all in the wrong business. Because they are competitive and discontented *and* they're living in a pressure cooker, frictions between personalities grow and fester. Never mind. At the end of the 1981 season there had even been speculation that Williams or McLaren might move for Mansell but this was only, as it turned out, a mark of his growing stature. A Lotus spokeman said:

'Nigel has signed with us for next season and I don't see that situation changing. He's just completed eight days' testing in the South of France and I hardly think we'd go to all that trouble just to let him go.' The talk was of de Angelis going. As it turned out, that didn't happen either.

But this needs to be said, and I am not contravening the Official Secrets Act when I say it: Nigel Mansell does not like Peter Warr.

Now 1982. Lotus had not won a race since 1978. Worse, they had no turbo engines and these, though not yet absolutely reliable, were giving a lot more power than the Cosworths. In a straight line the turbos were lovely and meaty and wished only for the other cars to get out of their way. Turbos no longer belonged to the future. The future was now.

Renault, Brabham and Ferrari had turbo engines. In the first race, South Africa, they filled the first two rows of the grid and the second, Brazil, the front row. The Cosworths would have to pant along behind them hoping they'd break down. Mansell finished third in Brazil – the winner, 36 seconds up the track was Prost, Renault turbo. Piquet (first) and Rosberg (second) were disqualified. Then he got nothing in Long Beach, nothing in Belgium. At Monaco, a place he always said he liked, he finished fourth a lap behind the leaders. Then Detroit nothing, Canada nothing except a badly hurt wrist in an accident. I met him for the first time in Canada. He sat subdued but sure of himself and said things like this:

'In a race I can sweat off half a stone. In Spain last year I lost 10 lbs. A day after the race I am absolutely shattered, drained. I have no more reserves to call on. My eyes are like sockets in the sand. I am battered to hell, I have bruises over my arms and legs. I've never raced and not had bruises. The main strain is the G-force on my neck – my neck is a size larger than it should be. It's muscle-bound now.' He stooped forward, deftly holding the collar of his shirt as if to demonstrate the point conclusively and added: 'Yes, the collar is one size bigger than it was a year ago.'

This was because of 'side-skirts', another of Chapman's ideas. It was absurdly simple and one more reason why Chapman was called, in hushed tones, a totally original thinker.

You put a thin strip, called a 'skirt', down each side of the car so that they trailed along the surface of the track. Air flowing at the car passed underneath but couldn't escape through the sides and this literally sucked the car to the road. Better, the faster you went the harder the suction. It allowed frightening speeds on corners – hence the G-forces which had enlarged Mansell's neck. His neck had developed automatically to cope with them. The bad news: suspensions were a disadvantage with 'skirts' and that made the ride in the car almost intolerably hard. 'Skirts' were finally banished because the corners on circuits couldn't cope with the speeds and worse, if a car took off for any reason, the skirt worked against it, making it into an aeroplane.

Mansell missed the Dutch Grand Prix – he hadn't recovered – and arrived at Brands Hatch for the British with his arm in a brace. He had had daily physiotherapy in a Birmingham hospital. 'Sometimes,' he said, 'the pain is unbelievable. I should have had a plaster cast on for another month.' Lotus sent the steering wheel of his car to the hospital so they could make a leather brace with a light-weight metal support – it covered the forearm to the knuckles. When he arrived at Brands he said, 'It is still extremely painful. I can't say just what will happen. I will have to see how it feels after a night's rest. I got a kick-back through the steering and the wrist was bent right back – which was the last thing I needed to happen.'

In the first session for the grid he was twenty-second and had to be helped from the car. He did race – and got nothing. Then, Germany nothing, Austria nothing, Swiss nothing, Italy nothing, Las Vegas nothing. If that reads like a barren journey, it was.

Towards the end of the Canadian interview – it was in one of those expensive hotels which cater exclusively to people with disconcerting hands of plastic cards, and seems curiously empty of spirit – I asked sheepishly if he wished he had a turbo engine rather than the faithful old Cosworth. His eyes altered at the mere suggestion of all that power the others had and he didn't; and it was answer enough.

It was also one reason why Team Lotus were struggling. Formula One is uniquely about winning (or trying to win) and if you're not, and the best chance you've got is that other cars will break down, you've a very discontented group – sorry, team – wandering the expensive hotels of the world.

And the friction? Peter Warr: 'The consistency of Elio was irking him. Elio was quicker but also more consistent because he drove his races to finish.' That de Angelis did finish was manifestly true. He had twenty-three points and was ninth in the championship, Mansell seven points, fourteenth.

Lotus did at last win a race that 1982 season, and thereby hangs a tale. Warr again: 'I have to say I know that Nigel thinks I was to blame a tremendous amount for his lack of progress or his lack of results but if you ask any of the 70-odd people who work at Team Lotus "Did he get exactly the same equipment?" they would say "yes". I went out and hired a second race engineer, he had his own set of mechanics, his own set of tyres and, in fact, the night before the race in Austria Elio had run out of engines. I went to Colin and I said: "Look, Elio's in bad shape, could we have one of Nigel's fresh engines to put in Elio's car?" Colin said "No, we agreed we'd give Nigel the same treatment and he'd have his own engines." '

In the race Mansell didn't finish. De Angelis held off Rosberg (Williams) in a desperate lunge for the line and got there first by a couple of feet or, if you can envisage fractions, 0.050 of a second. And that was the first win since 1978. Chapman flung his famous black cap in the air and set off running towards de Angelis, lost in the moment.

The result was deceptive. Lotus would require a major overhaul before they would win again and by then everything would have changed fundamentally and forever.

On 16 December 1982 Colin Chapman died of a heart attack.

Peter Warr inherited the running of the team. Months before his death Chapman had negotiated a deal with Renault to use their turbo engines in 1983. That, of itself, promised much but it created more friction. Renault initially could only supply enough engines for one car. Which driver would get them, Mansell or de Angelis?

To appreciate the full scale of this, you must understand quite why equal equipment means so much. You have two drivers in a team and both, by definition, are those very competitive beings we've spoken about before. The only way they can accurately measure how fast they are is against each other. McLaren, say, may have evolved some way of making their car go faster which is not available to you. So you can't compare yourself to a McLaren driver with absolute accuracy. His car is faster anyway. But your team-mate, the one you spend hours with at endless de-briefing sessions in the privacy of the motor home, the one who's always around and about you at race meetings – if his car is the same as yours, you're going to know who's quicker. No escape.

It makes for the most curious relationships and they are born of the closest personal conflict. It imposes great and often intolerable strain. And in the whole world of sport, it is certainly unique. No escape.

Warr says: 'We went into the Renault engine era and Renault could only give us engines for one car. And then a choice had to be made between whether Elio got them or Nigel got them. In fact, it wasn't Team Lotus or Peter Warr personally saying it; Renault said: "We feel de Angelis is the better and more consistent driver and we think he should have them." You don't argue.'

And in general terms, in the way things were going with Mansell, 'It didn't help.' And it may well be that after Chapman's death Mansell felt an understandable isolation.

Warr hired a Frenchman, Gerard Ducarouge, as chief engineer in June 1983. At that stage, after eight races, Team Lotus had a single point – Mansell had come sixth at Detroit.

Ducarouge knew his trade and knew, as part of his trade, the urgency of Formula One. He had trained at France's National Aeronautical Institute and worked on missile programmes before coming to motor racing in 1966. He was an integral part in French team Matra's victories in 1972, 1973 and 1974 at the famous and gruelling Le Mans 24-Hour race. In 1975 he had moved to Ligier in Formula One, had moved on to Alfa Romeo in 1981. It was the right pedigree and Warr allowed him the freedom he needed. OK, so his English – at first, anyway – was *Franglais*. So what? Formula One is international – and a drawing on a board is a drawing on a board.

Within five weeks Ducarouge had designed and Lotus had built an entirely new car. Even Formula One was astonished by that. (Joke at the time: At least we've kept the steering wheel the same.) It was ready exactly on the eve of the British Grand Prix at Silverstone. At last, at last a turbo engine beckoned to Nigel Mansell to see what he could do – and it sat nestled in a car which looked smaller, lighter, sleeker, faster.

On the Thursday, the first session for the grid, an electrical short-circuit hampered him and the mechanics worked straight through the night changing the engine and just about everything else they could think of. The mechanics finished at six in the morning and at seven the Renault engine was fired up, waking the vast tented village and Mansell himself. He was staying with his family in a caravan. The car was ready for this second day of qualifying. It was Friday. Bloody Friday. Before the session, the cars went out in the morning practice.

Mansell's car didn't complete a lap. The problem hadn't gone away. He had to take the spare car out to qualify eighteenth. The spare car. You know, the old car, the one with the Cosworth non-turbo engine . . .

The problem was traced to a faulty wiring loom and in the very best heroic traditions a message was dispatched to a small company in Diss, Norfolk: Make another one fast. They did, it was rushed to Silverstone and it was on the car for the race.

It worked.

Once more in his life Mansell had a little bit of something nobody can control – luck. Just after the end of the first lap de Angelis pulled limply off, his turbo on fire. Mansell was tenth then and, virtually handling the problems of a turbo engine for the first time – throttle lag, more speed – was moving up. By lap nine he was eighth, by lap seventeen, seventh, by lap thirty-two, fifth. And on lap forty-eight Mansell had one of the most magnificent moments of his career. At Club Corner he was swarming all over the famous Ferrari with René Arnoux in it. Arnoux was fast and uncompromising and would this season go all the way to the last race as a possible world champion.

They went down to the Abbey Curve in lock-step and were travelling through the left-hander which is 'flat'. That means you don't brake at all, you keep your foot flat down. Mansell jinked left, out from behind the Ferrari. James Hunt, commentating on British television, was saying wildly: *'Don't do it now, Nigel . . . wait . . . oh, he's done it.'* Mansell had. He was through and he was in fourth place.

He held that to the end. It was very, very emotional and he is a man who does not fear or conceal his emotions. The crowd swarmed and stampeded over the track to be near him. Women marshals were voting him 'Dish of the Day.' He gave interviews behind the pit, leaning against the wall of breeze blocks. His voice was heightened and he spoke in a strange, slow, artificial way as if he couldn't quite cope with it all – his fourth place, his emotions, and the interviews. Once I was sure he was going to cry and you couldn't have blamed him. In one sense, if he hadn't vindicated his career, he was closer to doing it. 'This,' he said, 'isn't the car of tomorrow . . . this is the car of the year. This year.'

'He was,' Warr says, 'on his way.' But after that, 'He started revealing a few flaws in his total make-up – which was that he made some mistakes and wasn't very honest with himself.' These are harsh words and they will be explored more fully later. They had implications, too.

Towards the end of the season – the second last race, in fact, the European Grand Prix at Brands Hatch – de Angelis put the Lotus on pole while Mansell was third fastest and on the second row of the grid. The race was sponsored by John Player and of course they sponsored the Lotuses, too. Perfect. Every dark-suited publicity person in the dubious Press Relations industry dreams – and I don't use the word carelessly – of such a conjunction of interests.

One way or another Britain was bathed in the name of John Player. Quite naturally the British daily press concentrated on Mansell's position rather than that of de Angelis. You may or may not agree with this judgement of news value; the motor racing follower would naturally be keenly interested in both men, the casual sports reader – outnumbering the former by hundreds to one – would be more interested in the Brit. Certainly the popular dailies reflected that. It saved Mansell, although he may not have been aware of that. Warr had a mind to replace him with the afore-mentioned Ayrton Senna, Brazilian, graced with the rarest skills. Senna had already been in Warr's office.

Warr opened the newspapers and the headlines screamed at him: *Mansell third*! 'John Player said we really ought to keep the Brit for 1984.'

Lotus kept the Brit.

Pit Stop

Late '83 and everyone was agreed Mansell had served his apprenticeship. He'd driven 43 races and won a total of 25 points. He'd been 3rd three times, 4th three times, 5th once, 6th twice. During your apprenticeship you are accorded a certain interest because, all else aside, you're out there on the track with the others at 200 mph and if you're not absolutely sure what you're doing in the car, that could have a very direct bearing on them. The apprentices represent the immediate future and when they're ready there's every chance they'll be looking for your drive. Sentiment is as rare as the milk of human kindness itself. You're out, he's in. Drivers are always in transition. Some are nearing the end of distinguished – or undistinguished – careers, some are in the solid middle years of achievement, some are just like you: trying to get there.

Late '83 and all the dramatis personae who would significantly affect Mansell were firmly in place for 1984 except one, and since they will all appear – even if fleetingly – hereafter, it is convenient and useful to examine them now with their curriculum vitaes. First, the missing man.

Ayrton Senna, then completing a season in Formula Three and already making people reach for extravagant adjectives. Brazilian. Born 21.3.60. During the season he had fought out an epic duel with Briton Martin Brundle ('We are not talking at the moment, but we have respect for each other and I admire him,' Brundle said). Of Senna, Dick Bennett, running the team, said 'He is really determined. I have never seen him touch alcohol.' Senna won the championship at Thruxton in late October and in 1984 would drive for the British Toleman team. Warr had already been watching him – fascinated. Later, Senna would say: 'The perfect lap? It's like tying your tie to get both ends exactly the same length. Practice tells you that you can do it, instinct tells you that you can do it – but you can't.'

Nelson Piquet: Brazilian. Born 17.8.52. Driving for Brabham.

Career began in Formula One in 1978. Ten wins, two world championships, 1981, 1983. He had just won that second championship in South Africa where he had been utterly laid back and had driven a calm, calculated, tactical race to finish third – all he needed. But was he laid back really? Once in Germany after a crash he'd clambered out of his Brabham and tried to kick and punch another driver.

Alain Prost. French. Born 24.2.55. Driving for Marlboro McLaren, who he had just joined from Renault. Career began in Formula One in 1980. Nine wins. Called the Professor because he was so clever on the track. The whole weight of France had been too heavy to carry in the run-up to the championship and he had ended it looking haunted and unshaven in South Africa where the Renault's engine went, giving it to Piquet. 'The perfect lap?' Prost would muse. 'You're always looking for it and when you think you've found it, you realise it's not perfect so you go out looking again.' He would also say: 'You never know if the hand slapping your back has a dagger in it.' At McLaren he would find . . .

Niki Lauda: Austrian. Born 22.2.49. Career began in Formula One in 1971. Nineteen wins, world champion 1975, 1977. Called The Rat, a term of endearment – this is Grand Prix racing – because his face looked that. (Joke for '84: Rats eat Frogs.) Survived one of the most horrible of all crashes in 1976, was given the Last Rites, recovered in weeks. In a car he was utterly controlled, precise, analytical. He would eye Prost, discover nothing sinister there at all and say so, adding only that Prost was a 'fast son of a bitch.'

Keke Rosberg: Finnish. Born 6.12.48. Driving for Williams Honda. Career began in Formula One in 1978. Two wins, world champion 1982. Classically combative, amusing or awkward, who thought about it all more profoundly than many. He would say typically: 'Being a professional is looking after your own bloody future. No one else is going to look after it for you.' He was always eminently capable of that.

Michele Alboreto: Italian. Born 23.12.56. He had just joined Ferrari from Tyrrell. Career began in Formula One in 1981. Two wins. Small, approachable, he had a schoolboy air and an elfin smile. He was now preparing for the Ferrari faithful to camp outside his Monte Carlo home day and night for a glimpse of him. He would say: 'I don't take taxis in Italy any more. The driver looks at me and tries to prove that he . . .'

Each of these men was different. Each of them was united in that they were driving against all the others – and Mansell.

5 Black and White

In an hotel room just off Hyde Park – it had been hired by the firm John Player Special used for handling motor racing publicity – Nigel Mansell was giving audiences. It was March 1984, only a few days before the first race of the season in Brazil. Audiences? The publicity firm were efficient and had invited lots of people: television, radio, local radio, women's magazines (the What-does-your-wife-cook-you-for-breakfast? interview), daily newspapers, Sunday newspapers, the specialist motoring magazines.

All have their own needs and so a general Press Conference is unsatisfactory. You cannot reasonably accommodate *Cosmopolitan* prying into your breakfast and *Motoring News* wondering what thoughts you have on the double-wishbone front suspension of the Lotus 95T. There is a cursory general Press Conference – TV likes that because it makes the thing look important, a stage, microphones, an audience – and the man himself says polite words and then he takes the lift up to the room and you book your five minutes with him.

In that room Mansell looked like a man so primed and ready to race that he could barely contain it. At moments he was speaking so fast that it became – nearly – an inspired gabble. The urgency of what he had to say was overwhelming him.

Listen:

'I think it is going to be a fantastic year because I've got vigour back, I've got enthusiasm, I've got the dedication, I've got the will and if you'd seen me training . . . I'm really fighting, I hope it is going to be the sunshine of my life . . . I've had three third places in my career, not fantastic, not bad either . . . we don't know if we will have reliability or the element of luck but it's going to take a lot to stop me if I get going . . . part of the job is coping with pressure, pressure doesn't worry me in the slightest, I think I perform better under a lot of pressure than none at all . . . what frightens me is not being successful, not measuring up to my own standards . . . that frightens me . . . but I am going to measure up.'

New seasons breed new hope (or you shouldn't be doing it at all) and this season bred more hope than any before. Lotus had unveiled their new Ducarouge car in December – a different hotel for that, but you get the idea – they had moved from Pirelli to Michelin for tyres, an important move and the right move, and they had Renault turbo power for both Mansell and de Angelis. The package seemed perfectly capable of winning races. Once the usual and tedious rumours of driver changes had died – this time it was John Watson for Mansell – he had only to concentrate on getting fit and getting ready.

But those words in that room would become like a handful of broken glass: sharp enough to break your heart. The year 1984 would be bitter, with undercurrents of unrest and unhappiness running all through it.

All this would start at the beginning: the Jacarepagua circuit near Rio. Peter Warr says: 'He made a mistake when he was lying third and we had carbon fibre brakes on and all the journalists were watching at that corner and they saw him fly off. Yet he came back to the pits and blamed the brakes. That had the effect that, because we had a report from the driver that the brakes were no good, we took them off the car and didn't put them on for the rest of the season. And that was, in fact, one of the half-second advantages McLaren had that season.'

Mind you, not all drivers come back – it's a long walk – and blame themselves. What did happen? On lap thirty-six Mansell was battling hard to keep Patrick Tambay (Renault) at bay, got off line and went into the catch-fencing.

The next race, South Africa, confirmed that Mansell and the Lotus were at least quick. He'd been on the third row in Brazil and now he was on the second. In the race he was fifth when he lost boost from the turbo (officially, a problem with the turbo inlet duct) and retired on lap fifty-two.

At Zolder he was on the fifth row of the grid. From the very start he was hampered by a slipping clutch and completed lap one in sixteenth place. By lap seven he was up to fourteenth but the next lap the clutch problem grew worse and he retired on lap sixteen.

At Imola, a scenic circuit in mid-Italy used to host the San Marino Grand Prix (San Marino, small principality down the road and a convenient title to give Italy a second Grand Prix; the real one is at Monza), he was on the ninth row after two horrors in qualifying. Jo Gartner, an Austrian making his debut, flew over his front wheels and left paint from his Osella along the flank of the Lotus and the next day a slower car suddenly moved across him forcing him, rotating wildly, onto the grass. (Always watch out for the apprentices.) In the race, on lap two, he braked hard, part of the brake broke and he went off . . .

That was a quarter of the season gone – already.

He flew to Dijon in a small plane. An unremarkable journey for a man like Mansell. It was 'buzzed' by a Mirage of the French Air Force which came very close indeed on its own racing line – apparently a mix-up over flight plans had brought it up to have a sniff round. The British within the plane were properly stoic and the pilot's young daughter took charming pictures of the Mirage through the porthole window.

At Dijon Mansell got on with the race. He put the Lotus on the third row of the grid and at last it went the distance. At the end of lap one, he was behind Tambay and de Angelis and soon enough Mansell himself was having a sniff round. De Angelis was less than charming, as he had every right to be, and shut the door firmly a couple of times. This was to be, in all senses, a proper race. Lauda was coming. Prost was coming. On lap fourteen Prost took Mansell and on lap seventeen Lauda took him. Warwick was now behind Mansell and Prost was in trouble. The two Englishmen began to duel and it was becoming captivating when, on lap fifty-four, they came upon a slower car which dutifully moved over. Mansell thrust the Lotus through, Warwick braked, locked up, slid, went off, taking the slower car with him.

Mansell kept on, as he was always going to keep on, and took the third place. Better than that, he wasn't at all far off the pace as the cars crossed the line. Lauda one hour 31 minutes 11.951 seconds, Tambay 1: 31. 19.105, Mansell 1: 31. 35.920. It was no time to celebrate. Unbeknown to almost everybody else, his mother had died and he would leave the circuit immediately to attend her funeral.

Then Monaco. It is an unforgiving place. In the first session for the grid he simply couldn't find a clear run to set a fast time; before the second session he crashed with Arnoux; the engine of his spare car wasn't right in the final session – it stopped at the tunnel up on the hill and he had to run back to try his newly repaired race car. 'I knew I would only have one good crack at it,' he said. He did have one good crack at it. Glorious, it was. Golden, it was, to accord with the livery of the Lotus. Prost was fastest of all, Mansell a whisker behind him (1 minute 22.661 against 1 minute 22.752). He was on the front row next to Prost.

63

And on race day it rained. Prost, his tyres cutting plumes of spray, took the lead, Mansell following. On lap eleven Prost was hopelessly hampered by a crashed Brabham in the middle of the road and Mansell was through. He was leading a Grand Prix for the first time in his life. It was to last five laps and when it was over beg the nastiest, most uncomfortable question: Was Mansell a winner or a loser?

You need to appreciate the special qualities – or more accurately the special disadvantages – of Monaco, particularly, as on this afternoon, in the wet. Monaco is deceptive. There are yachts for hire in the harbour and all you need is a loan from the International Monetary Fund to secure one for the week-end; there are topless women on their decks who might or might not be French film actresses; there are droves of normally dark-suited PR persons who here, chameleons, mill and jostle in tee-shirts or safari uniforms nursing uniform hangovers from the Tip Top Club. There is also, threaded through all this like a ribbon, a circuit which uses ordinary streets and is hemmed by metal barriers. If you make the smallest error you hit the metal and you get to Nice Airport before all the others because you're out of the race. In the wet, it's difficult *not* to make an error.

Mansell, leading, had no particular need to hurry. Prost was somewhere back there but overtaking, even if he drew up behind, would be all but impossible. Monaco is too narrow, it's almost all corners, and you can block the car behind comfortably for an hour if you want. That's in the dry. In the wet, when you're trying to peer through the plumes of spray the car in front is flinging at you, forget it.

Mansell led until lap fifteen. It was intoxicating, it was moments many people had waited years to see. Only the hardened, sanguine observers noted that Mansell was pulling away from Prost far, far faster than he needed to: at a rate of almost two seconds a lap.

On that lap fifteen Mansell came through the corner at Sainte Devote just past the pits and went up the rise towards the Casino on the hill. On the way up the car seemed to touch the white marking in the middle of the road – the ordinary, unremarkable line you get on any ordinary, unremarkable road – and was pitched into a semi-spin against the metal.

Welcome to Nice Airport. Have a nice flight home.

What really happened is still a matter of dispute in the closed and claustrophobic world of Formula One, where arguments still rage about the smallest moments in battles long ago. Was Mansell really

64

pushing too hard in the wet? The theory of the white line was treated with some derision. The subsequent photographic image of him sitting on the metal barrier, head bowed, the Lotus directly in front of him, left rear tyre hopelessly deflated . . . that told the whole story of his life, didn't it?

Constant replays on video convince me that the Lotus certainly touched the white line and that hardly helped. Immediately after the race Mansell said, 'I did make an error but that error was about three inches on a piece of white on the road with no grip (paint, of course, is smooth) and the conditions were so bad that even a good driver cannot get a racing car back. You're just in trouble.'

Mansell could – but did not – point out that the journalists who would castigate him had been sheltering in their press room out of the rain, not driving the car in conditions like these. As in all things, the judges don't commit the crime, they only judge it.

Mansell could – but did not – point out that conditions were so bad the race had to be stopped after 31 laps, Prost gesticulating from his cockpit to stop the damned thing *now*. Or that of the twenty drivers who started, only nine would be still churning round when, mercifully, the damned thing was stopped.

If he felt the world was against him, maybe he had his reasons . . .

He was sixth in Canada and everybody journeyed down to Detroit, like Monaco a street circuit. Here you don't hit metal, you hit concrete blocks. Welcome to Detroit Airport.

Within split seconds of the start, it went desperately wrong. In the first session for the grid he'd been quickest, in the second session still quick enough to put the Lotus on the second row. Let's look at the geography of that. He had Piquet directly in front of him, Prost to the front and the right; he had Alboreto alongside him. As the light went to green, Mansell aimed between Piquet and Prost – it is this moment and these risks which can give a man the lead, it is a legitimate thing to do if there is room to do it. You only find out if there's room afterwards.

The Lotus wobbled slightly as its snout bored into the gap and it brushed against Prost's car. With the ferocious acceleration – 0–60 in under two seconds – this brushing is enough to disturb the equilibrium of both cars. The Lotus lurched away into Piquet. Instant mayhem.

Piquet's car was flung helplessly across the track, left and then right, ramming Alboreto's Ferrari with his rear. These two hit the concrete wall – about waist high – with shirt-sleeved spectators behind it. As they struck, bits of bodywork, furious debris, were scattered over the wall and people turned away, heads dipped, arms shielding their eyes as if they were suddenly under fire. Now, with nowhere to go, Marc Surer (Arrows) came into Piquet, jarring Piquet's neck. Astonishingly nobody was badly hurt.

Mansell went quietly down to the waterside and sat on a concrete mooring-post under a parasol, gazing across at peaceful, sleepy Windsor in Canada on the other side of the Detroit River, and waited for the re-start. He was scarcely a man to be unnerved by what had happened. He went to the re-start and was running second behind Piquet when, on lap twenty-five, he lost second gear and retired two laps further on.

(A month later FISA's executive committee fined Mansell six thousand dollars for dangerous driving and did the equivalent of putting him on probation. They didn't take his licence away subject to his future behaviour. It was, I suppose, in ordinary human terms like an endorsement for speeding.)

Two weeks after that everyone had moved to Dallas for the first Grand Prix there. Being Dallas, the preceding publicity was enormous and entirely predictable, just as the actual build-up to the actual race was. The problems: the drivers strongly objected to how bumpy the track was, that the run-off areas weren't enough. And there were those concrete blocks, à la Detroit.

Mansell put the Lotus on pole and de Angelis was there beside him on the front row. This had not happened to the team since the Dutch Grand Prix in 1978.

But the track was breaking up. That such a thing could come to pass may appear absurd but very little prepares newcomers to circuit building for the destructive power of Formula One cars whose wheels churn along impelled by over a thousand horse power, especially when the temperature is edging ever nearer to a hundred degrees. That alone softens surfaces. An hour before the race, fresh concrete was being laid. Only an hour before the race . . .

There was talk of a driver boycott . . . shortening the race . . . postponing it. Formula One lives by images, sedulously created by clever people. In Dallas, of all places, that went terribly wrong. The race went on, as they generally do. (Factual footnote: only one race in modern times hasn't gone on, Belgium, 1985, when they'd relaid the surface of the track and you could pull chunks out with your hands. Very little prepares *oldcomers* for the destructive power of . . .)

From the green light Mansell took the lead and as they crossed

66

the line to complete lap one, de Angelis was behind him, Warwick third, but the engine in de Angelis's car wasn't running smoothly and by lap four Warwick had him. Warwick was with Renault and Renault were a formidable team. The expectation was that Warwick could become the first British world champion since Hunt. Here was a chance to make a move towards that.

On lap eleven Warwick ducked out and ran along the outside of Mansell into a right-hand corner. To get to the corner first – and consequently get himself back on the racing line – Warwick had to be completely past Mansell and he never did quite get that far. He was half a car's length clear and the corner was rushing at him. He touched the brakes and – was it the surface which betrayed him? – swerved across Mansell's front but travelling so fast that he simply skimmed away from Mansell sideways into a tyre barrier. Mansell, untouched, was still in the lead.

De Angelis, engine running smoothly now, attacked but Mansell held him off and, further down the race, Rosberg would attack, too, swarming all over Mansell but not getting past. Rosberg was not happy about this. Mansell clipped a wall and that was all Rosberg needed to nip by. Mansell came back at him but now Rosberg blocked and, as he did, shook his fist at Mansell. Mansell drifted away with tyre troubles and at the end glanced a wall again, finishing the gearbox. He got out and tried to push the car over the line. In the heat he collapsed. While he was being taken to the medical centre, Rosberg attacked him over the public address system for 'unprofessional driving.'

Mansell said: 'I just felt I had to get the car across the finishing line. I started to push it and then it was as if someone had turned out all the lights. I don't know how long I was unconscious.'

Warr was less than pleased. 'He collapsed in a big heap and was a hero and the stories were full of what a hero he was, but he only had to push it because he bounced it off the wall and broke the rear of it.'

Mansell could – but didn't – point out that of the twenty-six cars which set off sixteen failed to finish and the reason is given neatly and cryptically for twelve of those: Hit wall. As at Monaco, the judges didn't commit the crime and, fully understanding the perspective of 12 out of 26 hitting the walls, I say it again: if he felt the world was against him, maybe he had his reasons.

Four races later – he scored points in one of them, fourth, Hockenheim, West Germany – the travelling circus was in Zandvoort, a most agreeable seaside spa where the circuit snakes through dunes and a strong wind from the North Sea drags sand on to it and occasionally the locals complain about the noise.

Normally that most interesting aspect of the circus, the magic roundabout, starts rotating the race before, in Austria. It is there that drivers begin to sound out the possibilities of joining other teams for the following season and these drivers can be seen, by experienced observers who know the strategic places to sit, entering or leaving other teams' motor-homes after brief, or not-so-brief, exploratory talks. In the weeks after Austria we all get to know who's got off what and onto what on the magic roundabout. This was now Holland and the roundabout was, as they say, in full swing.

What we got, in fact, was a taste of farce.

On the Saturday prior to the final qualifying session, Lotus had a proper sit-down luncheon for the Press. The food was excellent but difficult to digest. Warr announced that Lotus had signed Senna for 1985 and presented each journalist with a properly presented description of all this. (Technical note: It's called a Press Kit.) Toleman, the team which had given Senna his chance in Formula One, believed that they had him under a most binding contract and just beyond the canvas walls of the luncheon area – it was under an awning against the Lotus motor-home – their publicity man tried to listen and hissed through: 'Remember what's being said in there, I want to know afterwards.'

Further away Alex Hawkridge, the Toleman team manager, paced to and fro murmuring incandescent threats about legal action. Then Mansell came in under the awning and he knew we knew it was over. He looked at us – a look was quite enough – and went into the motor-home itself. The door closed. It was almost symbolic. It had closed on him. For a long and awkward moment none among the journalists – hardened men, let us say, men who had reported other men dying in racing cars – had any idea what to say. Small talk would have been obscene.

In the race itself Mansell was third – ahead of de Angelis. He'd started it on the sixth row of the grid, de Angelis on the second. He worked his way slowly up, and on lap fifty-two, while de Angelis was flirting with overtaking Rosberg, Mansell overtook *him*. It must have been a sweet moment.

Jean Sage, a leading member of the Renault team and a most civilised man – who had no particular interest in this move on the magic roundabout and consequently can be seen as an impartial observer – smiled in his own wry way:

'They tell Mansell they don't want him and then he goes and drives like that . . .'

Warr, who is not the best understood of men by people who sit in judgement on *him*, says: 'Nigel had developed, he was getting faster but we had to make a difficult choice. In the end, because I was convinced, I managed to convince everybody else that Senna was the man we really ought to have and one of them had to go. It was my lot to tell Nigel we weren't going to renew his contract. In motor racing you can't build programmes and packages without people getting to hear about it so he had some advance notice of things going on. He didn't take it badly.' (In time, Warr would construct the whole team around Senna – it was a logical move or a gambler's throw, depending on your viewpoint. Certainly, if Mansell had stayed and de Angelis been sacrificed, this would have been intolerable to him. In time, de Angelis would be sacrificed, anyway, and Warr vilified as much as Mansell had ever been. When the magic roundabout starts rotating, some change places, some get flung off.)

And, yes, Mansell took it with considerable dignity, although his aptitude for seeming to moan even when he was happy might have masked that.

I happened to be in the Bowes Hotel that evening – it's in Zandvoort itself, a brisk walk from the track, and slightly olde worlde rather than plastic money. It's where the drivers instinctively stay because of its proximity – and Mansell was sitting on a barstool sipping a soft drink. He doesn't need alcohol, even when he has to watch his own world breaking up. Through the window the North Sea tossed breakers. Somewhere – is it a trick of memory? – piped music moaned and meandered. I don't remember the conversation, although it was as awkward as the lunch had been. But I do remember thinking: This is a man who won't give up. It was hardly an original thought. For a decade he hadn't given up. He had been humiliated, physically damaged, he had cleaned windows, he had known the (masculine) agony of watching his wife support him while he spent *that* money on a very expensive ego-trip with no assurances except that he might again be humiliated, physically damaged; and a total failure. He had sweated for his precious moments and, in the round, they were meagre in number and scope. Perhaps only he and his wife thought they were precious at all.

But give up? He was the sort of bloke who was never going to give up, anyway.

The rest of 1984 drifted into anti-climax. He spun off in Italy after thirteen laps, his engine blew after fifty-one laps at the Nurburgring in the Grand Prix of Europe and if his fate was largely

69

unlamented, it was also largely unnoticed. Lauda was challenging Prost for the championship and Lauda had come back to the Nurburgring – where he had almost died in 1976. It was not the same Nurburgring, it had been rebuilt so comprehensively – and with, incidentally, the aid of Lauda and computers and ultimate safety in mind – that any passing resemblance to the rolling, undulating, turbulent old circuit was an insult.

Prost won, Lauda fourth.

When Mansell's engine blew he did what most drivers do in the situation. He sprang out amidst billowing smoke and showed the hesitant fire marshal exactly where to point the extinguisher. Much ado about nothing.

One race remained of this 1984 season, at Portugal. The McLarens had dominated all of 1984 and now either Prost or Lauda would be world champion. If Prost won the race but Lauda finished second, Lauda got it by half a point. That is an impossibly dry mathematical way of setting the scene for a mere race which would inevitably become something vastly more.

Lauda, savagely burnt at the Ring in 1976, had been an emotive presence ever since. In the world at large – you know, that strange one beyond the claustrophobia of Formula One – he was arguably the only current driver just about everybody had heard of and would, if only because of the burning which still showed on his face, be instantly recognised.

If there is genuine mythology in Formula One, that October day at the Autodromo do Estoril, just inland from the holiday resorts, Lauda *was* its mythology. And it got more poignant as the meeting unfolded and the mathematics changed in the most subtle way. Prost was on the front row of the grid, Lauda lost and abandoned on the sixth row. Lauda was going to have to go a bit. He would have seventy laps to do it.

Prost took the lead on lap nine, Lauda ninth. But Lauda had driven 157 races before this and he was working out his own equations, risk balanced against risk. He owned an airline. He owned his own mind. He was his own man, win or lose. No external force could influence him, no pressure could be brought to bear except the pressure he himself wished to have imposed. He would not permit anything else.

(Before the race, drivers had milled nervously in the presence of this event. One of them said, 'Would you want to be the man to get in Lauda's way? Or wouldn't you get out of his way and let him go into history, you know, into *history*?' Senna had said, 'I won't get out

70

of his way.' Lauda himself would have appreciated, and expected, that. He might not have done it himself to another in the same circumstances, but he would have understood the reasoning. And now you know why Peter Warr would construct a whole team around Senna. No disrespect to Mansell.)

But the race, set amongst the barren hills of an unremarkable piece of land within hailing distance of the beaches . . . the race was being run. Prost led. So Lauda required second place and second place was firmly occupied by Nigel Mansell. This was still only lap twelve. The logic and symmetry of Niki Lauda and a racing car were to be restated: lap thirteen, eighth; lap eighteen, seventh; lap twenty-seven, sixth; lap twenty-eight, fifth; lap thirty-one, fourth; lap thirty-three, third.

He was thirty seconds behind Mansell and that second place. Worse, he was moving in amongst back-markers. They might try and get out of the way of history but it wasn't that kind of track. Getting out of the way wasn't easy – you know, corner following corner and you have to have your car somewhere and you can't be seen to be surrendering completely, and limply, and lamely, not you, not a *racing* driver. You do your best discreetly to allow the passage of history.

Mansell, half a minute up there beyond the back markers, held the fate of the world championship. How absurd. How absurdly cruel that a man whose fate was unlamented and unnoticed should now, going about his legitimate business, have become extremely noticed because he was getting in the way.

Lauda, third.

Mansell, second.

Prost, still leading.

The symmetry. Lauda coming, but too far away. He was going to lose it on the mathematics, even if he ever got through the back-markers trying to get out of his way.

Mansell spun. The television cameras didn't catch it and the photographers didn't catch it. But he spun. His brakes had gone somewhere out there at the back of the circuit and he'd spun. Lap-charters waited for him to come round and noticed that he was late. They didn't know what had happened but he was late.

He crept round the right-hander feeding on to the long straight in front of the pits – it was lap fifty-two, not that that matters – and turned into the entrance to the pit lane. He cruised that. He came to rest at his own pit. He stepped out of the black and gold Lotus for the very last time.

As he did, shaking his head with bemusement, Lauda went

cleanly and clearly down the long straight, unencumbered, free, in perfect control – went into the second place Mansell had just had to vacate to him, settled himself there, stayed there, circling long behind Prost. It was enough. Niki Lauda, world champion, 1984. Everybody was emotional about it – including his wife who had broken the habits of a lifetime to be here, charming, concerned – everybody except Niki Lauda. He grinned his toothy grin and said things about helping Prost to do it next season, and grinned his toothy grin and nobody knew what he really thought. He certainly did, we didn't. He didn't tell us. He was never going to do that.

Mansell, unlamented, unnoticed, was close to tears though not for Lauda – who required nobody else's tears. He still hadn't finished higher than third. He was thirty, which was – and is – old for starting again.

The Autodromo do Estoril. He went quietly away.

6   The Key and the Door

Jackie Stewart, thrice world champion and arguably the most articulate sportsman of all, sat one day explaining it patiently: winning motor races is like having a bunch of keys. One of those keys opens the door and you must first find it among all the others, *then* you must know precisely the feel of turning it, *then* you must remember *how* to turn it.

In Formula One, of course, there are many, many keys in everyone's bunch. Each track is different, each shifting moment in a race is different, there's the complexity of the car itself, there's the tyres to worry about, there's the fuel limitation to worry about, there's the mental arithmetic of where every other driver is on the circuit, who's coming at you, who's dropping back, who's likely to move over to let you through, who's got a history of *moving over* in front of you at all the wrong moments, there's your own state of mind. Endless keys on the bunch.

Winning? Alain Prost, *before* he beat Stewart's all-time total of wins, twenty-seven, also explained it patiently: 'I know when I'm going fast because everything seems *slow* and I look *slow* . . . when I look fast I'm hurrying too much, I'm not neat, and I'm actually going *slower*.'

Mansell had negotiated with the Williams team in late August 1984. An announcement was made on 10 September that he had signed a two-year contract. His career, which might conceivably have been over when Lotus didn't want him any more, was now safe until the end of 1986. As Warr had said: 'He was in trouble for a while.'

Now he had a drive and it was a very good drive. Williams knew all about winning. Since 1973, when they had entered Formula One, they had had two world champions, Alan Jones (1980) and Rosberg (1982). The question was: could Mansell ever win a race let alone a championship? He had driven 59 times for Lotus between 1980 and 1984 and hadn't finished higher than third. Memories of Monaco wouldn't go away. He had seemed to hold the right key in his hand. He hadn't.

Frank Williams believed he could win races and once when I asked him about that he gave me a hard, almost severe stare which said: Of course I believed it. How dare you pose a question like that? (Two years later, in an interview with a Press agency, he would expand on this: 'When he signed Nigel it was as a good team man and a good journeyman who would pick up points and win some races.')

Both Mansell and Williams had known the intensity and loneliness of struggle and that united them. As a school boy Williams had hitch-hiked to races and when he left school he went to a track and saw a man working on a car. The man casually handed him a spanner and, 'I had begun in the business'.

By 1973 he had his own Formula One team and was building cars. In one of them his friend Piers Courage was killed at Zandvoort and Williams had to ask himself most profoundly: Can I go on with this? It is not a new question but it is an extremely complicated one and each man must find his own answer. Williams decided to go on.

He found hard times. When the telephone was cut off at his Reading factory – unpaid bills – he made calls from public boxes. Like Mansell he wasn't the sort of bloke to be beaten by things like that. By 1978 he achieved a genuine and major coup by getting Saudi Arabian Airlines – not a company, we must assume, short of cash flow – as a sponsor. And in 1978 he hired a rugged, ambitious Australian, Jones, as his only driver. There were good vibrations that year. Jones had already set the fastest lap at Long Beach and, in the second last race, finished second at Watkins Glen. In the last race, Canada, he set fastest lap again.

The next year Williams hired Clay Regazzoni, a very experienced Swiss, to partner Jones and it all came right at once like a thunderclap. Regazzoni won the British at Silverstone. Jones won the next race – West Germany – with Regazzoni second. Jones won the race after that – Austria – with Regazzoni fifth. Jones won the race after that – Holland – and again in Canada, Regazzoni third. Williams were second to Ferrari in the Constructors' Championship, 75 points to 113, and Jones himself was third in the Drivers' Championship, Regazzoni fifth.

In 1980 Jones had total momentum. He won five races, came second in three and took the world championship by a distance, 67 points against Piquet's 54. The Brazilian was then with Brabham. He knew, of course, Mansell from Formula Three days. No doubt in the Austrian Grand Prix of that year, 1980, he had looked with a knowing eye towards the very back of the grid and seen a third Lotus there, perhaps even seen Mansell within it. Formula One drivers note details like that. They could be, often are, important later on.

Jones left in 1981, to be replaced by Rosberg and in 1982 Rosberg was champion, this same Rosberg who, in 1984 at Dallas, had publicly blasted Mansell, this same Rosberg who now, going into 1985, had Mansell as his partner at Williams. There was much speculation about how two such men might co-exist, if at all. This had been unmercifully fuelled at the very last race of 1984 – Portugal – when, for the briefest of moments, something had happened which had distracted everyone from watching Lauda win the championship. Rosberg's Williams and Mansell's Lotus had been going into a corner together and they had banged wheels hard. Maybe it was a normal, unremarkable incident, the sort of thing which does happen in races. Maybe they were giving each other messages, loud and clear.

Rosberg would subsequently write that privately he liked Mansell. 'My objections to Nigel were purely professional. The team was already under considerable stress and I felt Nigel would bring to the team a new factor which was only likely to increase that stress.' And: 'The one time I was asked my opinion by Frank about taking on Mansell, the discussion was perfectly calm and open. Frank asked his Number One driver (Rosberg, of course) what he thought, and I told Frank what I thought. Frank listened to me and I'm sure he understood what I was saying. "You'll get along," he said, "it won't be a problem." '

So Mansell went to the factory at Didcot and saw there the beautiful beast they had waiting for him. It was 8 ft long, it sat an inch and a half off the ground. Its total weight was six times his own. Eight seat-belts would hold him rigidly because if, in the words of a Williams spokesman, 'he could move more than half an inch in the seat he would risk breaking his rib-cage.'

He would wear, of course, flame-proof undergarments (the same spokesman: 'Most drivers are naked beneath them except for a tee-shirt because it's macho like that.'). He would have a telephone in the car, actually a two-way car-to-pits radio which was a microphone built into his helmet allowing him to speak whenever he pressed a button on the steering wheel.

He would have six forward gears, the gear nob shaped into the palm of his hand and he would be able to change those gears like a gunfighter, as fast as the hand could move.

As he sat his feet would be an inch and a half from the tip of the nose-cone, and this nose-cone would be made of a compound giving absolute strength: a layer of carbon, a layer of kevlar, a layer of nomex honeycomb, another layer of kevlar, another layer of carbon, the whole heat-treated until it had become a laminate as hard as rock.

And then there was the factory itself. A total of ninety-five people worked there and on a conducted tour once, the same spokesman – surveying the banks of high-tech machinery, the body-shop, the wind-tunnel, the computers churning out their calculations – said in sudden astonishment: 'You've got to remember that all this is just to produce our racing cars – we don't produce anything else here . . .'

('The mechanics are a very, very strange breed of person. They have to be prepared to work up to seven days a week and up to eighteen hours a day for a relatively small salary. Good race mechanics don't often make good mechanics on ordinary cars. They're too specialised. They are very good at improvisation but they are even better at thinking quickly and working quickly without rushing things.')

Within the factory, Patrick Head designed the cars while in an adjoining factory – but screened off – Honda put the engines together. This may seem bizarre but Formula One is obsessively secret about its secrets, even when they're sharing them with you.

Williams himself was the steady hand on the wheel. He was almost fanatically dedicated to fitness – he had an abhorrence of smoking and drinking – and used to change to shorts on the evenings of race meetings and jog round the track. He spoke with the articulation of a well-educated man and in securing sponsorship – without which you can't really go racing at all – he had the touch of Midas himself.

By 1985 he had the camera company Canon as a sponsor as well as the jean company Denim. The car was actually called the Canon-Williams-Honda.

Williams was a man constantly on the move. He once calculated how many hours a year he spent in aeroplanes and it was a *staggering* amount. (He also gave a celebrated interview to a motoring magazine, where he outlined all the aspects of what he called The Fear of Falling – not from aeroplanes, of course, but falling from the top, falling from grace.) At bottom he was a perfectionist – you hear the word a lot, but it really did apply to him – and the ninety-five people at Didcot, Oxfordshire were there to ensure it. He knew them and they knew him as he moved constantly among them, watching, monitoring, advising. He knew, too, how important the winning was to their morale, collectively and individually, even the ones who

76

didn't go to races, he knew the sort of banter they got in the pub when the team lost races. He knew the banter hurt.

That hand on the wheel was steady enough to avoid any possible problems with the Honda workforce – who were, of course, Japanese, locked into another culture and another language, both difficult to penetrate, but who, in the heat of the battle of race meetings, would have to blend imperceptibly with his own people. He had secured Honda engines by 1983 and now, going into 1985, Mansell's first season with Williams, the Sino-Didcot entente was functioning smoothly. Frank Williams was too worldly and too shrewd to have permitted anything else and the subsequent differences were scarcely of his making.

Mansell himself was living in the Isle of Man in some splendour, a hilltop house with a magnificent view of the sea. Electrically operated gates opened onto a curving drive flanked by more than three hundred conifer trees. Rosanne had a full-time nanny to help with the children, Chloe and Leo. There was a general help, too, and a full-time gardener. There was an indoor swimming pool (remember?) with a handy 18-knot current to swim against; plus those little knick-nacks which do make life more tolerable; a gymnasium, sun room, whirlpool bath. Mansell used them and used them hard because he understood the necessity of being fit. Perhaps memories of the garage and the blown-up photographs of Brands Hatch, 1977 hadn't gone away. But fitness? Frank would appreciate that.

If you are tempted to wonder how a racing driver who hadn't finished higher than third could afford all this, you must pause and reflect. Nobody truly knows how much money is awash in Formula One, but it comes in big waves on every tide. It comes from sponsors who get their names on the cars and in certain cases (if they pay enough) who get the cars jointly called after themselves. Hence Canon-Williams-Honda. Someone has done this calculation: over a year 650 hours of race coverage reach 935 million people in 41 countries because of television. If you're a sponsor, especially a multinational sponsor, the odd few million dollars you put into a team are in the nature of a bargain for global exposure 16 races a year. You can't really buy this sort of exposure any other way. It is very nearly beyond money.

The drivers operate a free market economy, which is a polite way of saying they take from the market what the market will stand, and the market will stand plenty – well over a million dollars per annum upwards if he's a top driver before he's started to sell advertising space on his own person: helmet, gloves, overalls, and the rest. This has

77

reached a point where a motor racing columnist much given to the wry comment wondered aloud if Rosberg was selling space on his pyjamas . . .

At some point you get your mansion in the Isle of Man or its equivalent some place else and it is not at all unusual for drivers to have three homes. (Monte Carlo is a favoured haunt for one home = tax relief = sunshine = proximity to Nice Airport to move around.) Are the drivers worth it? Leaving aside the market economy – and Formula One *is* capitalism – every driver risks his life every time he gets into the car. The list of those who have died is monstrously long and however much a driver may exclude such thoughts from his mind and his mental processes, it is there, a sort of subdued spectre which can never go completely away.

In taking the risk the driver earns the money and if you object to that either get in a car yourself or have a look at the list: Bob Anderson, Elio de Angelis, Alberto Ascari, Lorenzo Bandini, Carel de Beaufort, Jean Behra, Stefan Bellof, Lucien Bianchi, Felice Bonetto, Jo Bonnier, Jimmy Bryan, Eugenio Castellotti, François Cevert, Jimmy Clark . . .

Drivers seek solace and seclusion when they aren't actually driving. Piquet goes home to Brazil and fishes, if he chooses not to go back to Monte Carlo; Jacques Laffite is a rare and wonderful sight in airport arrival areas uncertainly clutching his tall bag of fishing rods; Prost plays golf and so does Mansell. He is good. That is partly steadiness of hand, partly co-ordination, partly a desire to beat the course and his opponents. He hints (darkly) that he'd like to play in the British Amateur Championship. After a round with him, Peter Alliss – no less – said: 'His grip, certainly, is not classic. The Mansell stance is a bit wide, too, rather on the quarter-to-three side of ten-to-two. But the hand and eye co-ordination is something to marvel at, and his inborn nerve and competitiveness shine through when he has to play the shot.' He is so well-known in the Isle of Man that in knock-out competitions the club secretaries are apt to be flexible about when he plays, so that he can still race the cars.

He flies helicopters. He is going for a pilot's licence, which means he can't fly unaccompanied yet. This private flying is quite normal to a Formula One driver. Some have their own aeroplanes and Lauda a whole airline. Others satisfy themselves with choppers they can land on the back lawn. If you feel a compulsion to move all the time, what could be more convenient than that?

But racing is the hard edge, the place you're invariably flying back to.

The 1985 season began in Brazil and on the first day of qualifying Mansell was eighth quickest, on the second day fourth quickest. It put him on the third row of the grid. He wasn't taking long to get used to the new car. He made a tremendous start in the race and going into the very first corner, a right-hander, was in the act of passing one of the Ferraris, driven by Alboreto.

This moment typifies so much of Formula One. Was the corner his or was it Alboreto's? Opinions generally differ – the relative angles of the cars in relation to the corner are all but impossible to establish *finitely*. Opinion does not assert itself but reality does. The Ferrari glanced the kerbing, returned and struck Mansell's rear wheel. Mansell was briefly airborne. He got the car back onto the track – last now – and set off again but on lap nine the exhaust pipe broke and that was that. Alboreto said: 'Mansell is crazy. He should know by now that you do not try to win the race on the first corner.'

Perhaps Alboreto should have known that, too . . .

The next race, Portugal, belonged entirely to Senna who, in a thunderstorm, took his Lotus to victory without making a mistake. This thunderstorm had broken before the race and drivers had been given some laps to get used to the conditions. Mansell went off – trying to clear a misfire, he gave the accelerator a good, hard dab and spun. He damaged the nose-cone. Once this had been replaced he had to begin the race from the pit-lane.

It meant starting at the back after the grid had set off. It is this sort of situation which makes Mansell go and he went. After ten laps he reached ninth place and this when it was almost impossible to see. By lap twenty-two he was up to seventh. He finished fifth but even then awful irony tried to claim him. He was a lap behind Senna. As Senna approached the line to win the race, Mansell was coming up to him. Senna slowed, Mansell jinked right where he saw somewhere through all the spray the Lotus mechanics swarming over the pit lane wall on to the track to acclaim Senna. They were in Mansell's path. He flicked the Williams left to miss them and, with standing water on the track, slithered wildly onto the grass at the other side. It was a nasty moment.

At Imola he had another nasty moment – but in qualifying. He got his braking wrong for the chicane and thundered down the escape road. The escape road was also the pit-entry road . . .

Imola was one of the thirstiest tracks and the 220-litre fuel limit made the race a public mockery, not a race at all. Three men who led during the final laps went away emptied – Prost, disqualified because his car was underweight, Senna and Johansson

79

(Ferrari) running out of fuel. Mansell was getting disconcerting messages from his fuel digital read-out on the dashboard and slowed down to finish fifth. Nobody was happy about Imola. 'It wasn't really racing, was it?' Mansell mused and that captured everything. It wasn't.

In retrospect his season could be seen to be building nicely if slowly. At Monaco he was on the front row of the grid next to Senna although during qualifying his throttle was sticking open so that, going into all those tight corners, he had the awesome power of the Honda engine thrusting him forward too, too fast. 'I don't mind admitting I was frightened today,' he said. He added that it was the first time he had felt that in a racing car.

You must, of course, establish the difference between an accident, which happens all-at-once and lasts a very short time, and this which went on and on for well over a minute. You must of course see it for what it is: metal barriers, and you're flowing into the right-left at Sainte Devote, you're up the hill to the left-hander, you're in Casino Square, bumping along, you have to turn sharp right, you're going down to Mirabeau, another sharp right, you're into the switch-back hairpin, then sharp right again, sharp right again after that into the tunnel, back down the hill with a chicane in the middle of the descent, sharp left at Tabac corner, left, right round the swimming pool, another hairpin at La Rascasse . . .

In the race – anti-climax. He was slowed by brake problems (not nice here) and came in seventh after holding sixth for a good long time.

He did finish sixth in Canada and at Detroit – he always did like street circuits – he was on the front row next to Senna again.

Affection didn't help. He was a front-runner until the third corner – called inevitably by Americans Turn Three – began to break up badly. It claimed several victims, among them Mansell. This happened on lap twenty-four and he had already spun. Now, deep into Turn Three – a right-angle right-hander – Mansell's car skittered helplessly across the broken surface and thumped the wall hard – the protective tyre-barrier had already been scattered by a previous victim. Mansell got out slightly concussed and was so angry he brushed aside one of the marshals trying to help him away. He had a badly swollen hand, too.

After six races he had only five points, Rosberg twelve, and in the next race at Paul Ricard he had the highest speed crash in modern Formula One. During qualifying a rear tyre exploded with the sound, as one witness said, of a 'cannon.' The car veered uncontrollably and hit a concrete post which tore off a front wheel. The wheel flew back and struck him on the head. He was knocked unconscious. He was flown immediately to a hospital in Marseilles by helicopters where a full examination, including a brain scan, revealed that he was suffering from no worse than concussion. The worry, of course, was that this was the second time in two weeks. (The analogy with boxers surfaced for the first time. They take punishment which is not immediately visible; it can – or used to – reveal itself in later years.)

It is a measure of Mansell that he said from hospital: 'I hope to be at Silverstone for the British Grand Prix in two weeks because I love our home circuit and I don't want to let people down.'

How fast had he been going? If it wasn't 200 miles an hour, it was close enough. 'I am lucky to be alive,' he said. 'I heard this explosion behind me when the tyre blew while I was going flat out in sixth gear down the straight. I closed my eyes when I hit the barrier. I was fortunate that there was a run-off area and the catch-fencing slowed me down.'

He went to Silverstone and qualified twelfth on the first day . . .

Rosberg, one of the most straight-talking people you're ever likely to meet, said: 'After Ricard I think Nigel's qualifying performance is absolutely magnificent.' Rosberg was magnificent himself in a quite different way and on the Saturday lapped Silverstone at 160.925 miles an hour, the first time that had been done. It was so thunderous you could hear the echoes of it a long time afterwards. It was so thunderous it demonstrated that the Williams could be the fastest car of them all in 1985. And certainly on Saturday, 20 July it was.

At Silverstone Frank Williams confirmed that he had taken up the option in Mansell's contract for 1986. Mansell was staying. He still only had the five points and Williams was perhaps offering him an act of judgement. Mansell was running fifth in the race when the clutch went. It was exactly the mid-point of the season. He still only had the five points . . .

He picked up a single point in Germany but nothing in Austria, although he'd started from the front row of the grid.

Nobody could deny that in qualifying he was among the fastest, and qualifying is, above all else, a matter of speed. It is speed over two hour-long sessions. There are special 'sticky' tyres made to last a single, full-out lap; soft rubber which clings to the track to give maximum grip. There are special qualifying engines which, when wound up properly, deliver 1200 horse-power. That's one-thousand-two-hundred-horses. And there is your sense of timing. You must time your run perfectly because other drivers are out there, some meandering round experimenting, others doing their flying laps but marginally more slowly than you. The trick: to come out of the pits and cruise for a lap warming up your tyres so that as you accelerate across the line to begin your run – and the clock begins to tick-tick-tick – you've as near a clear lap as possible. You don't want the others in the way. Or if they are, you want to meet them where you can overtake them.

Drivers come back after their flying laps and constantly bitch that they were blocked by so-and-so, why doesn't he look in his mirrors, he must have seen me coming? Even if this blocking lasts only as long as following a slower car through a corner before you can overtake it, think about what that means. At Silverstone, on the Saturday, these were the times:

> Rosberg: 1 minute 05.591 seconds.
> Piquet: 1 minute 06.249 seconds.
> Mansell: 1 minute 06.675 seconds.
> Senna: 1 minute 06.794 seconds.

They are fractions so slight that they can have little real meaning to ordinary people, especially when lost or gained over a circuit almost three miles long.

Qualifying is not, of course, racing, although, interestingly, the people who do well in one invariably seem to do well in the other. That Mansell had mastered qualifying would suggest, then, that he could and would win races. Rosberg had. Piquet had. Senna had.

He finished sixth in Holland and recorded the fastest lap in Italy but the ironies hadn't done with him yet. Rosberg took the lead and Mansell followed, the two Williams cars visibly faster than anything else. Until lap four. Mansell's engine began to misfire – it's not a pleasant sound – and he was forced into the pits for repairs. He rejoined twenty-second and last. He went for it, carving his way up and his progress is worth detailed study: fourteenth on lap 43, twelfth on lap 44, eleventh on lap 45, tenth on lap 46, ninth on lap 47. In its context it was one of the best drives of his career so far. The pity was that there was time for no more. Prost won the race. Ah, that Prost. Now he's a winner . . .

Of course inspired changes from the back assume a context of their own. You have nothing to lose – you've lost it all already – and in your immediate vicinity are the slower cars. Most of them are easy prey on a fast, wide circuit, if you know what you're doing. Many and great are the heroic charges from the back where, if it goes wrong, you can walk back to the pits and say quite truthfully: So what? But those heroic charges have to be done, they don't do themselves, and you have to care enough to try and do them.

The unbelievers in Mansell would point out that to lead a race, command it from the front with all the power and pressure of the rest concentrated behind you, that wasn't the same at all. Look at Monaco in '84 . . .

But now, with only four races remaining in 1985, Mansell had seven points. At this same stage the year before with Lotus he had had nine. Beyond that no comparisons were valid. The sum total of 1985 was that he had become an accepted and established frontrunner and consistently so. The real question had become much, much more interesting: what's going to happen when his machinery holds up?

Spa, almost concealed in the rolling woodland of the Ardennes, is a beautiful place and a beautiful circuit. The track has everything, a really tight hairpin, a descent to a left-right twist which pitches you uphill and now you are out into the country, between the trees. It is a rare and profound examination of a man, his nerve and his machine.

Once upon a time it was 8.7 miles long but modern day safety requirements had outgrown it. You might remember the feature film *Grand Prix,* which seated such celebrities as Yves Montand and James Garner in cockpits. Part of the film was shot at Spa – during the actual race – and the crowd sat unprotected just beside the track. It was authentic. And if a car went out of control and missed the people, it wasn't going to miss all those trees. By 1983 the circuit had been extensively re-built without sacrificing any of its grandeur. It was safe, it was 4.3 miles long and the only discordant section (aesthetically) was a chicane precisely the shape of a bus stop which quickly became known as just that: The Bus Stop.

In September 1985 the Formula One cars were there for the Belgian Grand Prix. The race should have been held earlier in the season – June – but the track surface had been re-laid with a compound of asphalt and rubber only three weeks before and it was so soft that drivers could, and did, sink their fingers into it. The surface was far, far too dangerous and the race was postponed amid much chaos. Now, in September, all was well. Mansell started on the fourth row of the grid after the usual misfortunes in qualifying: clutch, a puncture, getting blocked.

Rain is endemic here – it was why the surface had been re-laid in the first place, the compound of asphalt and rubber preventing aquaplaning – and it did rain, stopping with a proper sense of timing just before the race began. From the grid, it is but a short way to the hairpin and there was a lot of bumping and barging there.

Once the traffic had settled the order was Senna, Prost, Mansell. On lap four Mansell attacked Prost and took him up the hill. The track was drying and what you needed was dry tyres, not the grooved wets you'd started on. Mansell came in for them on lap eight, so did Senna and Prost. Mansell called his pit stop 'fantastic' and he actually came out in the lead but Senna got past him. The traffic settled again. Senna, Mansell, Rosberg, Prost. It would stay like that until lap thirty-two, although Mansell did have a spin at the hairpin but kept the engine alive and kept going.

Spa is beautiful – and treacherous. Rain fell, but only on certain parts of the track. You try driving at those speeds with tyres for the dry – bald, no grooves at all – and you come upon the wet parts. You're into ice skating. On lap twenty five Marc Surer (Brabham) went off and Mansell said: 'He came back right in front of me and almost side-swiped me off the circuit. I had to go almost off the track to miss him.' Rosberg profited by that and drew up to Mansell.

Rosberg, combative, shrewd, is not the man you want stalking you but without any warning he slowed on lap thirty-two. Brakes. Exit Rosberg. Mansell felt the pressure melt away but he made a mistake up at the top of the hill, braked too late and the car lurched through the chicane. No damage.

It didn't help that the chest was painful – he'd hurt it at Monza – and this had been aggravated during qualifying here when he'd had to make a sudden correction. It didn't help but it wasn't going to stop him.

There was no real possibility of catching Senna, though Senna did have a misfire. Senna crossed the line 28 seconds in front of Mansell. He was second. It was his best result in seventy-one races and this might easily have been overlooked immediately after the race. Senna was The Coming Man in Formula One and knowing people spoke of him as being capable of true greatness *soon*. Prost, who finished third behind Mansell, was going for the championship and his four points took him further along that road – 69, and a lovely 16-point gap to the next man, Alboreto. These were the potent topics of the moment.

We didn't really see, I think, that Mansell had found the right key in his bunch, nor that all he had to do now was turn it. We did see that Brands Hatch and the Grand Prix of Europe was just three weeks away.

Pit Stop

The scale of the thing is impressive enough. Grand Prix races don't run themselves and more or less the moment they finish and the transporters have lumbered into the night it is time to begin work on next year's race. In Britain, in fact, that had been on a two-year cycle, the race alternating between Silverstone and Brands Hatch; in 1985 the cycle was broken when Silverstone held the British Grand Prix in July and Brands got the Grand Prix of Europe – an umbrella term, and very useful – in October.

But the scale of it . . . someone has estimated that at least 20,000 people travel from abroad, spending a couple of £million. The total attendance, Friday, Saturday, Sunday, may be as high as 150,000, which is half as big again as the Cup Final. To handle this number of people you must have a large and well-trained workforce, catering measured in tonnage, space enough for helicopters so numerous they give a passing resemblance to Vietnam, acres of car parks. There are the hospitality suites hired by companies and densely packed with their guests, there's a village of marquees, some holding several hundred other guests; there's the hard sell of the cigarette girls, the food caravans with their queues waiting for doner kebabs or the ubiquitous hamburgers. At any given moment, except when the race is actually in progress, everywhere will be busy, bustling, jostling, elbow-to-elbow. That's the atmosphere.

There are the periphery people wearing, like sophisticated sandwich-boards, company insignias on anoraks, seeming important and involved, scurrying somewhere – picking up the managing director from his chopper or looking vainly for Taiwanese business-men they've lost. That's the atmosphere.

But the people there are the merest fraction of those who will see the race. That's television, and this October the BBC would get an audience of eight million in Britain alone. You can be careless about statistics – this is an age of far too many statistics – but eight million remains a lot. Traditionally the host country provides the television coverage for the world – the eight million becomes ten-fold globally – and standards vary. If you're watching a race and wondering why the cameras are trailing after a French car so often, that'll be the French Grand Prix, with a French producer, and you see what he decides you see, wherever you are in the world.

The BBC has established a reputation for covering sport better than anybody else (we think) although they have the enormous advantage of no breaks for advertising so that they can spread the whole feast before you rather than course by couse. This week-end they would have fourteen cameras at Brands Hatch, one on a 170-foot hoist, another in a helicopter.

What, of course, the unseen millions can't do is lend the place any of their own atmosphere. They only give it a sense of importance because they are so many. Odd. Of those who come few are noisy – there is simply no point in shouting at Formula One cars whose engines drown everything for miles around – and violence is all but unknown. A handful of police suffice to control the 150,000 and it is done in the best benevolent traditions. The people who come are the widest cross-section of our national life, many of them families who sit all day in the sure knowledge that they won't hear a four-letter word or see a punch thrown, especially at themselves. This may seem idyllic and it is.

There used to be a theory that a lot of people were drawn to motor racing just to see accidents. It is manifestly not true in Britain. People go, if one may generalise about a cross-section of 150,000, because they like watching the cars, always have, always will. And, better, they understand what they are watching. That's the atmosphere. It is very, very special.

7 An English Country Garden

To reach Brands Hatch Place, you must go down a narrow, leafy lane. It is less than a mile from Brands Hatch circuit but you probably don't know it's there. It's as secluded as that, lost somewhere behind the trees. When you do find it, it has the presence of a small stately home: landscaped gardens, a pond with ducks fidgeting. It is an hotel now.

On 3 October 1985 Nigel Mansell was staying there with his family. The weather – for England, anyway – was acceptably warm. Well, it wasn't raining. Mansell wandered the gardens slowly and casually as if all the tautness you need in a car can be shed and you can make yourself almost loose-limbed. He was in shirt sleeves and was spending his time casting up fallen branches to get his son conkers while Rosanne took their daughter down to the duckpond to have a look at what was going on there. Not much.

Mansell was a family man utterly at peace.

Rarely have I seen anyone more trim, more fit. He protested that he was overweight and that was so absurd that everyone laughed except him. Pressed to say more, he moved into that curious language which is governed by self-defence.

'Before, it was a forty per cent chance that I'd win a race, now it's a seventy per cent chance. It may not be here – I'm not thinking about that – but I know it will be somewhere.'

Here, of course, was Brands Hatch circuit. Tomorrow he would ease himself into his Williams for the initial session for the grid.

Seclusion was important for Mansell because this Grand Prix of Europe would be like no other race he had known. A crowd approaching 100,000 would be there on race day, the faithful who love cars, any cars, but deep down yearn for a Briton to win. Astonishingly, that had not happened at Brands since Jim Clark in 1964. It had been a long wait, spanning two complete generations of drivers. It had been very nearly an intolerable wait.

On the Friday Mansell left his seclusion at the hotel and there they were, the faithful: they walked doggedly towards the circuit with their tents and sleeping-bags and backpacks. Of course they wanted to see the race, wanted to see a good race, but what they really wanted to see was *him*.

And of course it started to go wrong. In the untimed warm-up that morning he was in the spare car. His race car had a misfire. That afternoon he took the spare out in qualifying then switched to the race car. Meantime it rained and he was baulked by de Angelis. This meant that he had one flying lap left on tyres which were 'unbelievably blistered.' Crossing the line after his flying lap he got his foot off the accelerator fast – Paddock Hill Bend was coming at him like a vision and would his tyres get round it? Yes. He was seventh fastest.

On the Saturday, when that wander in the garden with his family was a distant memory, it all came right. He didn't like something about the car in the warm-up so the mechanics did what they do and started changing things. The moment he got it out on the track for qualifying he knew it was fine. He thrust in a thunderous lap and was third quickest. He would start from the second row of the grid.

Some context is necessary. The world at large was watching Prost. He could win the championship here and he was on the third row.

On the Sunday the weather was at its best; sharp autumnal sunlight spreading from between running clouds; and the faithful were here, the 100,000 in the grandstands and on balconies and on grassy banks.

Brands Hatch is like the Osterreichring, a natural amphitheatre. The nature of the terrain makes it so. From the start line, just along the straight, the cars go into Paddock Hill and dip so sharply that you lose sight of them altogether. They flow up the hill to Druids, a U-turn fringed by trees, the leaves turning to russet. They flow down the hill to Cooper Straight which runs along the back of the paddock so that any team member agile enough can watch the start, clamber down the metal stairs set into concrete behind the pits, scamper a few yards between the transporters and see the cars go by. Those cars turn left – uphill – and go out into the fast sweep up to Hawthorn Bend, go right – they are far out into the country now although it's only taken thirty seconds to get there – towards Westfield Bend, come down through Dingle Dell, right, left, along into Clearways where the circuit unfolds in a long, lazy loop towards the start-finish line. It is here, travelling under the bridge at Clearways, that the 100,000 see the cars. Because it is a long loop, the 100,000 can see the whole field spread back. It is a majestic spectacle.

The start was more frantic than majestic. It is always going to be that when you have twenty-six cars surging into the compression of Paddock Hill Bend. Senna went for it, Mansell after him and they got to Paddock together, but Senna with the decisive advantage of the inside line. Senna held that line, forcing Mansell to brake. As they went up to Druids, that braking had left Mansell momentarily vulnerable. Rosberg got by him – Mansell edged on to the grass – and Piquet got by him, too. Mansell – pitched back to fourth! When they came under the bridge at Clearways Rosberg was attacking Senna, Piquet was closing on Rosberg and Mansell was attacking Piquet. And that was a spectacle, all right.

The Senna–Rosberg duelling dominated the early laps, Senna blocking, blocking, blocking. On lap seven, Rosberg – was he pushing too hard? – went into a spin and Piquet, directly behind, crashed helplessly into him. Piquet's Brabham was damaged and out of the race. Rosberg, wheels spinning, was on the grass, back off the grass, heading on. Mansell had slipped through and was up to second place . . .

Rosberg limped towards the pits with a puncture.

And now the irony which had stalked and haunted Nigel Mansell all these years became Senna's irony. While Mansell went after Senna, Rosberg was in the pits having the tyre changed. As Rosberg emerged from the pits he saw Senna coming along from Clearways. The exit to the pit lane fed Rosberg out onto the track just as Senna reached him. Rosberg blocked him into Druids, did it again going down the hill. Every instant, Mansell was catching up. When he'd done that he struck hard. It was lap eight. Mansell went through into the lead and the 100,000 were making wild noises. It happened like this: Rosberg slowed at a corner, Senna had to back off him, Senna accelerated and went for Rosberg's right. Mansell saw the gap to the left and grabbed it.

Could Mansell stand the pressure and could his car stand the pressure over sixty-seven more laps?

On lap twelve, Alboreto's Ferrari caught fire and he coasted down the pit lane, having loosened his seat belts and risen in the cockpit to jump clear if the fire spread; and he looked then, wreathed in smoke, an unreal, almost surreal figure. He was the only man who could have caught Prost for the championship. But, on this lap twelve, that was one plot among many. Mansell commanded the race and Senna could do nothing about it.

What Mansell had to do was keep absolute command of himself. That is a lonely discipline when the 100,000 are with you and want you to win it so much. Somewhere around four laps to go the team withdrew their board – the one habitually hung over the pit lane wall so that as the driver passes he gets simple messages about who's behind him and how far they are behind. The board was deliberately withdrawn so that Mansell wouldn't become intoxicated and make a mistake. The team just wanted him to keep on in calculated ignorance until he saw the chequered flag.

The crowd beat the team. At every corner Mansell saw ranks of people holding up four fingers. Four laps to go. Next time round, three fingers, three laps to go, then two. He'll never forget that last lap. Chill sunlight played across the car. He came under the bridge at Clearways and the 100,000 were on their feet, howling and howling. He crossed the line and both his hands were raised from the cockpit, fists clenched. Somewhere along the pit lane his father was in tears. He was not alone. Nearby, Rosanne cuddled Chloe. 'I keep telling her Daddy has won but she's not taking it in.' And: 'It's such a shame Colin's not here to see this . . .'

Senna came in twenty seconds behind and if you take, as Longines do, times to a hundredth of a second, that's a lifetime.

Mansell cruised up the incline to Druids and he was intoxicated. And then – time itself had no meaning now – many hundreds of people were surging towards the control tower because they knew that up there on the balcony Mansell would appear.

When he did the howling began again. He was dressed in red overalls and a blue cap somebody must have given him. He stood for an instant, tired, consumed by what had happened, while the result was officially announced. That brought another howl which echoed and ebbed, like a reverberation, into the woodlands of England. He held a microphone and said: 'I've been trying so hard for so long to sell England and now we've done it.'

Prost emerged from the doorway nearby and although he'd finished fourth and was not strictly entitled to be on the balcony he *was* world champion and he got a howl for that as big as Mansell's. It touched Prost who, all else aside, had become France's first world champion. 'I like this country and its people very much,' Prost said. 'I would almost rather win here than in France.' He, too, was in red overalls and a blue cap which matched Mansell's. Were they left alone on the balcony deliberately, Senna and Rosberg – an amazing third – sensing that this was not their moment? It is certain that Mansell and Prost were the only two at the rim of the balcony. Mansell clutched a magnum of champagne and sprayed Prost. Prost returned fire from his magnum. Spray covered both of them. And the crowd howled again. Both men smiled, turned, sprayed the hundreds gathered beneath them.

As Mansell came down the stairs to cross the track to give a Press Conference, a woman rushed up and embraced him. He smiled politely at her – she was, I imagine, a total stranger – and continued. As he came into the Press tent the applause was very nearly emotional. He did look tired now; drawn, wrung out mentally as well as physically. Very few people in their lives get to know such moments of total vindication and it has to be difficult to cope with, especially if it involves 1 hour 32 minutes and 58.109 seconds of the most intense effort in front of the 100,000; especially if, over almost a decade, many thought you'd never, ever make it. How had he known how many laps were left? Those fingers. 'At every corner it was incredible. There were Union Jacks all over the place and thousands of people jumping in the air. It was so amazing I found it difficult not to be distracted.'

When the Press Conference was over he threaded a way through the crowd and went quietly back to Brands Hatch Place. His family were there and a few old pals from Birmingham came along. They were all soberly dressed. It was as it should be. He drank a few glasses of champagne – not more – and said: 'I've never been happier in my life.' Someone who knows him well said: 'He had a kind of glow on his face.' He watched the televised highlights of the race and the instant he overtook Senna he cheered himself. He went to bed at 11.30. He had to be at Heathrow early to fly home.

When he did get home he said his hands were blistered, his body ached but the happiness took all that away. And he ventured – the intoxication was still potent and for once it overwhelmed the prudence: 'Now we can go for the world championship.' That would be next season, of course. 'The team is right and Nigel Mansell has the potential to do it.'

The aftermath of every Grand Prix is purest anti-climax. The motor-homes and transporters get away from the circuit as fast as they can. The drivers get away as fast as they decently – or indecently – can. If they crash during the race they sometimes leave before the end of it, into the private helicopter and away. Two hours after a race you can be virtually alone at a circuit with the waste paper which the wind drags over an empty track.

There are several reasons for this exodus which is really a stampede. Formula One is always about the next race. Sentiment is mistrusted, people who linger . . . well why aren't they in their chopper, moving, moving, moving? As darkness came in at Brands Hatch that Sunday evening the circuit was emptied. It was a moment for reflection. Nigel Mansell had altered his career in the most decisive way. Second in Belgium. First here. He had turned the key and the door was wide open.

Peter Warr must be quoted again: 'What happened is exactly what happens to most racing drivers. After a long struggle they finally finish up winning a race and once they've done that they know what has to be done in order to win races. They suddenly realise that you don't have to try flat out from the first corner, what you can actually do is control the pace.'

Mansell had done all that.

But now, in the darkness, it was time for the reflection. The choppers which flatten the grass in the fields where they are parked had spirited their precious cargoes away long before. The transporters with *their* precious cargoes were already deep into the traffic jam on the A20.

In two weeks they'd all be in Kyalami, South Africa, and they'd have to go through it all again. The next race is always the big one.

South Africa could be no ordinary race. Civil unrest began to make some teams wonder if, on moral or physical grounds, they ought to go. This, of itself, is instructive. If other sportspeople or even entertainers go, they appear on Blacklists and their governments become embroiled. Quite why this hadn't happened to Formula One, which had been going to South Africa regularly since 1962, may not be such a mystery after all. The international business community had been trading there on a vast scale. Maybe Formula One was seen as business, not sport . . .

Between Brands Hatch and Kyalami, Formula One got as near as it can get to agonising over an external factor. Was it morally right to go? Was it physically dangerous to go with the unrest gaining in intensity. Would FISA call the race off? In the end only the two French teams, Renault and Ligier, didn't go. Two minor teams, RAM and Zakspeed, weren't going anyway. It left twenty-one cars, soon reduced to twenty when Jones (Lola Hart) fell ill. Mind you, several cars which did compete had had their sponsors' logos removed so that, presumably, the global audience would see that they weren't there although the cars were . . .

All this was slightly sad for Mansell, if one may be allowed to make a judgement like that in a situation of such broad human concern. It was sad, furthermore, because as sportspeople constantly point out they are sportspeople not politicians, and really all they wanted to do was race.

So Mansell went to Kyalami, a circuit in the veldt ten miles north of Johannesburg, and at 2.55 miles shorter than average. It is at an altitude of 6,000 feet. It has a bleached air about it as if it had been laid in bare countryside and burnished by a southern sun.

Of course, Prost had won the championship at Brands and that took a whole dimension away from the race. Because of the absentees, a small grid wasn't going to help either. As is the way of things, any sense of loss perished the moment the red light went to green and the cars set off along the famous straight towards Crowthorne Corner.

In qualifying Mansell had demonstrated that he had kept his momentum from Brands. Rosberg had a fastest lap of 1 minute 03.073 seconds, Mansell 1:03.188, Piquet 1:03.844. That was the first session. In the second Mansell broke free of them all. About fifteen minutes into the hour-long session he did a 1:02.700 and a few minutes later a stunning 1:02.366. Stunning? 'At one point I was up on the kerb next to the wall but managed to bring it back on the track. I think I clipped the wall.'

He was in pole position for only the second time in his Formula One career. The grid: Mansell, Piquet; Rosberg, Senna; Surer, de Angelis; Fabi, Lauda; Prost, Boutsen . . .

When that red light did go to green Mansell was away, clean and clear, into Crowthorne. Rosberg had a bad start but the two Alfa Romeos had worse, crashing into each other.

And then there were eighteen left. Lap one: Mansell, Piquet, de Angelis, Senna, Rosberg, and it was sure sign of Mansell's growing maturity that he turned the boost down to save fuel even though he was up there in the lead. The days of panic had gone.

Meanwhile Rosberg started to tear the field apart in front of him. By lap three he had overtaken Senna, by lap four de Angelis, by lap five Piquet. Only one man remained and that was his team-mate, Mansell. By lap six he had reached Mansell and the two cars ran together, by lap eight Rosberg was through into the wide open spaces of the veldt. Mansell wasn't unduly concerned. There were sixty-seven laps left. Time enough. He held the key to the door and he knew *when* to turn it.

In fact – and races can be curious like this – time started to move very quickly. On lap eight an Italian called Piercarlo Ghinzani driving a Toleman blew up, belching oil over Crowthorne Corner and leaving a dense pall of smoke, too. The next man through, Berger, was lost in the smoke, hit the oil and all but plunged off. The man after that, another Italian, Pierluigi Martini in a Minardi, came onto the oil and left it sideways. Then Rosberg, travelling like a missile. He was on the oil. He scudded off it into deep, deep sand laid just off the track to slow cars. Mansell, perhaps ten lengths behind, saw all this instantly and was on his brakes, swivelling the snout of the Williams towards where he thought there would be *less* oil.

He got through somehow, just keeping control of the car, that snout wavering wildly in front of him. If Mansell had been in the lead he'd have reached the oil first and been into the deep, deep sand himself. But he wasn't and he hadn't . . .

Out came Rosberg from the sand, wheels spinning and churning – out came Rosberg in a rare and fearsome mood back onto the track, away went Rosberg at very high speed. But he was fifth now and, at least for the moment, no longer a factor in the equation. By lap ten something very familiar and ominous was happening. Prost was up into second place, Lauda was up into third place. The McLarens, majestic in their might, were coming hard at Mansell. Lauda was retiring and this was his next to last race, his farewell to South Africa. Would he make one last great gesture and go for the win? Only a fool would doubt that he wouldn't.

Further back Rosberg was handling his car like people used to do in the old days, flinging it at corners, bouncing crazily over kerbs, urging and urging more out of the Honda engine, locking his brakes, unlocking his brakes, attacking and passing de Angelis. By lap seventeen Rosberg was fourth and coming at the rest like a train.

Prost and Lauda began to slice into Mansell's lead, taking fractions here and there until whenever he glanced in his mirrors he could see both of them. And he was their prey. He would say later that this was when the real pressure began. By lap thirty Prost was within striking distance but maddeningly for the Frenchman the McLaren simply didn't have the speed on the straights to overtake, however much quicker it was in the corners.

Mansell fended Prost off and Lauda turned into the pits for his tyre change on lap thirty-two. It was a slow sixteen seconds. Prost was in on lap thirty-four and his was slow, too, almost twenty seconds. As they settled again Lauda held second place, Prost third. In came Mansell on lap thirty-seven and his mechanics changed the tyres in a crisp 11.7 seconds. He emerged still in the lead and – all at once – the immediate pressure was removed.

Lauda's turbo had gone and with it his great gesture. Prost remained. Between Prost and Mansell there was now only the blink of an eye. Mansell used the back-markers as his minions, selecting with exquisite judgement the instants when he could dart past them and leave Prost to follow the minions through a corner losing touch.

This, more than anything else, was the real measure of Mansell's growing maturity.

Prost was unrelenting, working out his way to another win and another step towards Stewart's record – the one he wanted so much, the supreme thing – but for long laps he would have to hover a couple of seconds behind Mansell until, with only sixteen laps to go, one of the minions – a Ferrari, mark you! – held him up and the gap became three seconds. It was too much without the straight line speed.

Mansell was going to win. Rosberg had been in for *another* set of tyres and although he was roaring and raging his way round he was ten seconds adrift. Rosberg was leaving Williams for McLaren. It was almost the end of the season, everything important had been decided long before and a comfy second place behind Mansell would be agreeable, wouldn't it?

No.

Rosberg thundered past Prost and now flung the car at the whole circuit rather than the occasional corner. Not content with riding the kerbs he had the car on the grass too – on full power. And he was coming, coming, coming. With a single lap left there was response and counter-response. Both men set their fastest laps, Rosberg 1:08.149, Mansell 1:08.518. That mattered little. The gap was too wide even for Rosberg in this mood. Mansell came across the line slightly more than seven seconds ahead and had won his second Grand Prix. That they had been consecutive made it infinitely more wonderful.

He had opened a much bigger door than mere winning.

Adelaide remained, a new circuit for the last race of the season. It was a street circuit and because it generated so much enthusiasm among Australians, a special race. Mansell started on the front row, next to Senna who had taken pole. It was hot. It would become hotter very soon. Mansell seized the lead, powered through the chicane just after the start, powered through the left-hand corner and on to a tight right-hander, then another left-hander. He put the car in the proper place to go round that and Senna, inside him, thumped him off. He limped on for another lap before transmission problems stopped him altogether. Mansell was extremely angry.

Rosberg, incidentally, won the race. That was *his* last great gesture with Williams.

And that was 1985. In the last few weeks Mansell had altered everything. With thirty-one points he had finished sixth in the championship but nobody cared too much about that. He had proved one great truth: that he was a winner, not a loser. The next great truth awaited the proving: that he was capable of winning the championship itself.

Piquet would be alongside him for 1986 in the Williams, making for fierce in-house competition. Senna would be in the Lotus – he had shown a certain immaturity in Adelaide but few doubted that he learnt as fast as he drove. Rosberg would be alongside Prost at McLaren – this same McLaren who in two seasons had won a staggering eighteen races. And then there would be the Ferraris. Who knew what magic they would conjure out of the winter, who could be sure that it wouldn't all come right for them again and the others would be at their mercy? And 1986 wasn't far away either. Adelaide had been on 3 November. Brazil would be on 23 March.

As he left Adelaide, Mansell did what any sensible man would have done. He took his family on holiday.

Mansell's first Grand Prix, Austria, 1980 – in pain in the cockpit from fuel burning his skin and before mechanical failure stopped the car.

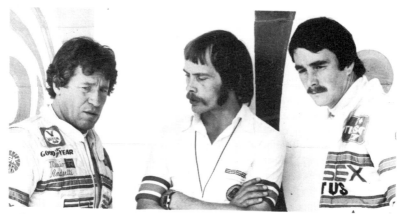

Before that first race: senior Lotus driver Mario Andretti, Lotus engineer Nigel Stroud and Mansell.

All smiles in the early days. Mansell with team-mate Elio de Angelis at Rio, 1981.

Mansell's first points, Belgium, 1981 where he finished third.

Early Mansell movement. Here he finishes the British Grand Prix in 1983 in the John Player Special Lotus.

He always said he liked Monaco and here he is enjoying himself there in 1982…

... but in 1984, when he was leading, he spun into the barrier and was out. Note the spray the tyres are throwing back from the rain-sodden track.

In an English country garden the day before the Brands Hatch meeting in 1985 which would make him a national celebrity. With Leo, Rosanne and Chloe.

One of Mansell's ruling passions is golf, and he is always happy heading for the fairway.

A putt that did go down ...

The family man.

Friend and contemporary. Derek Warwick and family.

Niki Lauda. Mansell unwittingly helped him to win the World Championship at Estoril when he had to drop out and Lauda finished second, all he needed. (Inset) Lauda in his Championship-winning year – 1984 – and his Championship-winning Marlboro McLaren.

Mansell and Rosanne at Brands Hatch in 1985 where he would win the Grand Prix of Europe and open the door.

8 The Inheritor

To understand it, you must have its perspective. As Mansell spent a quiet Christmas and the children opened their presents, the hype which would threaten to become something approaching hysteria was only a few weeks distant.

If he'd been just another British winner in a sport which is, truth to tell, not major like soccer or cricket you could have asked, and been forgiven for asking, just what is all this fuss about, anyway? Motor racing? That's the one we don't do well at any more, isn't it? Motor racing? That's the one on TV, isn't it, and don't those cars look funny going round and round and round all afternoon? Foreigners win the races, don't they?

Forgive the casual spectator. Television, even with a BBC commentator as highly charged by boyish enthusiasm as Murray Walker, captures the incidents during a race but misses the essence. The essence is speed and you have to be physically present to catch that. A long-range camera shot directly down the straight at Kyalami flattens the speed so that if 200 miles an hour doesn't actually look *slow* it doesn't look all that ferociously fast either. But when you go . . .

Generations of British people had been going since the first Grand Prix of modern times at Silverstone in 1950. We had a vast car industry then, as befitted a great industrial power.

If the age of national decline had already begun in 1950, that decline was hidden from most ordinary people. When Roger Bannister broke the four-minute-mile barrier at Oxford in 1954, Harold Wilson, who was there, said people weren't particularly surprised. After all, one expected British people to achieve those things first.

It was true, and was to remain true for a long time, in motor sport. Stirling Moss began in 1951 and although paradoxically he was never world champion his name became deeply embedded in the national sub-conscious as meaning speed and style with it. He

97

drove for, among others, Cooper Climax, BRM and Vanwall, resonant names, just as his was. In 1952 Mike Hawthorn began – blond, an adonis, who drove wearing a bow tie, and he was of his time when chaps were good chaps and a post-war generation was proving that they had that war-time jauntiness in the face of great danger themselves.

He overlapped with Graham Hill – 1958 was Hawthorn's last season and Hill's first – and Hill with his moustache *did* look as if he had just wandered in from the Battle of Britain. Hill would make Monaco his own principality, winning there five times. And Monaco was then a place where British people could afford to go, just as they went to Switzerland because it was so wholesome and cheap. Britain still mattered and here were our young men proving it in the cut and thrust of motor racing. Maybe they did drink wild amounts of champers, maybe they did dance on the tables, but that was just high spirits, wasn't it?

Jim Clark started two years after Hill – 1960 – and driving only for Lotus was world champion in 1963 and 1965. His name is still remembered far beyond the confines of motor sport. He overlapped with another Scot, Jackie Stewart, who would win the championship in 1969, 1971 and 1973. Consider it: between Hawthorn's win in 1958 and Stewart's win in 1973, Britons won the championship seven other times and British cars all but three. But Stewart was a technician, not a fighter pilot. And he behaved like one, precise and prudent. The emphasis in Formula One was altering and soon enough drivers would become remote beings much more anxious about whether the armco was in the right place than what came out of champagne bottles. Particularly Stewart after a bad moment at Spa.

Into the middle of this came James Hunt, public school boy, who overlapped Stewart, and journalists unashamedly fed the British public's desire to see just that – a public school boy – beat the world again. Hunt was a hard, professional driver although he had driven, at the beginning, for *Lord* Alexander Hesketh and Anthony *'Bubbles'* Horsley – Hesketh of Falstaffian proportions who lived quite naturally in a stately home. To the British – and others – who have a strange idea that this is what the British are really like, it was all irresistible. Hunt joined McLaren in 1976 and in the very last race at Mount Fuji, Japan finished third after a dreadful rainstorm when others had dropped – or pulled – out because they said it was too dangerous. True Brit, Hunt. The Right Stuff. And he was world champion. Hunt had joined the heritage and maintained much of its early character.

That early character had been spiced by the one race everybody knew outside Formula One and that had been British, too: Le Mans. That it was run in France was a fortunate geographical accident mollified by the availability and price of vin rouge and the chance to get away from your wife for a week-end. Spread over 24 hours, Le Mans attracted a pilgrimage of uncounted thousands of British spectators every year. Jaguar won it in 1951 *and* 1953 *and* 1955 *and* 1956 *and* 1957. Best car in the world, eh? In 1957 they took *five* of the first six places. But that had been the 1950s, not the 1970s.

Hunt retired in 1979 and by then the drivers almost all came from distant places and were technicians and Formula One was no laughing matter, it was Very Big Business Indeed. But those memories of great and golden days lingered. Who followed Hunt into the heritage?

Nobody.

It was difficult to accept although by then Britain had had to accept much like that – a car industry going, a motor cycle industry gone as obvious symptoms among many. Virtually within the span of Formula One's lifetime from 1950, Britain had lost an empire which contained one person in every three on the planet and joined the European Economic Community as a modest power beset by problems the Continent didn't want.

This placed, whether people knew it or not, very real pressure on sportspeople to win to show that – at least in *this* – we were still worth something.

Hence the adulation of Coe and Ovett and Cram, the open surrendering to Torvill and Dean, the tears for McGuigan, the symbolic value of Botham, and 'Enery's left hook which put Ali on his behind, and holding on, year after year, to memories of winning the World Cup in 1966 . . .

That was what the fuss was about. And more. In motor sport the memories of the golden days fed expectations, safe in the knowledge that while *foreigners* were winning all but four of the seventy-seven Grands Prix between Hunt's retirement and the end of 1984, Britain still remained the epi-centre of Formula One. Of the fifteen teams competing in 1984, nine were based here, mostly round the Home Counties. Every race was started by an Englishman, Derek Ongaro. An Englishman, Professor Sid Watkins, attended every race and sat in a car ready to get to any accident within seconds. An Englishman, Bernie Ecclestone, spearheaded FOCA, the Formula One Constructors' Association, and he guaranteed at least twenty-six cars on every grid and he made sure the races stayed on the world's television screens and the sponsors liked that and the money came in to keep the teams alive to keep the races going to stay on the world's television screens . . .

Britain lacked only one aspect and it was the one which mattered most to most people: a driver to win the championship.

And that was what all the fuss had been about when Mansell finished third in Zolder in 1981. Forty men would drive Formula One cars that year, only four of them British: Mansell, John Watson, Brian Henton and Warwick.

Henton and Warwick were in the Toleman team, then fighting desperate rearguard actions to actually qualify for races.

In 1982 Watson, from Northern Ireland, finished joint second in the championship but he was somehow too polite a man for his achievement to spill over and excite the appetite of the millions. In 1983, while Mansell was getting a bare ten points, Warwick was getting nine and making a name for himself because Toleman had no pedigree and if he could do this in a Toleman, what might he do in a big team? He joined a big team, Renault, in 1984 and it seemed clear that he, not Mansell, had a real chance of joining the heritage. He got twenty-three points – but was never able to seize a race by its throat. He didn't win a race. And when Mansell started to win in 1985 the Renault team was distintegrating. Warwick got five points from fifteen races – one less than Mansell got from Belgium alone.

There were two other Britons now, Jonathan Palmer and Martin Brundle. Palmer, a qualified doctor, had more of a struggle than Mansell had had. In 1984 he had driven for the RAM team, who were not competitive. In 1985 he had driven for the new German Zakspeed team and they weren't competitive either. Palmer was learning, Zakspeed were learning but it was always going to be a long slog. Brundle had fought out a season-long duel with Senna in Formula Three before joining Tyrrell. Ken Tyrrell had made the cars for Stewart but however much he dreamed of another British champion he couldn't give Brundle the machinery to do it. At moments Brundle was outstanding. It was scant consolation and, taken all together, this was an age away from Moss, Hawthorn, Hill, Clark, Stewart and Hunt.

In the 1980s it was left to Derek Bell to dominate Le Mans, but in Porsches. And Le Mans wasn't the same either. Even the locals said it: When are the Jags coming back?

I remember a Press Conference given jointly by Mansell and Warwick when both said that, as the matured and experienced

100

Formula One drivers they had now become, they fully intended to pass on whatever help they could to promising young British drivers. ('We're friends of course but we still aim to beat the hell out of each other on the track.') They were both sincere because they both fully understood what the fuss was about and they both knew the depth of the yearning from the thousands who actively support race meetings – not just the pampered and prosperous at Grands Prix in hospitality suites but the people who go in all weathers to small and distant circuits to watch competitors who have minimal sponsorship (if any) and tow beast-like racing cars of all shapes and sizes on trailers to these small and distant places; them, and the amazing enthusiasts who keep immaculate lap charts of races nobody will remember except themselves.

In many significant ways motor racing is a closed community, so closed that one British columnist remembers going to a race in upstate New York and reading in the local paper: 'Nobody at the track would have known if America had been neuked – or *cared*.'

The fuss, of course, starts when – nuclear wars aside – something happens which brings motor racing out of its closed community. In Britain that is quite simply a British driver going for the world championship.

This championship is by nature panoramic because its sixteen races embrace four continents and places as different as Monaco and Detroit, Budapest and Rio, and each of the sixteen is a quite different kind of hurdle.

As Mansell prepared himself for this in early 1986, he could reasonably assume that the worst of his particular struggle – getting to a position where he could go for the championship – might now be safely forgotten. Long before he had drawn a startling allusion about living with a car which simply wasn't good enough. 'It's like being shut up in a dark room and stifled, it's like a writer being put in prison without a paper and pen, so he can think, he can dream, but he can't write.'

For 1986 he could think, dream and have the car. Nobody is ever quite sure at the start of a season which car will be best because all of them are 'new' – re-designed, anyway, or honed – and this has been completed in elaborate secrecy during the short gap between seasons. Engine development is incessant, fuel limits change (the 220 litres had come down to 195) and the chassis of the car is widely regarded as a work of art in itself. The whole, when assembled, is a creature of enormous strength and sensitivity and, as I say, nobody knows which one will be best. But it was certain: The Williams would be, in the word Formula One treasures almost unto itself, competitive.

It was also certain that Mansell would be competitive. It had always been hard to mistake that, whatever he'd been driving, from the Austin 7 all the way here.

It was something inside him, although at moments he could appear moody – perhaps downcast would be more accurate. He always found difficulty concealing that and Birmingham is not noted for its *joie de vivre*. It is a solid town, a town of substance, just as Mansell himself is. Of all the bones in his body one was never broken: backbone.

He was not and is not dour. He has a slow smile which spreads softly somewhere under that moustache. He resembles, partly because of that moustache, a subaltern and someone once remarked: 'He wouldn't have looked out of place in a uniform defending Mafeking.'

He did, and does, greet you in a way he has made his own ritual: either an arm-lock round your neck from behind (it doesn't hurt but don't try and move) or a tap on your knee from behind which momentarily tips you forward off balance. When you turn to see what the hell's going on, there it is, that slow smile spreading, naughty as an urchin.

He did, and does, play jokes. Behind the pits at Zandvoort Murray Walker was filming for Australia where he, the BBC and Grand Prix racing all have considerable followings. The scene: Walker standing in a clearing between tyres talking urgently to camera a few yards away. Mansell stalked up behind him and dipped his head, thrust it between Walker's legs and lifted Walker completely off the ground by the strength of those neck muscles alone. Mansell stood erect. Walker dangled like a doll wobbling helplessly. It was a long way down.

Everybody – you know how camera crews can be – got a belly laugh out of that, Mansell leading it.

This was the man who, in March 1986, caught the plane for Rio and the start of the hurdle race. But even before this something had gone terribly wrong.

9 Descent, Ascent

Frank Williams left the Paul Ricard circuit in a hire car. Another session of pre-season testing was over and now he was going for the airport and home. Alongside him sat Peter Windsor, presently working for the team.

Somewhere on that descent from the circuit – Ricard is set in hills – Williams made a mistake, the car rolled several times and came to rest in a field. Williams, functioning like the professional he was, switched the ignition off – to prevent any chance of a fire – although he was suspended upside down by his seat-belt. He felt searing pain. He thought, again like a professional: *I've been in crashes before, it shouldn't hurt this much.* While Windsor struggled to get out, a farmer came up and found a 'very big rock' and smashed a rear window. It took some doing. Toughened glass is tough. The farmer and Windsor got Williams out as carefully as they could and laid him on his briefcase 'which contained all my worldly possessions.'

He would spend days in a Marseilles hospital fighting for his life. He was crippled but that could wait. The most immediate concern was a build-up of fluid in his lungs. Windsor said: 'He's got this advantage that he's so fit and all the running over the years has enlarged his lung capacity.'

Formula One, hardened to all manner of tragedy, waited aghast. Frank, the man who was super-fit. Frank, the man who looked after his body as he looked after his racing cars – with infinite care. Frank, an utterly familiar figure in every pit lane.

Frank, immobile in Marseilles, fighting.

They operated and they operated again and Formula One was full of ugly rumours and when it became mercifully clear that he was going to win the fight it became decent to ask the inevitable question: What happens to the team? The question became more pressing because he was moved back to England and word filtered through about the extent of his back injuries. He was virtually paralysed from the neck down and the recovery from that might take years.

'It was,' Mansell said, 'a huge shock but I have gone through something similar before' – he was of course at Lotus when Chapman died – 'and I know the whole team will pull together.' That was the general feeling and everybody at Williams said the same thing. They all sensed, too, that 'the best medicine' – Mansell's words – would be to win the Brazilian Grand Prix, then only a week away. Patrick Head would run the team.

As the team prepared to leave, Williams had recovered enough to be asking penetrating questions from his bed in the London Hospital, Whitechapel about what the team were doing. It was a good sign. To the team it was a wonderful sign.

This was also a time for careful words. 'I don't,' Mansell said, 'accept that we are favourites. Just because we did well at the end of last season doesn't make us that. Let's see how we go.'

The start of every Formula One season is a step into the unknown. Over the winter the closed world has opened up a little bit to let people out to say hello to their families and play their golf, or fish, or promote themselves – that's apart from any promotional tours for sponsors, and testing, and nipping along to the factory to see how the new car's coming along . . .

That first morning of the first meeting the world closes in again until the end of October and every aspect of the circus is back where it belongs again. Over there is Kaspar Arnet from Longines checking the timing devices, and Derek Ongaro smiling benignly, and Barry Griffin from Goodyear stalking the heaps of tyres making sure all is well. Men in overalls are laying television cables.

At some moment the first engine is fired up along the pit lane, all thunder and lightning, and everybody thinks: Here we go again.

Well, here we did go again.

Brazil (Jacarepagua, near Rio). A flat circuit but with an interesting variety of corners. Length: 3.126 miles. Race over 61 laps. Seventh Grand Prix to be held here. Speeds well over 100 miles an hour.

It was grey that first morning, unusual for such a place, as the cars went out for the traditional ninety minutes of untimed practice. It is always called untimed, although Kaspar and Longines give the times to three decimal points, out of interest, you know . . .

The important session lasts from one o'clock to two o'clock and it is always at this time, will be for all sixteen races. Same thing on the second day of the meeting: untimed ten o'clock to eleven-thirty, final session for the grid, one o'clock to two o'clock. The rule is simple: your fastest lap in either hour-long qualifying session determines your place on the grid.

Mansell was all but unobserved on the Friday. Senna and Piquet, both of course Brazilians, excited an already excitable crowd by challenging each other for pole position. Piquet would hold it overnight with a lap of 1 minute 26.666 against Senna's 1 minute 26.983. Mansell, hampered by an electrical problem and a sixth gear not quite right for the long straight, was third.

The Saturday was hot and the two Brazilians chased each other again. Piquet was baulked, tried another run and at 200 miles an hour put a rear wheel off. The car went into catch-fencing, bruising his wrist. At this point Piquet was still on pole – his Friday time remained fastest – but Mansell had drawn up alongside him on the front row with 1 minute 26.749 despite the engine cutting out three times. Senna waited. Piquet was back in his pit with an ice-pack on his wrist, tightly hemmed by security men. Then Senna went out and caused tumult. One minute 25.501. Mansell tried to respond towards the end of the session but as he was warming his tyres up he noticed a slower car coming up behind him. It was important not to let it go by because he'd have to re-take it and that would cost time. So he accelerated. It warmed the tyres too quickly – they are made to last only one lap, remember – and they didn't last. He would start the race on the second row of the grid. Senna and Piquet on the front. 'With two Brazilians there,' Mansell said cryptically, 'I might be better off behind them anyway.' He could hardly know he was saying it very prophetically.

The race was generating hysteria with thousands chanting for Senna and thousands chanting for Piquet. It was Senna who seized the start and Mansell who tucked in behind him down the straight to the first corner. Mansell ducked out and took the inside line, Senna abreast of him. There wasn't room for two. They touched and Mansell went off onto the grass, then into a barrier. His race was over. Piquet went by and won it comfortably and when he was interviewed he said: This one was for you, Frank.

Mansell had to live with the questions he knew people would be asking, the same, eternal questions they had always asked. Why go for it so early in a race? Why go for it against Senna of all people, a Brazilian in front of all those Brazilians? And what had happened in the very last race last time around, Adelaide? The same thing. That had been Senna, too. Maybe Mansell wasn't as matured as we thought. But that Piquet, now there's a driver. When he

105

overtook Senna he picked the moment, gave him a wide berth, none of this nudging wheels, thank you. That's the way to do it.

Spain (Jerez). A new track, narrow but with challenging corners. Length: 2.621 miles. Race over 72 laps.

Senna does learn fast. He was quickest on the Friday with Mansell behind him and Piquet behind *him*. On the Saturday Mansell dropped back to the second row of the grid. As at Brazil Senna and Piquet were in front. Mansell, cryptic again, said: 'All I'll say is that I had a small accident in Rio on my own to avoid a big one involving both of us. I won't do that again.'

He didn't. Senna got clear away with Piquet following, Mansell third. From lap two Mansell drifted back a couple of places quite deliberately. The on-board fuel read-out – only 195 litres available – was giving him messages he didn't like at all. He would wait and see, wait until the read-out was giving him messages he did like after he'd eased off, saved a bit of fuel. In fact he waited until lap nineteen to reclaim fourth place, lap thirty to reclaim third. Senna and Piquet remained ahead of him. At the beginning of lap thirty-three he went effortlessly past Piquet. Senna was a couple of seconds up the road but thirty-nine laps remained to catch him. On lap forty Senna was behind Brundle (Data General Tyrrell) and Mansell saw a gap, went right, was through into the lead. Now Senna would wait and see. He came back carefully and was with Mansell when there were ten laps left. He harried Mansell and took him at the hairpin, timing, judgement and courage perfect.

Mansell had to brake hard and Prost, lurking close by, stole through, too. Mansell made a decision which was a risk. He came in for new tyres. Once he had them and the read-out was still giving him messages he liked he put his foot hard down. That was lap sixty-three. Nine to go. Senna had a lead of twenty seconds and somewhere between Mansell and Senna was Prost. With the new tyres, Mansell carved into those twenty seconds at a rate of four seconds a lap. It was as if the man was announcing himself for the whole season by the length and depth of the gesture.

Three laps to go. He reached Prost but couldn't afford to stay there long. He attacked on the pit straight and Prost responded, put *his* foot hard down! Mansell had to wait as the two cars moved out among the smoothed hillocks of southern Spain, did get past Prost, but had had to linger. The lingering cost a good second – a long time now, with only two laps to go. The gap was 4.6 seconds. Mansell, freed of Prost, charged and when the two cars crossed the line into the final lap the gap had become only a second and a half. Senna was nursing tired tyres. Mansell was still charging.

And it came to this: the end of the last lap – a right-hand corner leading to another right-hand corner, then a short run to the hairpin which contorted left, left, left, then the sprint to the line. Senna was still clear at the right-handers but as he braked for the hairpin Mansell swarmed all over him. Out of the hairpin the track seemed to broaden in front of the two men. Mansell plunged down the left, coming up level with Senna – or almost level. As they crossed the line Mansell was moving away from Senna.

Both men thought they had won it.

It needed Kaspar and Longines' refinement to settle it finally. Senna: 1 hour 48 minutes 47.735 seconds. Mansell: 1 hour 48 minutes 47.749 seconds. It was almost certainly the closest finish of all time. How far in real distance? After 188.708 miles, no more than a couple of feet. Think of it. 0.014 of one second.

Senna: 15 points. Piquet: 9. Mansell: 6. Prost: 4.

San Marino (Imola, 'near' Bologna, Genoa, Rimini). Set in charming parkland with good, fast corners and invariably a big crowd to see the cars going round them. Length: 3.132 miles. Race over 60 laps.

Imola was feared as the thirstiest of all tracks. Even with 220 litres in 1985 the race had ended in bitter chaos with front-runners running out. What would happen with only 195? The grid lined up Senna, Piquet, Mansell. Third race, third time. Mansell had no fuel problems at all. The Williams went only as far as lap eight after two pit stops. Misfire, electrics, finally a cloud of smoke. Prost won, Piquet second.

Senna: 15 points. Piquet: 15. Prost: 13. Mansell: 6.

Monaco (Monte Carlo). A street circuit which the cars have long outgrown. Too tight to overtake easily. And it has a sharp edge: because it is so cramped – claustrophobic, really – only 20 cars start instead of the usual 26. That makes qualifying tense and sometimes downright cruel. But the place seems necessary to the image of Formula One. It is the only race where qualifying is on Thursday and Saturday, Friday being kept sacred for wine, women, song and Press Relations. Length: 2.068 miles. Race over 78 laps. Speeds – average speeds anyway – well under a hundred miles an hour.

The first session was a nightmare. No other word will do. Piquet's car blew up, Mansell's car blew up and the spare car blew up. Amidst all this Piquet had at least managed one flying lap to be thirteenth quickest and that would get him into the race. Mansell was twenty-second. It meant he was not yet in the race at all. And it rains in Monaco. If it rained in the second session on Saturday, Mansell would have absolutely no chance of gaining the time necessary to hoist himself into the top twenty. Rain slows even Formula One cars. (This happened in 1983 when McLaren lost both their entries, Watson and Lauda).

Monaco is a harbour and a hillside and you can see the cloud gather up there over the hills. As they walk from their hotels, the drivers habitually cast nervous glances up to those hills. But for the Saturday session the weather was . . . good. Mansell went out in the untimed hour and a half and was repeatedly baulked by Arnoux (Ligier) and finally, trying to force his way through, they touched. Thankfully the Williams was basically unhurt, as was its driver.

Now the actual qualifying. A car spilt oil and while this was being dealt with all the other cars went back to the pits. It meant that nobody, nobody at all, was out there on the track. A clear lap beckoned to anyone brave enough to try it. *Faites vos jeux*, as they'd say up the hill in Casino Square. Mansell gambled, came out, got safely round and was at last in the race.

Later during the session all would come right and Mansell would set the fastest time, only to be subsequently bettered by Prost. Never mind that. Mansell was on the front row of the grid and at Monaco there is no better place – in fact nowhere else at all – to be. He didn't get the best of starts and slotted in behind Prost and Senna. It stayed like that: no retreating. Typical Monaco.

Mansell's engine wasn't delivering power smoothly at the endless corners and the driving was harder work than usual. The trio ran in their lock-step for twenty-five laps when Rosberg – combative here as elsewhere, rarely accepting the constriction of not really being able to overtake – edged by and Mansell came in for new tyres. He ran fifth to lap thirty-eight when Alboreto dropped out and he was fourth. Senna was ahead and Mansell gave chase, coming upon two cars he would have to lap. Patrick Tambay (Lola) was in one, Brundle in the other. These two were approaching a right-hand corner and braking from around 135 miles an hour, side by side. Tambay's car suddenly rose over the Tyrrell and flipped, smashing into a guard rail. It landed the correct way up and Tambay astonishingly wasn't hurt. It might have been – and did look for a fleeting instant – infinitely worse. Brundle's helmet had tyre marks on it.

Mansell held fourth place, which was all he could realistically anticipate anyway, and Prost finished an eternity up ahead for his third consecutive win at Monaco. 'Once I had the car in pole position it was always *logical* to win,' the Professor said.

He was defending his world championship with consummate control and towards the end of this race, when Rosberg flirted with an attack, set the fastest lap three times without ever sacrificing that control. A glance at the table suggested that he was entirely capable of retaining the championship.

Prost: 22 points. Senna: 19. Piquet: 15. Rosberg: 11. Mansell: 9.

A few days after Monaco, the Brabham team were testing at Ricard. During that testing the car of Elio de Angelis went out of control – it may have travelled through the air for as much as 100 yards – and came to rest upside down. This is no place to examine the facilities, or lack of facilities, present at Ricard that mournful Wednesday but discussion of them became bitterly intense when de Angelis died in hospital the following day.

Nigel Mansell had been at Ricard when de Angelis crashed. He would say subsequently that he and de Angelis had become close friends and that when de Angelis died he asked himself the most profound question: what am I doing in this? He drew a kind of answer out of that question: that if I am in it, I might as well do it properly, try to be the best, win races.

Close friends? That had only happened after Mansell had left Lotus and it is fair to say, necessary to say, that when Mansell had his crash at Ricard in 1985 de Angelis was one of the few who rang him up to see if he was all right.

Belgium (Spa, near Liège). Scenic, wooded, with a hairpin – La Source – where you can (if you have the right pass) stand just inside the armco – please don't stand outside the armco – near enough to see the helmeted heads bobbing and banging under the G forces. Once the cars are round that hairpin, jud-jud-juddering away, they go downhill into a left-right kink which is as spectacular as anything in the whole hurdle race. Length: 4.317 miles. Race over 43 laps.

And they came to Spa, the circus, and none could conceal their sadness; Mansell himself was a sombre figure in the paddock, lost in his own thoughts. These are brave men but when one of them is missing it is very, very close to home. Part of the sadness is the sure knowledge that the next race will go on and the world will go on. And it did.

Mansell qualified fifth after another moment with Arnoux which brought some very pungent words out of him. Fifth wasn't at all bad because Spa is not Monaco. Here you can overtake. The problem is the initial problem: La Source, which the cars reach just after the start, jostling and struggling, and if there's trouble there it spreads in all directions at once. Piquet, on pole, gunned the engine and was gone safely through. There followed a complicated *carambolage* although both Mansell and Senna escaped it. Prost's car was damaged. He had to go into the pits and lost a whole lap. By then Piquet was away and Mansell was moving against Senna.

The third time they came round La Source and into the descent to the left-right kink Mansell made his move and got him. But Piquet was more than five seconds ahead – already. And on lap five, in the Bus Stop, Mansell made a genuine mistake: 'I was too fast. I braked late and I had to bounce the car off the kerb to keep it on the road. The car went up in the air.' It came down undamaged, Mansell wrestled it round so that it was pointing the right way and set off again. By then Senna had gone through and one of the Ferraris, too. The mistake had left Mansell fourth.

Piquet had a lead of almost ten seconds over Senna but his engine blew up on lap sixteen and now Senna led and Mansell was past the Ferrari into second place. He stopped for tyres on lap twenty, Senna on lap twenty-one and as Senna emerged from the pits he saw Mansell go by into the lead. The gap was three seconds. It would remain so for almost an hour while much, much further back Prost was making a charge to sixth place. Whenever Senna threatened, Mansell responded. He said (cheekily): 'I thought I'd upset him a bit by turning up the boost and going quicker.'

Ah, the boost. That can drink fuel. 'With three laps to go Patrick Head was giving me an ear-bashing on the two-way radio from the pits. "*Watch the fuel! Watch the fuel!*" On the last lap I heard the engine cough and I thought: No fuel . . .'

And Senna was still there, still that bare three seconds behind; close enough to take the race if Mansell slowed.

But Senna was nursing fuel problems of his own. He accepted that he would finish second and pragmatically – or was it inevitably? – drifted back. Mansell crossed the line, clambered out and said: 'I think I only had fresh air in the tank at the end!'

He also had nine points.

He stood on the rostrum and sprayed a little champagne but what he really wanted to do was slake his thirst and when someone handed him a bottle of mineral water he drank avidly. It had been a long, hot afternoon. 'I am,' he announced to those below, 'very, very happy.' A car was waiting to take him up the hill to the Press tent. There, on a makeshift stage and with a dozen tape-recorders and microphones rammed towards him, he spoke of this and that, the way he does. It was only at the end that he said slowly, solemnly, sombrely: 'I would like to dedicate this race to Elio de Angelis.'

Senna: 25 points. Prost: 23. Mansell: 18. Piquet: 15. Rosberg: 11.

Canada (Île Notre Dame, a subway ride from downtown Montreal). On an island with artificial lakes and the ghostly edifices of Expo '76 – edifices which loom out of the trees. Sections of the track are spectacularly fast. Length: 2.74 miles. Race over 69 laps.

Any lingering questions over Mansell were swept aside – surely forever. As if winning at Spa had made him impatient, he went out in the untimed session – in the wet – and was a massive two seconds quicker than all-comers.

It was an omen. He was fourth quickest in qualifying on the Friday and on the Saturday Senna gave him a target. One minute 24.188 seconds. Fifteen minutes of the session remained when Mansell went for that and beat it. One minute 24.118. He was on pole, happy as he had been in Belgium. He was suddenly the man. It had been a long time coming. And still he was handling it all with his customary prudence, making little jokes and no predictions.

At the start of the race he broke away, Senna following. As they crossed the line to complete lap one, the timing computers blinked out an amazing series of quartz numerals: Mansell was almost three seconds in front of Senna. He added another second to that at the end of lap two and suddenly Senna was slipping back, holding up the cars following him. Prost at last got by and went looking for Mansell, couldn't find him, did find Rosberg in the other McLaren coming up at him. Rosberg went through and now he went looking for Mansell. On lap seventeen he overtook Mansell and, just like at Jerez, Mansell permitted someone else to go by because the fuel read-out was giving him messages he didn't like.

At Jerez, of course, he had been third when he decided to save a little fuel. He had grown in confidence and stature to the point where now, against Rosberg – a man everybody knew to be formidable – he was happy to let him go. We are not, really, talking any longer of confidence and stature. We are talking about mastery.

The cars, incidentally, do something like four miles to the gallon and that consumption is measured with agonising accuracy to take them to the line. If you back off a little bit the saving quickly becomes appreciable. Mansell did precisely five 'fuel economy' laps and started to get good readings again. Immediately – and this *was* mastery, all right – he surged past Rosberg and stayed there. Apart from his tyre change he held that to the end.

On lap fifty-nine he saw something wonderful in front of him, the black and gold of Senna's Lotus. Mansell lapped him. He finished an impossibly comfortable twenty-one seconds ahead of Prost with Piquet third, Rosberg fourth and Senna fifth.

In the last three races he had won twenty-one points out of a possible twenty-seven. In the six races so far, he had scored points in four. He was, then, consistent, but far, far more significantly he had put himself in a position where he had as much chance as anybody of winning the championship.

Prost: 29 points. Mansell: 27. Senna: 27. Piquet: 19. Rosberg: 14.

Detroit (in Detroit City). Mo-town. Street circuit lined with concrete blocks so it's all a funnel. Sometimes they leave the manholes in place which do interesting things to the suspensions of Formula One cars. The track runs along the Detroit River and the organisers drop wrecks in and see how fast they can bring them back up in case an F1 car goes in, too. The drivers stay in the Westin Hotel in the futuristic Renaissance Center in the middle of the track so they never get to see downtown Detroit at all. They're lucky. Length: 2.50 miles. Race over 63 laps. Speed well under 100 miles an hour, which prompts unknowing Americans to say their own cars go quicker on the freeways. When they see the power of F1 in corners they don't say that again.

The race is a game of chance. Anyone can clip the concrete at any moment and a lot do, so that the running order on *this* lap might well not be the running order on the *next* lap although nobody has done any overtaking. This means paradoxically that pole is not all-important. There will be casualties.

Better for Mansell, Prost has always said he dislikes Detroit (Prost is candid enough to say these things on the record). The point is that Formula One – if it is to sustain an image of a world championship – must visit the United States at least once during the hurdle race. Long Beach had been a great success between 1976 and 1983; there had been a flirtation with Las Vegas in 1981 and 1982, the great Dallas disaster in 1984. Watkins Glen, the established home of the United States Grand Prix between 1961 and 1980, was now only a memory. Whatever the drivers thought, Formula One needed Detroit. It was all that was left in the biggest market in the world.

Mansell's form guide was hardly encouraging. He'd finished sixth there in 1983 and been on the front row in 1985. It was no time to dismiss Prost, either. However much he professed his dislike, the

112

Frenchman had been on pole in 1982 and the front row in 1984. He'd set the fastest lap in 1982. He had, though, only finished in the points once, fourth, 1984.

Senna put the Lotus on pole – he seems to like *everywhere* – with Mansell alongside him on the front row. Piquet was on the second row, Prost on the fourth.

Senna took the lead, Mansell following, and on lap two Senna missed a gear. That's not difficult to do here. Mansell seized the moment and overtook him. He cruised away. It was going to be Montreal again . . .

On the fifth lap he pushed the brake pedal at the end of the pit straight and the brakes weren't there. Detroit is all corners and all braking. From this moment on, 'Sometimes I had brakes, sometimes I didn't.' It was like being stretched on a rack.

You cross the line and you're into a sharp left followed immediately by another sharp left; then a right-angle right followed immediately by another right-angle right, then a left, another left, a bit of a straight, a right-angle left followed immediately by a right-angle right; another bit of a straight to a left-right, then a left followed immediately by another left, a right-angle right, a hairpin-like left, up the pit straight along the River to a right-angle right right-angle left, through a kink and back to the finishing line to begin again. With brakes which might or might not work, Mansell would have to survive this assault course another 58 laps. That's 145 miles. That's 870 corners . . .

He couldn't possibly hold off Senna, who went through on lap seven, nor Arnoux on lap eight, nor Laffite (Ligier) on lap eleven.

On lap fifteen Senna came in for new tyres – 'The car had been behaving strangely, I was going nearly sideways in a straight line sometimes' – and that put him back to eighth. Mansell ran a cautious third from laps fifteen to twenty-six. It was an absolute test of nerve. At any moment he might ram the pedal down and find nothing at all, and the concrete, like a whitened tide, would be coming at him. He was briefly into second place during the pit stops for tyres, briefly down to sixth after his own stop for tyres. Towards the end he settled into fourth. This certainly wasn't Montreal. Senna lapped him and towards the *very* end Alboreto nipped by so that Mansell finished ultimately fifth. Prost – never underestimate the man or you'll pay a terrible price – brought the McLaren in third. Mansell said: 'I was never so glad to see the flag in my life.'

Senna: 36 points. Prost: 33. Mansell: 29. Piquet: 19. Rosberg: 14.

Immediately after the race Mansell flew home. He was very,

very tired. And if you think that Formula One drivers are pampered and over-paid, consider: he went virtually straight to Silverstone to do a demanding test session. In the morning they wanted him to experiment with a thing or two, in the afternoon run a full Grand Prix distance. He was still so tired he sat in a corner of the motor-home drifting between waking and sleeping.

He completed the morning session although it's almost impossible to prepare yourself for that. Work on a car can take an age and you have to be ready, the moment it's suddenly done, to get yourself in and go round at 150 miles an hour, maybe for a single lap, get out, hang around for two minutes or ten minutes or two hours while they have a close look.

At lunchtime, he set off in a helicopter to collect Rosanne and the children from a nearby airport. He was not yet qualified to fly on his own so he had a pilot with him. Airborne, they both heard a Mayday from a light plane which was actually in the process of going down near Cheltenham. They asked the control tower at Cheltenham if there was anything they could do to help and within minutes were standing beside the man who had crashed. He lay not far from the light plane in a field. Rescue services arrived and someone asked: What's the best, quickest way to get him to hospital? In a helicopter. They took the rear door off it to get him in lying down and during the journey Mansell held on to him to stop any chance of him slipping out. The man was in pain and might have become unconscious. That would have been dangerous and Mansell knew it. Mansell talked to him constantly so that he wouldn't lose consciousness. 'I'm a racing driver,' he said. 'I know what it's like.'

He was back at Silverstone on time to resume testing . . .

The next race was at Paul Ricard. It was in his thoughts already. 'You don't,' he said quietly that day at Silverstone during the testing, 'actually look forward to a place where there have been so many unfortunate happenings.'

10 Pressure Point

The track had been altered. The S-bend where de Angelis had crashed was gone and, in its place, two new right-hand corners which in effect took the cars from the pit lane straight to a point somewhere along the world-famous Mistral Straight, reducing the length of that. The alterations had more substance than the merely cosmetic, although it was reasonable to ask if the central problem had been squarely faced: was the standard of marshalling and the speed of response to an incident adequate? The race would re-state the question in an alarming way.

France (Paul Ricard, near Toulon). Purpose built and fast; still fast. Length reduced from 3.610 miles to 2.369 miles. Race over 80 laps. The alterations would drop the average speed from around 125 miles an hour to around 117 for the winner.

Of all tracks, Ricard is – superficially at least – the most difficult to put hard questions into proper focus. This is the South of France, this is golden July. The beach people have made the short journey up on trendy motor bikes or mini-mokes or hot-cars of their own. Outside the main entrance carefully chosen girls wander among the columns of vehicles handing out leaflets or programmes or invitations to the very latest disco, and their limbs are a source of wonder.

Inside, in the paddock, the standard of cuisine, mingling with the herbs of Provence and the inescapable garlic, can tempt strong men away from looking at the cars at all. That, and even more limbs.

The French have an instinct for the right place to be at any given moment. More than any other European nation they feed off the temporal, the fashionable and the ephemeral, and Ricard in July for the French Grand Prix is the right place to be. And the right place to be seen to be. If all the film actors of France don't come in person, their children certainly do. Isn't that Jean-Paul Belmondo's son over there?

The pit lane can and does resemble the Left Bank with chic

115

photographers taking their endless pictures of chic people. All this has no measurable effect on Formula One except that the chic people do get in the way of the mechanics. Another race, another place.

Of what had happened in the past, Mansell said only this: 'There's no problem facing life because the day you don't face life and the facts of life you might as well not exist on this earth. You've got to get up in the morning, you've got to go to work, you've got to do your job. So you control it and you do it.'

If he chose to remember – and it would have been inhuman if he had not – that very first time he got into a Lotus here, his own crash in 1985, Frank's crash in the spring, Elio's death – it was not necessary to speak in public about it. Better to conduct himself in the necessary way: another race, another place.

The changes had created a potential problem which exercised the minds of the drivers. The new right-hander along the pit straight meant that from the grid a lot of cars were going to congregate there. Senna, who uses words as sparingly as Mansell, said: 'The track is much shorter and safer. The only doubt is the start because everyone will arrive there together at high speed.' Pole position assumed an importance it had never had here before. If you were on pole you could get through the corner first, leaving any chaos safely behind.

Mansell and Senna fought for that pole across the first session, Senna quickest with 1:06.526, Mansell just behind him with 1:06.755. 'I'm on the front row, so that's not bad, is it?' Mansell said, sparing words again. Curiously, almost freakishly, weather conditions on Saturday for the second session – wind, hotter temperatures – slowed the cars, so Friday's times were decisive: Senna holding pole, Mansell with every chance – well, fifty-fifty – of getting to that first corner first.

The Williams team felt that Mansell would need two tyre stops. Ricard would be hard on tyres. But that was in the distant future – half an hour away, anyway – as the cars stood on the grid, and rain, that awful imponderable, lurked in grey cloud over the hills. At the green light Senna was away like a hare, running hard for the corner.

Steady, Nigel, we thought, all holding our breaths. Remember Adelaide, 1985. Remember Brazil, 1986. Senna both times. Remember? Mansell drew up level, cut across and took that first corner all for himself. He went round it comfortably enough and the race was already spread in front of him. He drew away from Senna. Behind him, there had been no chaos at the corner. Everybody let their breaths out together.

116

On the fourth lap de Cesaris blew up and his Minardi gushed oil onto the track. Mansell reached it, the Williams wobbled but he was through. Senna, following, slithered wildly and went off, crashing heavily. 'There was a lot of oil,' Senna said, 'and I got caught out, I lost it.' Arnoux was second now and beginning to nibble at Mansell's lead: Arnoux, Frenchman in a very French Ligier at the French Grand Prix . . .

And Prost, Frenchman in a very English McLaren, but at the French Grand Prix . . . Prost was beginning to move. He went past Arnoux on lap fifteen – the two men didn't like each other, anyway – and ran some distance behind Mansell until lap twenty-five when Mansell made his first stop for tyres. It was completed in a magnificent 7.2 seconds and when he got back out he was third. Prost, of course, hadn't been in yet. Mansell reasserted himself and when, on lap thirty-six, Prost did come in Mansell took the lead again. The nagging question was: would Prost stop a second time for tyres, as Mansell was planning to do? If Prost didn't, Mansell would have to build a substantial cushion to come in again and still get out near Prost.

The time a tyre change takes is deceptive. The stop-watch measures it only when the car is stationary between the strips of tape the mechanics have laid, like boundary lines, to show the car exactly where to position itself. The total time is much longer, perhaps as much as thirty seconds. Leaving the track, the car has to slow, enter the pit lane – sometimes the entrance to the pit lane is a tortuous, twisting sideroad a hundred yards long – halt, have the tyres changed (that's the 7 or 8 or 9 seconds you see on your television screen) and accelerate out again. While all this has been happening the other cars have been pressing on at high speed.

Mansell now tried to get himself that cushion but Prost, as he always does, held steady and on lap fifty-three Mansell had only a thirteen second lead. He came in. The actual stop was 8.05 and when Mansell did come out Prost was in the lead again – but only by nine seconds. With new tyres Mansell could attack that at will. He did. The lead came tumbling down to 8.8 seconds, 6.7, 4.2 and then Prost was directly in front of him – and vulnerable. On lap fifty-nine, going past the pits, Mansell ducked to the right of the McLaren and was clean through. But Mansell knew all about Prost and every time he looked in his mirrors Prost was still there, clinging on, waiting, hoping. Mansell couldn't know that Prost was being restrained. He didn't like the messages *his* fuel read-out was giving him.

Prost simply dared not risk the counter-attack.

Towards the end Prost lost touch and Mansell was left in splendid isolation. Once, passing the pits, he gave them a good old thumbs up. It was going to be all right. He finished seventeen seconds ahead. Now *that* was a cushion. Prost, still battling, was second, Piquet third, Rosberg fourth. Mansell said: 'My one bad moment was when I hit the oil. I thought I was going to be into the guard rail. And before the end someone cut me up – I won't say who because he is a fellow-countryman (chuckle). But he wasn't looking in his mirrors and I could have gone off. Towards the end I thought Prost was conserving his tyres to come back at me.'

So there it was.

But what about that hard question which had been re-stated? On lap forty-four Philippe Streiff (Data General Tyrrell) came round the corner to the pit straight with his car on fire. He got the car off the track just beside the entrance to the pit lane. After a long time – maybe ten seconds, you ever seen a fire burn in a racing car for ten seconds? – a tentative marshal came up and skirted it with a small extinguisher. He was not wearing fire-proof clothing. A second marshal arrived, who was. Then, roaring up the pit lane, came a fire engine. I repeat: *up* the pit lane. If any car had come in it would have met the fire engine head on. When the fire engine reached the burning Tyrrell, and its water was switched on, the pipe at the back blew clean away and the water flooded the pit lane entrance.

Because, mercifully, Streiff was long out of the car we could afford a good laugh. And indeed the next day the daily sports paper *L'Equipe* devoted a whole story to the incident with the headline 'Clochmerle Continued' after the famous French farce. But everybody knew, deep down, that it was no laughing matter at all. Formula One, the world which Mansell and the others inhabit, is dangerous enough without ineptitude on this scale. If Streiff had still been in the car . . .

By then, of course, the beautiful people had ebbed away and the entrance of the circuit was carpeted with the discarded leaflets, sad as autumn leaves, and the light planes were scudding along the runway, next to the circuit – Paris, the next right place to be, or Nice, or Cannes, or wherever such people go. The mechanics were picking up their pieces. In the paddock, as the motor-home staffs cleared away the carcasses of barbeques and hoarded what was left of the rosé wine – not much – the name Mansell ran like a shiver. How good was the boy? Could he really go all the way? Why not? Well, go on, tell me, why ever not? It was exactly half way through the hurdle race and he was jumping them like a thoroughbred, one after another.

That was the evening of 6 July. Brands Hatch lay a mere week away. The British Grand Prix. It wasn't exactly a fuss, that wouldn't do it justice at all. Mansell had set up something cataclysmic. I know sportswriters are extravagant – but he had.

Prost: 39 points. Mansell: 38. Senna: 36. Piquet: 23.

Britain (Brands Hatch, near London). The best of English pastoral water-colours fringing a pastoral circuit, but tricky to get a racing car round, uphill, downhill. It's almost a rock-'n'-roll place (in technical terms, of course). Many drivers say it is the place they measure themselves against. Jonathan Palmer: 'You don't do a perfect lap anywhere, but here you're more aware of that.' Length: 2.613 miles. Race over 75 laps.

He set the tone as he was always going to set the tone, with a few of those sparing words. 'The better I do, the more I want to keep doing well. It's got to the stage where I think I can keep on improving.' It was hardly a cataclysmic thing to say; but then he wasn't that kind of bloke.

Britain had the yearning, this was the British Grand Prix, this was high summer . . .

The Thursday was quiet. The circus was gathering. Metal-on-metal chimes as the mechanics worked on this or that, the tinkling of teacups from motor-homes, subdued laughter. Thursdays, during the gathering, guard their solemnity. The cars are already nestled in their pits, held there, wheel-less, on stout steel tripods. The cars won't be going out today. And the cars seem curiously chunky, curiously functional without the bodywork which can be attached in a couple of minutes by a few screws and makes them, before your very eyes, into the beautiful beasts you know so well.

Another race, another place.

Well, not this one.

Senna sat under the clear plastic awning of the John Player motor-home locked into deepest conversation, charts and technical papers being passed round, his eyes missing no detail. Ducarouge was there beside him. Warr sat opposite. Nearby a pretty girl dispensed coffee from polystyrene cups to a few journalists who gazed at Senna's table, not daring to go near.

Was Senna the man to beat Mansell, here, of all places? 'Brands Hatch has always been good to me since my early days,' he said. 'In my first Formula One race here I was third, last year I was second, so it is a very good progression.' But this was publicity-speak, and only marginally to do with the race.

119

Senna didn't have to elaborate on anything. He would do all that in the car.

Prost, also deep into publicity-speak, said: 'I had only 26 points at this stage in 1985, now I have 39 and the second half of the year will be better for me.' Well, he would say that, wouldn't he? But was The Professor the man to beat Mansell, here, of all places?

Piquet said little. For him nothing changes. Another race, another place. But he had the same car as Mansell and, more important, as the number one driver at Williams, he had their spare car, too. Was he the man . . .?

Then – the Friday and words had no currency any more. It was time to go for pole, time to think about that. In the untimed morning session Mansell had engine trouble and the mechanics changed the engine. It is a ritual, not a crisis. They've done it before.

Frank Williams was there, the first time he'd seen cars in combat since his crash. He had followed the season very closely and there was little happening he didn't know about, although he insisted that he wasn't trying to run the team. He was a poignant figure in his wheelchair, his formidable intellect unaffected and he would permit himself no self-pity. The crash, he would say, was my fault. And he still had that warming smile. Nothing could take that away. The day, he said, was 'emotional but great fun.' As he was wheeled by, 20,000 people in the grandstand opposite the pits applauded long and deep. It was the only way they could say it: Welcome back.

But the cars were in combat. With the engine changed, Mansell went out in the first session for the grid and didn't get close to a clear lap. He had to overtake three cars. It left him third behind Piquet and Gerhard Berger (Benetton).

Berger, a slim, almost wan, young Austrian, was in the process of building himself a reputation – fast. Everyone knew he was going to win races, nobody, of course, knew where the first would come. It wouldn't be long. Was he the man . . .?

Piquet waited for the Saturday session knowing that everyone had to fear him. They were right to do that. On that Saturday he went round Brands Hatch in 1:06.961 and none of the others could live with it. Mansell, at 1:07.399, was on the first row, then Senna, Rosberg; Berger, Prost. It could hardly have been better balanced.

The session was marked for Mansell when, really going for it, he came upon a slower car and went off. It is (almost) a ritual, not a crisis. He'd done it before. The car was mildly damaged.

e smile on
the lion.

n-Marie
hen
of the
body,
he
id, talking.
es what
erally did,

ansell
lion at
, he was

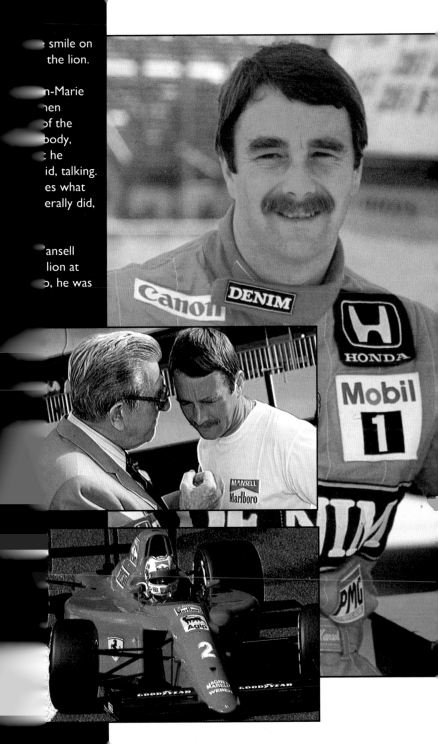

The sweep on Monaco in 1990 where Mansell ran a strong second until the engine failed.

(*Left*) Ferrari folk chewing over the nitty-gritty. Alain Prost (back to camera) makes a point, Steve Nichols the designer (in sunglasses) ponders it.

(*Above*) Mexico '90 and Ferrari folk celebrating the team's first win-double since 1988. Prost has just won the race, Mansell 25.351 seconds behind him.

(*Below*) Any pit stop is a precious handful of fraught and fleeting seconds. This one in 1990 went right...

(*Left*) Race four, 1991 and the great title challenge begins. Thus far Mansell's Williams Renault hadn't finished a race. Now at Monaco he takes second place.

(*Bottom left*) Mansell majestic at Monza, autumn 1991. Prost looks bemused, Senna does what people generally did (again), listens to Balestre.

(Below) The man of '91: power, poise, concentration, judgement.

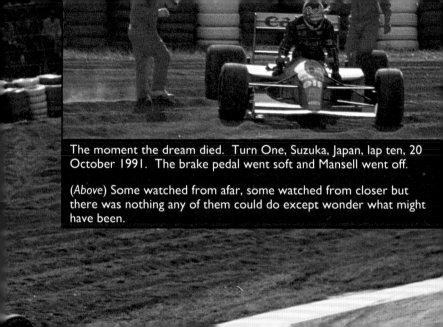

The moment the dream died. Turn One, Suzuka, Japan, lap ten, 20 October 1991. The brake pedal went soft and Mansell went off.

(*Above*) Some watched from afar, some watched from closer but there was nothing any of them could do except wonder what might have been.

Sunday, 13 July 1986.

Brands Hatch is not an easy place to reach if you are one of 120,000 trying to do that. You meet the queue at the Dartford Tunnel, eight miles away, and the M25, designed to cope with a lot of traffic, can't begin to cope at all. That's *before* you turn off on to the narrower road which goes up the long hill to the circuit. By then you've got the atmosphere. The helicopters bank and wheel above you, probing for the landing pads behind the village of marquees. Even a couple of miles from the circuit every grass verge is cluttered with parked cars, tightly packed, and the occupants are making the walk up the hill. Already, six hours before the race, the pace is quickening, the atmosphere building.

Sunday, 13 July 1986, and by mid-morning Brands Hatch presented an astonishing spectacle. Even the vast grassy bank facing the rear of the paddock was completely enveloped by people. Thousands and thousands of heads. Down Paddock Hill, temporary stands were full. Just past the bridge at Clearways, temporary stands were full. It made a bowl of people from Clearways to Paddock – maybe 80,000 of them.

They did get the smell and sound and might of the cars before the race: in the morning warm-up.

Mansell went well in that and was second quickest. Not that that meant much. Piquet had a small turbo fire, so small that it could be comfortably repaired. The race didn't start until 2.30. He wouldn't need the spare car. Not that that mattered much.

The crowd settled again. They cheered when Derek Bell, world sports car champion, was driven round like an emperor, pausing only to make explicit gestures towards where, in the Elf motorhome, the Press were drinking the last of the rosé which had been hoarded from Ricard. Bell, much loved, got explicit gestures back.

The crowd had the strength of their ear-drums sharply tested by Concorde, hired to make a low fly-past. The crowd had their credulity tested when a party of British soldiers fought a mock battle against a party of mock German soldiers and – surprise, surprise – beat them. This is family entertainment for 120,000 people? One of the drivers, Christian Danner, was German. He was far too polite to say what he thought.

At last, mercifully, the sound of gunfire died.

It was time, high time, for sounds just as sharp and potent. It was time, high time, to get the cars out on the grid. They cruised round as imperiously as Bell had done and settled. Each was on its appointed place, each surrounded by that milling, jostling horde who seem to find a way onto the grid to gaze at them. There is still time, but only a few minutes.

And this is the countdown which bears, inescapably, all the inherent strands of a pace which is gathering more and more quickly.

With thirty minutes to go – at two o'clock that Sunday afternoon – the pit lane was opened so that the cars could go round to their appointed places.

With fifteen minutes to go – at 2.15 that Sunday afternoon – the pit lane was closed.

With five minutes to go – at 2.25 – a board was held out. It meant only: Five minutes to go . . .

With three minutes to go – at 2.27 – a heightening, urgent voice over the tannoy said: *Clear the grid, clear the grid.* The horde melted away leaving only, like sentinels, the mechanics who would actually start each car.

With one minute to go – 2.29 – a board was held out, a klaxon sounded shrill and godless, and the voice over the tannoy was saying: *Start engines.*

With thirty seconds to go, a green flag was waved and the cars moved slowly away for the parade lap which would bring them back, in precisely the same formation, for the start. They weaved violently as they went. Friction warms tyres.

And, as they moved in a cavalcade up to the end of Cooper Straight and out of sight, out into the country, a hush fell. Everybody knew the symmetry:

	PIQUET (Williams)
MANSELL (Williams)	
	SENNA (Lotus)
BERGER (Benetton)	
	ROSBERG (McLaren)
PROST (McLaren)	
	FABI (Benetton)
ARNOUX (Ligier)	
	WARWICK (Brabham)
DUMFRIES (Lotus)	
	BRUNDLE (Tyrrell)
ALBORETO (Ferrari)	

	BOUTSEN (Arrows)
JONES (Lola)	
	PATRESE (Brabham)
STREIFF (Tyrrell)	
	TAMBAY (Lola)
JOHANSSON (Ferrari)	
	LAFFITE (Ligier)
NANNINI (Minardi)	
	DE CESARIS (Minardi)
PALMER (Zakspeed)	
	DANNER (Arrows)
GHINZANI (Osella)	
	ROTHENGATTER (Zakspeed)
BERG (Osella)	

They came round under the bridge, still slowly, still in perfect formation. It was necessary for each car to be stationary before the race could begin. *There* was Piquet, coming to rest on pole, *there* was Mansell stopping beside him.

Waiting.

There was the tail-end of the cavalcade flowing round the loop, each snout of each car being slotted into its appointed place. When Berg settled, a marshal ran across the very back of the grid waving a green flag so that Derek Ongaro, high up in the control tower, would know they were all stationary. He reached for the button and pressed it. The red light came on above and to the right of the twin columns of cars. As it did every engine began to rev.

Every driver knew – and every one of the 120,000 knew – that at some instant between four and seven seconds away Ongaro would press the green light. All that power, all those engines revving so hard they made concrete tremble and vibrate in the pit lane, would be unleashed at once.

Green.

It was mad, mad movement, surging and churning, surging and churning at the unleashing and Mansell got the nose-cone of his car just in front of Piquet, thrust the small knob into second, let the clutch out – a stab of the foot – and felt the drive-shaft 'explode'. The momentum he already had took him round Paddock Hill Bend and down the drop towards Druids. He was cruising. Uselessly, hopelessly cruising. The surge went past him: half a dozen cars. It was all over and he was very, very angry. He thought: *I'm out of the race, I'm out of the race*. He moved politely to the left to allow the surge to go by unimpeded. He could do nothing else.

He had no way — absolutely no way — of knowing that the world had gone crazy behind him. As the rear of the grid came into Paddock, Thierry Boutsen lost control of his car, veered left, smacked into a guardrail, was flung back across the track. Johansson was going straight for him and fast. Johansson — it was all reflex, all unconscious reaction — flicked his Ferrari to the right to miss Boutsen. Laffite, already on Johansson's right, veered *further* right to miss Johansson. He went off. He went across the grass and into a barrier head-on. Even as Laffite was travelling across the grass the rest of the grid was arriving — and fast. Six of them went into the carnage.

Mansell, out on the circuit, was shouting into the two-way radio: 'It's over, it's over. It's all over, I'm out . . .'

He saw a black flag. And another. Incredible. The race was being stopped. He had no idea why. But the race being stopped: he just couldn't believe it. He came back to the pits, got out of the car and stood.

Laffite was trapped. Palmer, a doctor, of course, rushed over to help if he could. Prost, a close friend, left his McLaren in the pits and started to run towards Laffite, It would take more than thirty minutes to get him out of the cockpit. He was eventually taken to Sidcup Hospital by helicopter, legs broken.

It could have been worse and for a long time it looked worse. Quite naturally it absorbed the attention of almost everyone. All unnoticed, came an announcement that the race would be re-run for the whole 75 laps as a *new* race. Even though this wouldn't happen until the helicopter returned from Sidcup — in case, of course, it was needed again — and that would take another thirty minutes, maybe more, it was simply not enough time to repair Mansell's car. Again all unnoticed, the team of mechanics who spend their lives waiting — they're the ones who care for the spare car — began to ready it as best they could. A new race. An entirely new race. There was nothing to stop Mansell having the spare, nothing at all. The *Daily Express* would capture it all in a headline which echoed round the country the next morning: THE GREAT ESCAPE . . .

It was easy to miss that in the confusion. Laffite was still in a mangled car, the drivers were back in the pits exchanging rumours and explanations. Boutsen would say candidly that he didn't know how it had happened, it had just *happened*. Others would recall their particular visions of going into the carnage. Three of them wouldn't have spare machinery to take part any more: Berg, Danner and Ghinzani.

Mansell looked at his spare car. It was, he observed very quietly, 'the one which hasn't been working very well during the week-end.' It was set up for Piquet and it had been set up *by* Piquet. That didn't matter. Nor that on a hot afternoon there was no bottle of water in it to slake Mansell's thirst.

He was back in the race . . .

Shortly before four o'clock the twenty-two cars left did another parade lap, came to rest on the grid in exactly the positions they had been. Derek Ongaro pressed the button. Red light. At some instant between four and seven seconds he pressed the other button.

Green.

Piquet leapt away, Mansell following. They all got round Paddock Hill, Piquet still in front, Mansell still following. He could afford to be in no particular hurry – yet. It was a strange car, imperceptibly different and when you live on small margins imperceptible differences suddenly become very perceptible indeed. Berger bustled through to take second place from him. Fine. Seventy-five laps to go. A hundred and ninety-six miles to go. Let Berger go after Piquet.

When Mansell was good and ready – and this is a *very* mature man we are talking about now – he would have another look at the situation. By then he would have the feel of the spare car, would be blending with it, would know what it would do and how it would do it. Then he'd make it move.

He gave himself two laps. He came upon Berger at Pilgrims Drop and had him. He began moving towards Piquet and as he did so both the Williams opened up a gap on all the others, a gap which would grow and grow until two quite distinct races were going on at the same time, Piquet versus Mansell, the rest versus the rest.

The 120,000 didn't care about that.

That vast bowl of people, tier upon tier of them all the way from Clearways to the bottom of Paddock Hill, watched hypnotised as each time Piquet came under the bridge Mansell was closer. Nervous fingers stabbed stop-watches on and off. The differences between the two cars was two seconds. The drivers could see each other with utter clarity. The two cars might have been locked together by some umbilical cord. And it went on and on until lap twenty-three when – in one of the great moments if you were British – Piquet missed a gear and Mansell was past him at Pilgrims

125

Drop into the lead. Piquet responded and they ran together in their lock-step again but Mansell leading, Mansell leading, Mansell leading.

Every time they came under the bridge the 120,000 were cheering, but that was partly the release of great anxiety. The pit stops for tyres were coming, and every moment brought them nearer. What if Mansell's people made a mess of it? He'd never catch Piquet again. Any slip by an errant hand, any instant the pneumatic hammer wasn't functioning as it ought, any wheel-nut which stuck . . .

Piquet turned into the pit lane on lap thirty going like a sling shot. He knew the importance of *his* tyre stop. 9.04 seconds. He came out in a flurry of angry wheel-spin. Now Mansell. He left it for another two laps – let the pit settle again, let them get ready. He came in on lap thirty-two. *He* came in like a sling shot. 9.57. You can do them quicker but no sane man can *demand* that you do them quicker under this depth of pressure.

Mansell gunned the engine and was gone along the short feeder lane, slightly uphill, which pitches you out into Paddock Hill. As he reached it Piquet was coming round the loop from the bridge towards him, foot hard down. If Mansell had come out a fraction later Piquet would already have gone and the race decided. But he hadn't.

Mansell had to defend desperately. His new tyres were cold. Piquet's had been warmed by three laps. Piquet would be faster – measurably faster – until Mansell's tyres had come up to the same temperature. By then Piquet would have overtaken him. Piquet would be long, long gone.

Mansell blocked him in Druids and blocked him coming down from Druids and blocked him in Cooper Straight and his tyres were already a little warmer. Mansell held him out in the country and as they came into the loop under the bridge the whole 120,000 were cheering again. Mansell was still in the lead.

But he was still vulnerable. They moved into Paddock Hill and the umbilical cord held them but Piquet took a wide line to position himself to get Mansell as they went up to Druids. At this moment Mansell was more than vulnerable. He was going to be overtaken. But . . . but there in front of Piquet was Nannini, minding his own business, scrabbling over to the right to get out of the way. Over to the right . . . in front of Piquet. And Piquet hit the brakes hard. Mansell went round Druids and was still in the lead.

His tyres were warm now. Piquet's moment had gone. Mansell set off and squeezed out a little lead. Piquet immediately responded and came close to smashing the lap record. Mansell responded to *that* by smashing the lap record. And there were forty laps to go . . .

With thirty to go, nervous fingers were working the stop-watches again. The gap was two seconds. You could see the gap as well as measure it.

Piquet: twice world champion, being paid a great deal more than Mansell, the number one driver in the team, the one with the right to the spare car and here it was, his spare car, maddeningly always that two seconds in front of him whatever he did. Back-markers loomed here and there like ghosts from another dimension and any one of them could have destroyed the race – by minding their own business, scrabbling to get out of the way, and going to the wrong place to do it. Mansell made no mistake with any of them and they melted away behind him like the ghosts they were. Piquet made no mistake with them and stayed hounding and hunting his own spare car with a Brummie people thought was a loser driving it . . .

With twenty-one laps to go Piquet smashed the record Mansell had set nineteen laps before. Now Mansell smashed *that* again. Nobody had seen anything like this for decades. You'd have to go back to the great heroes and the great days to glimpse anything of this intensity, this scale, this skill, this bravery, this pressure . . .

And still Piquet was there.

The 120,000 were murmuring: Mansell can't stand much more of this, nobody could stand much more of this, and it's the damned spare car, the spare car can't stand much more of this. *We* can't stand much more of this.

And still Piquet was there.

With less than ten laps to go Piquet launched a savage assault and went round quicker than he had done before. Mansell smashed the record again. It may have been the ultimate, decisive gesture. It brought a wild outburst – much more than cheering – from the 120,000. People were on their feet. The commentator on the tannoy was baying into his microphone and nobody could really hear the words.

And still Piquet was there.

All at once the 120,000 fell silent. It was absolutely unreal. It was as if some terrible, communal, childlike superstition had seized them, every of them at some unstated moment and if they *spoke* they would disturb the spell and Mansell's car wouldn't come bursting into view under the bridge this time round.

With three laps left, suddenly Piquet wasn't there, he was further back – not much further back, but further back! To hell with the stop-watches! Look, he's further back, he's further back! Just as suddenly everybody was on their feet making baying noises of their own. Piquet was broken!

As Mansell crossed the line and bored deep into the last lap, thousands of arms were waved, a whole, rippling, turbulent sea of them. This was not the count-down at Brands in 1985, this was not the upraised fingers telling him how near he was. This was ecstatic.

He came under the bridge one final time, smooth, clean, easy. He crossed the line this final time and Piquet was six seconds behind him. It could just as easily have been sixty seconds – which would still have made Piquet second. Prost, running third, was a complete lap behind. Arnoux, running fourth, a complete lap behind *that*. Brundle, running fifth, a complete lap behind *that*.

Mansell had destroyed the most powerful field the world could put against him.

Up on the rostrum he was unsteady. He had driven the race without a drink, without anything to even moisten his lips. Dehydration, he'd say, *as well as* exhaustion. Some said he was close to tears. He was.

'We had,' he would say, when he had had a drink, 'no team orders. It was completely left to us and there was no backing off. It was push, push, push and the person who was going to win was the person who pushed hardest.' However you care to measure it, he had driven one of the great races – and pushed hardest.

It took time to find any perspective. Too much had happened. It had happened in a sort of overwhelming profusion. Someone in the Press Room said they'd heard a hospital bulletin that Laffite was not seriously hurt, although the broken legs were confirmed. Everybody knew it: In Formula One you can be lucky to get out with broken legs, which will of course mend. But Laffite's accident seemed from another age. It *was* from another age.

And you could have been forgiven for not realising – not really realising – that Nigel Mansell, for the first time in his life, led the world championship.

Mansell: 47 points. Prost: 43. Senna: 36. Piquet: 29.

There were seven races left and a four-point lead could be swept away at the very next one, in Germany. None of the 120,000 cared and, I'm sure, none of them were doing mental arithmetic as they went away. What they had was a glow. We all did.

You have to come down with a bump, of course. A proper bump and a real one – preferably several of them. Long before Mansell crossed the line another Williams car had left the factory at Didcot and was being transported to a small, discreet, anonymous track in northern France, called Croix en Ternois. To do some testing. On the Monday morning after the race, while Britain was still intoxicated, Mansell flew there. 'We're doing *bump* testing,' he was told, 'so find as many bumps as you can on that track and see how the car reacts.'

I repeat: if you believe drivers are pampered and overpaid, think about it. And think about Laffite in Sidcup Hospital, too.

Germany (Hockenheim, near Frankfurt). Many drivers say this is flat, tedious and predictable in a Teutonic sort of way. It is. It rains frequently. Length: 4.223 miles. Race over 44 laps.

This one was delicate. He would be subjected to two kinds of pressure, one off the track, one on it. On the track he would have to defend his world championship lead, although only Prost could actually get past him here. Senna and Piquet, who knew all about pacing themselves across the hurdle race, could close the gap. Off the track, the urgency of re-signing for Williams for 1987 was to be communicated to him, although he wouldn't let it reach *into* him. This was a matter of fine tuning and it could hardly have come at a worse time.

Piquet was earning a lot more. If Mansell stayed, could Williams afford to give him financial parity, however much they wanted to? Other teams were actively interested in him, among them Ferrari – who would subsequently claim that on a visit to them he signed a contract and threaten legal action.

If Mansell hesitated, now, Williams might sign somebody else. If he signed *now* and didn't become world champion, he'd sacrificed that enormous bargaining chip. Not that he could wait until the end of the championship before he opened negotiations. That would be too late. It was, as I say, a question of fine tuning, complicated by the fact that other teams were interested. Mansell said he was in no hurry. More privately, after so much struggling, he was enjoying – as any reasonable man would – this courting by the other teams. What made it all more pressing, and brought some strange moments, was a complicated external pressure. But that wouldn't be brought to bear – publicly, anyway – until the Saturday.

In the Friday session Rosberg was quickest with Mansell just behind him. Rosberg announced his retirement that morning and was now driving as if he wished to demonstrate that he had ten good years left in him yet. Typical Rosberg. Typical to go out and do the quickest lap amidst all the interviews he's giving in the pit lane in

English, German, Swedish and Finnish telling the world why he's stopping . . .

In the Saturday session Mansell had engine problems and would start the race from the third row of the grid. Behind all this the complicated dealing was going on and a great deal of complicated dealing had already gone on. It is important to understand it because it had a direct effect on Mansell, his future and his peace of mind. And to understand the dealing you must understand the 'packages.' Formula One teams regard themselves as packages and each component is a part of the package. Thus a winning package is the right designer, the right chassis, the right tyres, the right engine and the right driver. Take a deep breath . . .

Lotus were leaving Renault and going to Honda for their engines for 1987. Honda (as part of their own package) were delighted to find that Lotus would field a Japanese driver, one Satoru Nakajima, instead of Johnny Dumfries. McLaren had already made a (reported) bid to get Honda engines, had been (reportedly) to Japan, but this had now foundered. Honda were (reported) to want to see what Senna could do with one of their engines and as a result of that there were (reported) chances that Senna would replace the retiring Rosberg at McLaren; but this had all foundered. Meanwhile, since Mansell hadn't re-signed, why not Senna for Williams, who already had Honda engines, anyway? Williams certainly weren't going to have Nakajima and if everything had foundered might have been tempted to go for the Renault engines Lotus had just – or were just about to – vacate. Or not, as the case may be.

Got it?

What is certain – indeed, the only thing which seems certain – is that at some stage while the packages were being wrapped and re-wrapped Mansell held the string.

After the Saturday session the Press crowded into their tent for the definitive Press Conference about the package. Much confusion. The Press Conference was temporarily delayed because Honda wanted everything neatly tied up – with the scale of their commitment, who can blame them? – and everything was not neatly tied up. In fact, Nigel Mansell wasn't tied up. What Honda wanted to announce was:

Lotus get our engines in 1987, and the cars will be driven by Senna and Nakajima.

Williams keep our engines in 1987, and the cars will be driven by Piquet and Mansell.

Pressure was on Mansell to re-sign now and then we can get on with the nice, neat Press Conference. What Honda didn't want to announce was that:

Williams keep our engines for 1987, and the cars will be driven by Piquet and Mr X.

Got it?

Mansell, to his great credit, did not bow to this pressure, made stronger because it was so immediate. The Press Conference was joint: Honda, Lotus and Williams. The announcement was made, complete with Mr X. You cannot blame Mansell for keeping his several options open and you cannot blame him for having been to visit Ferrari – as someone said, everybody should drive for Ferrari once in their lives, to which someone else said, Yes, but only once . . .

What Mansell now had to do was exclude all this from his thinking and concentrate on the race. The race wouldn't wait, the race was tomorrow. He had the four-point lead to defend. He had a championship to try and win.

And it went wrong.

From the start it was Senna, Berger, Rosberg, Piquet, Prost, Mansell. 'On the second lap the balance of the car went completely and at every corner it tried to go into a spin. You know when your fuel tanks are full and you're still getting wheel spin in fourth and fifth gears that something is really wrong with the car.'

He could do nothing except keep it going and hope. One consolation, and one only: Rosberg, now virtually out of the championship, took the lead from Piquet on lap fifteen and for virtually all the race would keep Piquet, Prost and Senna at bay. After seven laps Mansell was running in sixth place – worth only a single point, of course – and had to stay a prisoner there until, on lap thirty-eight and the end of the race in sight, he hauled the Williams past Arnoux and was fifth. He'd get a couple of points. Now Piquet made his move. It was this same lap thirty-eight. He went round the outside of Rosberg but Rosberg, driving as he had done in qualifying, came back at him and stayed there, harrying, until the second last lap. While Rosberg clung on to Piquet, Senna went past Prost. As they circled, heading towards the last lap, it was Piquet, Rosberg, Senna, Prost, Mansell, Arnoux.

That last lap would change everything.

Going to the first chicane, Rosberg kept straight on, braking as he went through the cones. He was out of fuel. The engine stammered briefly and he meandered on, stopped completely. All three of Mansell's rivals were now in the big points – nine for Piquet, six for

Senna, four for Prost. Well, at least Mansell would get three points and would keep his lead in the championship. It had been an interesting race as races go; not more.

Piquet came smoothly into the curved concrete stadium which flows all the way round to the line. He crossed the line. The crowd waited for Senna. Now he came into the stadium, round the loop to the right-hand corner and the line a couple of hundred yards away. As he cleared the right-hander the Lotus began to weave violently from side to side.

He was literally trying to slosh whatever fuel was left in the tank to the engine. Somehow he reached the line. He was second. Now Prost. And he was weaving, too! The McLaren crept reluctantly round that right-hander and stuttered for a hundred yards, stopped. No fuel at all . . .

Prost sprung out and began to push the car. The crowd loved that. Prost pushed hard, marshals nearby watching, astonished. *Go, go, go*, the crowd cried at him. He abandoned trying to push and steer it, went behind the car, dipped his head and pushed the rear with both hands.

Mansell was coming. As Prost pushed, Mansell went by and over the line. He, of course, had been running more slowly all afternoon. He had plenty of fuel left. Prost suddenly stood up and walked away from the McLaren towards the pits. 'When I remembered that pushing over the line doesn't count, I gave up,' he said.

He had made a very public spectacle of the farce of fuel restrictions and however much the crowd had loved that, the point was made. This was not racing.

Mansell had noticed Rosberg's retirement, had noticed his immobile McLaren back there and thought, as he passed that, it might be a 'lucky day.'

But he certainly didn't know, as he crossed the line, that he was up to third.

Mansell: 51 points. Prost: 44. Senna: 42. Piquet: 38.

Hungary (12 miles from Budapest). A new track set in gentle hillocks, built quickly at great expense and a genuine unknown quantity. First penetration of the Iron Curtain by Formula One. Everyone on their best behaviour. Slow track, lots of sharp corners set at interesting Engels. Length: 2.494 miles. Race over 76 laps.

To have the race at all was an Ecclestone master-stroke and the little man was clearly delighted. So was everyone else. To have it was almost *logical*. Every year at the Austrian Grand Prix – a comfortable journey from both Hungary and Czechoslovakia – you could pick out the Skodas which had come with their tell-tale H for Hungary and CS for Czechoslovakia stickers. Now, a much shorter journey from Budapest, the Hungarians had something all their own, although, being entrepreneurs, they were delighted to share it and on the motorway between Budapest and the track you could pick out – couldn't help picking out – a lot more stickers: BG for Bulgaria, R for Roumania (whole ancient bus loads of them), DDR caravans (they're from the wrong side of the Berlin Wall), PL for Poland, all heading for the track. They all wanted to see and smell and taste the most extreme form of capitalism outside Wall Street.

Only the Soviet heavy lorries were going the other way, towards Budapest. The race would be televised live in the USSR but sadly Ivan and his family were not to be allowed to see and smell and taste from closer range . . .

By nature this was an extreme week-end. It would certainly be that for Mansell. Because the track was new, there was a special exploratory session for drivers on the Thursday. Martin Brundle was moved to say that it was so tight it reminded him of Monte Carlo without the houses. Once all the drivers had been round, the muttering started about lack of grip. Over the years, tyres leave a thin film of rubber on tracks in regular use. Here that film of rubber was missing and consequently adhesion. During qualifying many, many cars would spin and Senna freely confessed that he'd spun more times than in the rest of his career. Mansell, echoing Brundle, said it was as important to be on pole here as it was in Monte Carlo. On the Friday he was quickest, in front of Piquet and Senna.

On this Friday, too, Williams announced that he had re-signed. There can be little doubt that he cost himself a million dollars – Ferrari were reported to be offering him £2.3 million and Williams couldn't match that. Mansell said, and these words are entirely typical of him: 'In the end there are more important things in life than money. This is a good team, I'm a driver and now I can concentrate fully on that and, I hope, keep on winning.' He had given himself peace of mind.

Williams himself was there, finding the hot day difficult to cope with but obviously – and publicly – delighted. 'I think,' Williams said, 'that he has proved his is truly world class.'

Almost everyone shared that sentiment.

Going into this eleventh round of the hurdle race, Mansell had won points in nine of them. It is worth emphasising, too, that he had won four races. Prost had taken the championship in 1985 with five;

Lauda in 1984 with five; Piquet in 1983 with three; Rosberg in 1982 with one; Piquet in 1981 with three . . .

That might, or might not, mean anything. It depended on your total points and when Lauda had won in 1984, Prost had scored seven victories. To have a chance, you have to be consistent. Mansell's eight finishes in ten races argued that. What he couldn't do was shake off the Piquet–Prost–Senna wolfpack. They were as consistent as he and on the law of averages alone one of them was going to do well every race.

On the track in the untimed Saturday session Mansell was badly baulked by Riccardo Patrese (Brabham) who, travelling much more slowly, moved over. Mansell struck the rear of the Brabham and went into the guardrail. ('I don't think he saw me.') Fortunately damage was light and in the afternoon he qualified fourth behind – you've guessed it – Senna, Piquet and Prost.

Race day seemed innocent enough except for a rumour that Soviet television hadn't paid its dues in dollars in advance and been told to go. Big Brother isn't accustomed to that behind the Iron Curtain (or most other places) and shortly thereafter we could all hear a heavy droning from over the nearby hills. Tanks? No, just an aerobatic display to keep the crowd – a staggering 200,000 – happy. But race day was not innocent, despite the absence of tanks.

Something *was* happening – or had already happened – which would break the season open in suspicion, doubt and acrimony and not a little mystery. It would call into question Williams as a team and cost Mansell dear. As the cars waited for the green light few suspected anything like that. As they went for it on the green, few suspected anything like that . . .

Mansell, surging, was past Piquet and Prost and following Senna. As they completed lap one, it was Senna, Mansell, Piquet, Tambay, Prost, Jones. But Senna, showing mastery of his own, was pulling clear and Piquet was gaining on Mansell. Piquet was gaining easily on Mansell. At the start of the third lap Piquet simply powered through at the right-handed corner beyond the line. Mansell, impotent, watched him go.

Something strange *was* happening. Although Piquet wasn't catching Senna, he was moving clearly and decisively away from Mansell. How could Piquet, in an 'identical' car, be so much quicker? More to the point, as careful observers noted, Piquet's car was smooth through the corners, Mansell's decidedly twitchy. Mansell didn't seem to be in any mechanical trouble, but of course, even careful observers can't always tell that. In can be hidden within the bowels of the car, only revealed when the driver gets out afterwards and tells you. But there was no concealing that Piquet was quicker, vastly quicker. It was compounded on lap twelve when Piquet caught and passed Senna. It was further compounded on this same lap when Prost passed Mansell easily.

Piquet stormed off, leaving Senna to fall back towards Prost. Mansell ran fourth and a memory of him returns, going hard through the loops and corners and undulations alone, gaining nothing. He would keep on, of course. He would keep going hard, of course. But he wasn't really going anywhere. He would have to try and pick up the pieces. Prost came in on lap seventeen – electrics – and that made Mansell third and he stayed there, circling and circling, making two tyre stops, actually being lapped by Senna and Piquet during the second of them. He had to circle three times more to un-lap himself. By then Senna and Piquet were locked in a fascinating and frightening duel – both Brazilians, remember, not exactly bosom pals, remember – which reached its consummation on lap fifty-five when, at that right-hander, Piquet moved out of Senna's slipstream but Senna wouldn't give way. Piquet did get through but was into the corner on the wrong line, braked, the Williams swung sideways under the braking and Senna was through again . . . Piquet gave chase and two laps later did it again, wheels almost off, opposite lock on the steering wheel, everything, was through and gave Senna a shake of his fist as he went.

If anyone should have been shaking fists, it was Mansell.

Not that 200,000 people noticed him, so much. The Senna–Piquet duel had – rightly – absorbed every attention. Ah, you could hear the 200,000 saying, so this is what it's all about, capitalism.

Senna tried counter-attack but couldn't catch Piquet. Piquet won and both he and Senna finished a lap in front of Mansell.

A lap?

Mansell, visibly angry, wasn't saying much at all. Subsequent inquiries revealed that Piquet had made full use of the fact that he had a race car *and* the spare to experiment with and he found a way of gaining stability on the corners . . . *and* his people hadn't told Mansell's people about it. The advantage had been that whole lap and nine points to Piquet, only four to Mansell. It was bound to strain relationships within the team and between the two men, and this as the run-in to the championship itself beckoned. The next race, Austria, was only one week away. Clearly the matter would have to be sorted out by then – or Williams risked a split, one half of the team competing against the other, and all that that would mean.

Prost's retirement eased the pressure a little.

Mansell: 55 points. Senna: 48. Piquet: 47. Prost: 44.

Rosberg, who hadn't finished here, was next on 19 and out of it. The Gang of Four would contest the remaining five races among themselves.

Austria (Osterreichring, roughly in the middle of Austria). Really fast. All loops in the hills which means that spectators can see a lot of the race. Spectacular moments as the cars go uphill from the start line, 'bottoming' out and sending a firework display of sparks as they do. Spectator drinking not discouraged. Sometimes hot, sometimes thundery, which can make the day into night. Length: 3.692 miles. Race over 52 laps.

And what, everyone wanted to know, had happened in the week between here and Hungary? What had been sorted out? Mansell would not be drawn into any kind of verbal struggle with Piquet, though he did disguise a barb – if that was what it was – by adding that his idea was to drive for a *team* and that was what he intended to do. He arrived at the track late on the Thursday afternoon – it was the sombre gathering of the circus, the same atmosphere as it had been on the Thursday at Brands, had been, for that matter, everywhere else – and seemed entirely relaxed. No point in looking back, he said, that's not my way, I'm looking forward. It was enough. Whisper had it that the Budapest Blunder would not be repeated. He turned from it all, and was happy to turn from it all, with words about actual racing. 'I think it is fair to say that some of the corners here are the most demanding in Formula One.'

If Silverstone is the fastest track, this is next. At moments, awesome. At moments, in the sweep of the loops, majestic. If you have anything go wrong, terrifying.

Friday's grid session demonstrated that. Warwick, going up the hill from the start line, was reaching towards 190 miles an hour when a tyre burst. 'I remember going through the air at an angle of 45 degrees. I wasn't worried about the car turning over. I was worried about it crossing the top of the barrier.' A lot of people stood and sat on a bank there. Warwick – artificially joking his way through his memory of what had happened – added: 'I'm not hurt, I can't see any blood anywhere.'

Mansell qualified fourth on the Friday behind Rosberg, Prost and Piquet. The familiar story. When Mansell was going for it de Cesaris blocked him going into the final corner. *That* familiar story. Then the Italian's engine belched smoke all over Mansell. He wasn't hiding behind that, figuratively or otherwise. Ominously he said: 'I'm a second and a half slower than the Marlboro McLarens, Nelson is a second slower.' And this on a speed circuit. On the Saturday it was worse, Mansell fifth fastest, Piquet sixth fastest. Little Teo Fabi and Berger, both in Benettons, took the front row. They were getting quicker and Berger was Austrian, the natural successor to Lauda. This was his home match. If you do the pools, you know what that means.

On race day, in the warm-up, Mansell was quickest, Piquet sixth. It's the last, final and so often deceptive clue you get to the race itself. This time it was extremely deceptive. That warm-up, in chronological order: Mansell, Patrese (!), Berger, Rosberg, Fabi, Piquet, Prost . . . and you had to let your eye stray down to twelfth to find Senna. All your instincts told you to distrust that.

(Very brief *Pit Stop*: Normally the aerobatic display here is a Harrier, courtesy of the RAF, which does amazing tricks, suspended in mid air, bowing to the crowd; not this time – only the Italian version of the Red Arrows who singe the trees up at the top of the hill from the start line and, because of accidents, are fewer in number each year. They are known inevitably as the *Arrivedercis*; but all this is only a marginal digression. It does not set the scene for the race or add to it in any sensible way. It only – because the planes fly low and are noisy – stops people speculating about the race. Merciful release, even though you can choke on the red and blue smoke trails the *Arrivedercis* spew out as they criss-cross so inconveniently above the luncheon areas.)

In the race Fabi and Berger set off as if they were demented – sorry, it's only an observation, don't sue – and astonishingly they were gone together, leaving the Gang of Four far behind in their wake and everybody else. Just when you think you've got Formula One into perspective, these things happen. But for how long? Berger in the lead, Fabi followed, Prost after that, Mansell after that, Piquet after that, Rosberg after that, Senna after that. Strange it was because Berger and Fabi were powering away and stranger still when on lap sixteen Fabi overtook Berger and slowed almost immediately with his engine in trouble. By then Senna was out – engine, too – changed into slacks, sat on the pit lane wall watching. That, whether he could guess it or not as the cars went by, had very likely cost him the championship.

Lap seventeen: Berger, Prost, Mansell, Rosberg, Piquet.

Then the tyre stops. But Berger pressed on without one and so did Mansell. When Prost came in on lap twenty-one Mansell was up to second place. He held that until lap twenty-five when Berger came in – but not for tyres, although these were instinctively changed. He had a misfire.

Mansell was now in the lead, Prost behind him. Mansell came in on lap twenty-eight – stationary 11.2 seconds – and Prost had gone by. As Mansell emerged, warming his new tyres, Prost was eleven seconds up the road. Piquet, fourth, pulled into the pits. Engine.

Of the Gang of Four, two would get nothing, nothing at all.

Mansell said his engine 'was fine. I was warming the tyres up and I knew I could catch Prost. I was just getting back into the rhythm.' Prost, in fact, was pulling away at a rate of a second a lap but there was still time, still plenty of time. They ran in that order between laps twenty-nine and thirty-two. With Senna and Piquet gone, this was a good day to get points.

Mansell felt the drive-shaft go out on the back of the circuit. The same problem as Brands Hatch. No Great Escape now. The race had been going more than thirty laps. He pulled the Williams on to a peaceful grassy verge, pulled his helmet off and began the long walk back, quite alone. 'At least,' he would say – and scant consolation it was – 'the car was going well when it was going.'

Prost won it . . . just. 'The engine started to die and I could only bring it to life by using the gearbox and the clutch. Then I had a misfire. I was afraid.' He was deeply sure, as he crossed the line, that the McLaren wouldn't have gone another lap.

Postscript: Mansell said: 'The last thing I wanted was Alain to win. He's the man I fear most.' Prost said: 'I think the championship is between Nigel and myself now, but . . .'

Mansell: 55 points. Prost: 53. Senna 48. Piquet: 47.

Italy (Monza, near Milan). Hysterical centre of Grand Prix where mobsters, morons and Ferrari missionaries mingle with 100,000 others and alsatian dogs keep them from the paddock in case they try to wrench bits off the Ferraris to keep as icons. Pick-pockets pick-pocket pick-pockets here and every woman for herself. The track is not particularly special but nobody notices that. Length: 3.603 miles. Race over 51 laps.

In qualifying – will nobody *ever* get a clear lap? – Mansell was baulked at the chicane by two other cars and was fourth quickest. Senna, of course, was quickest. On the Saturday Mansell moved up a place but there had been changes. Fabi was on pole, Prost unusually alongside him. (Ron Dennis, who runs McLaren, once said: 'Who wants to be remembered as winning all the qualifying sessions? You want to be remembered for winning the races.') Mansell and Berger shared the second row, Senna and Piquet the third.

Prost was in trouble before the start of the race, coming into the pits after the warm-up lap. He changed cars and would start from the pit lane after the rest had gone. Meanwhile, Fabi's car wouldn't go and when the mechanics had feverishly corrected that he sped round but would have to start from the back of the grid. That had taken away the front row. Mansell was in reality on pole.

But from the green Berger pulled ahead, Mansell behind him, Piquet behind him. Senna's transmission had gone on the grid and the two columns of cars moved past him, Senna waving his arm in the traditional signal that he was in trouble and *miss me, please*. They did. As all this was going on Prost pulled out of the pits for what would have to be a long and arduous race, making up the ground he had lost already.

Berger moved away, Mansell tracking him, and it was clear: The odds were much, much heavier now against Senna winning the championship. It would surely happen one year. Not this year.

Mansell stalked Berger and on lap seven overtook him. A lap later Piquet took Berger and Mansell and Piquet ran one-two all the way to lap thirty-seven. Ten laps *earlier* Prost had been black-flagged – he had changed cars after the signal to begin the parade lap, that was clear, nobody was disputing that. What nobody knew was why it had taken twenty-seven laps to decide it and pull him from the race. No matter. By an irony his engine had gone anyway. Prost was truly out of it.

Piquet was the problem and for several laps he had been catching Mansell – quickly. By the end of lap thirty-seven Piquet had caught him and now overtook, powering past. Mansell's seat-belt – well, one of them – had come undone and that made him move around a little in his seat. A little is a lot. It affected the precision of controlling the car. Piquet, also, had experimented with a different rear wing and this gave him greater speed in a straight line. Taken together, it was decisive.

Piquet ran comfortably to the end and finished ten seconds in front of Mansell.

Mansell: 61 points. Piquet: 56. Prost: 53. Senna: 48.

Portugal (Estoril, near Lisbon). An interesting selection of corners but a circuit lacking real atmosphere because the admission cost represents a large sum of money to one of Western Europe's poorest countries. (Near the airport you can see slums which would never be tolerated in Hungary.) Weather guaranteed golden, so bring your waders. When it rains, it rains – and it does rain. Length: 2.703 miles. Race over 70 laps.

Mansell was outstanding on the first day of qualifying, quickest in front of . . . Piquet. On the Saturday Senna took pole, Mansell behind him, then Prost, Berger, Fabi and . . . Piquet.

Significantly Mansell now had his own spare car and this cannot be underestimated. It gave him parity of opportunity, it emphasised his growing stature, it was only fair anyway, and it was useful for harmony within the team. A spare car. *His* spare car. To experiment with, maybe, or make ready to suit himself as a back up in case anything went wrong. The way he was driving one car would be quite enough. But peace of mind? The spare car was good for that. Therapeutic. Reassuring. Nice.

Senna had taken pole with a lap of 1 minute 16.673, the only man under 17 seconds. Piquet was back in the one-18s but over seventy laps that was hardly a factor.

Mansell joined in the general admiration of Senna – you *had* to admire what he did in qualifying, *had* to – but sincerely added that he hoped he wouldn't be that quick in the race. He need not have worried. Mansell made a perfect start and by the first corner was clearly ahead. On that first lap Senna had a look, as they say, but Mansell held him and they settled. By the third lap Mansell was moving fractionally away and would continue to do this. Better for him, Berger, third, was holding up both Piquet and Prost. This was valuable. Piquet and Prost took until lap nine to overtake Berger, and by then Mansell was almost ten seconds ahead. Senna, of course, was still behind him.

All four completed pit stops for tyres efficiently and by lap thirty-four were running: Mansell, Senna, Piquet, Prost. It did cross Mansell's mind that if he made a mistake now . . . well, three of the Gang of Four were just *there* and they'd swamp him. He made no mistake. What he did was break the lap record – more than once. Piquet had a lunge at Senna but Senna wouldn't be budged. Prost waited, watched, waited. On lap fifty-three Mansell broke the lap record *again* and was now uncatchable. The final laps were an agony. Would the car last?

Piquet made the mistake, spinning, and that let Prost up to third. No, wait a minute . . . Senna's in trouble, look at him coming round the last corner, he's only just going to make the line . . . Prost's gone past him, Piquet's gone past him.

Senna: no fuel. Whatever he did now, he couldn't be champion. And then there were three.

Mansell: 70 points. Piquet: 60. Prost: 59.

Pit Stop

Someone, I think it was a French journalist, made the interesting discovery first, and it was this: the ground rules of Formula One had not been changed. Ground rules? You have the sixteen races but you can only *count* the points you score in eleven of them. Absurd? Yes. Artificial? Yes. Worth changing? Yes. (Lots of people said, that rule was abandoned years ago, wasn't it? No, it wasn't. It was just that it hadn't been needed for so long. The rule was introduced, of course, so that one driver couldn't run away with the championship half way through and render the rest of the season meaningless. There are tickets to be sold, you know, and who wants to pay a lot of money to see a championship which has already been decided?)

Once the truth of the interesting discovery had been ascertained beyond doubt, the rush for pocket calculators began in earnest. Two races remained. Mansell had seventy points but had already used up his quota of eleven races. If he scored in Mexico and Adelaide, he would have to drop his two worst results. Approaching the Mexican Grand Prix, they were the fifth place at Detroit (two points) and the fourth place at Monaco (three points). Piquet had sixty points but from only nine races. Whatever he got in Mexico and Adelaide would count fully. Prost had fifty-nine points and had used up his quota of eleven races. If he scored in Mexico and Adelaide, he was better off than Mansell – he would drop two sixth places, worth only a point each. Still the pocket calculators gave their deliberations, and nervous journalists – who would have the onerous task of explaining this to their readers *and* superiors (I tried and failed) – checked and rechecked.

If Mansell won in Mexico, he would have 79 points minus the two from Detroit = 77.

If Piquet was second in Mexico, won in Adelaide and Mansell didn't finish in Adelaide, he would have 60 + 6 + 9 = 75.

If Prost was second in Mexico, won in Adelaide and Mansell didn't finish in Adelaide, he would have 59 + 6 + 9 minus 1 minus 1 = 72.

Somewhere in the middle of all this, a great truth revealed itself and none could doubt it, however they arranged the figures.

If Mansell won the Mexican Grand Prix he would become Britain's seventh world champion. It didn't matter a hoot about the Brazilian or the Frenchman or the pocket calculators. 77 was a winning score. Adelaide, afterwards, would be a milk run.

And another great truth.

If neither Piquet nor Prost beat him in Mexico, second place would be enough.

Mansell: 70 + 6 minus 2 = 74.

Piquet, third Mexico, winning Adelaide: 60 + 4 + 9 = 73.

Prost, third Mexico, winning Adelaide: 59 + 4 + 9 minus 1 minus 1 = 70.

Wait a minute, wait a minute, this is better than we thought.

If neither Piquet nor Prost beat him in Mexico, third place would be enough.

Mansell: 70 + 4 minus 2 = 72.

Piquet, fourth Mexico, winning Adelaide: 60 + 3 + 9 = 72.

A tie. Now let's look at the tie-break. Most Grand Prix victories gets it. Both have five. Most second places gets it. Both have two. Most third places gets it. Both have three. Most fourth places gets it. Both have one. Most fifth places gets it. Mansell has one (dreaded, not now discarded, Detroit), Piquet none – none at all. Mansell would win the tie-break, and the game, and the set, and the match. On *fifth* places.

Whatever happened to Prost? Fourth Mexico, winning Adelaide: 59 + 3 + 9 minus 1 minus 1 = 69. *Goodbye.*

Whether you can follow all this or not doesn't matter. It doesn't matter that hoot we mentioned before. The sum total of it was getting clearer and clearer by the minute.

If you were British, and particularly if you were Nigel Mansell, it was looking good.

11 · Out of Gear

The headline said enough: MANSELL UNDER THREAT. It was late September, it was Maranello, headquarters of Ferrari, and it was a Press Conference given by Enzo Ferrari himself. Ferrari, at eighty-eight, was the seigneur of Formula One.

'Mansell,' he said 'signed a regular agreement on 10 June after coming here twice on his initiative.' The meaning was clear. Enzo Ferrari believed that Mansell had signed to join his team for 1987, and claimed the document was comprehensive, reaching all the way down to how many tickets Mansell would want for each race. 'Then his behaviour astonished us. Our lawyers will take proper action in the case.'

Mansell, of course, had re-signed for Williams.

What actually happened when Mansell visited Maranello? He was entirely free in July to join whom he wanted and he was, perhaps, exploring one option among several. Since Ferrari is almost a sacred name in Formula One, Mansell was pleased at their interest in him – Enzo Ferrari would use the word 'admiration' for him at the Press Conference – and when he did re-sign for Williams he was careful to stress, and formally asked the journalists to stress on his behalf, that by re-signing for Williams he intended no slight whatever on Ferrari. Quite the reverse.

This begs the question: what did he sign at Maranello? It does seem certain that he signed *something*.

It was a good story for the national papers on its day, although nobody had any idea what Ferrari's lawyers might try to do or where they would try to do it. Such international cases can last a long time, cost a lot of money, and bring with them who knows what else? Much later, the matter would be resolved and Mansell would thank his lawyers for clearing it up.

As he had had to do so many times – for different reasons – in the past, Mansell needed now to banish it from his mind and concentrate on Mexico, then only a couple of weeks away.

143

Nobody knew quite what to expect there. No Grand Prix had been held in Mexico City since 1970, a complete generation away. The Marlboro Grand Prix annual guide records, cryptically, that only one driver had an 'accident' then, Jackie Stewart. He was driving for Ken Tyrrell, who explained that a dog ran across the track 'de-ranging Stewart's front suspension' and presumably the dog's front suspension, too.

Truly, nobody knew quite what to expect.

The World Soccer Cup had been staged there a few months before and from that had come tales of impossible smog, impossible traffic jams and the inescapable problems you get at an altitude of 7,500 feet. Worse, before the World Cup there had been a major earthquake which tore a canyon of chaos through the city and may have killed as many as 50,000 people. Nobody knew. Nobody knows how many people live in the city because a couple of million are in an endless shanty town near the airport and who's counting? The Mexicans aren't.

Mansell went to Austria the week before to do some testing because Austria is at least at altitude. He was calm and becalmed there, saying all the right things. It was no time, no time at all, to start changing himself. He was obeying Stewart's dictum, stated so clearly: *You read the book you are reading, you go to bed at night, you don't become a hermit, you don't try and alter yourself.*

He flew out on Concorde to New York where one of the team's sponsors, Mobil, wanted him to give a Press Conference. He was impressive. He had lunch with the President of Mobil, which is all but unknown and evidently like touching the Holy Grail. The President was impressed. Frank Williams went too, although he would return home and watch the race on television. However much he wished to be in Mexico – he did, after all, have both his drivers leading the championship – his health was not yet robust enough for a place like Mexico City. Before flying on to Mexico, Mansell appeared three times on television. He was impressive; and much impressed by the sudden realisation that the forename Nigel doesn't exist in the United States. He was introduced as Ni-g-el with a hard g.

He arrived in Mexico 'knackered', posed dutifully for a photographer friend, drank exactly one beer, went to bed and slept like a baby.

Prost had flown in via Amsterdam where he had contented himself with saying: 'I am not thinking about the championship, but I know it will be very difficult,' Publicity-speak again. I was on the

Mansell, pensive at Brands Hatch.

The tense time. Getting ready to come out of the pits.

Brands Hatch 1985 and after all the waiting he wins his first Grand Prix.

Brands Hatch 1985 and all England smiled with Mansell after he won the European Grand Prix. The clenched fist salute ...

BRANDS HATCH
RMULA ONE WORLD CHAMPION

ell Oils   She' ils   Shell Oil   Shell Oils   S

Brands Hatch 1986 and one of the great duels of all time, Mansell versus Nelson Piquet. Mansell took all the pressure – and won it.

(Left) The hardest race of his life, Brands Hatch 1986 and the British Grand Prix. He was so exhausted anxious hands held him on the balcony. (Right) But he recovered enough to hold the champagne and spray it over the hundreds below.

Mansell, vintage '86, harnessing all the fearsome Honda power even on the kerbing.

The 1976 World Champion, James Hunt, with Mansell.

The moment the emotion got almost too much. Mansell embraces his wife – and doesn't care who's watching.

The Williams team had a special day at Brands Hatch to raise money for charity after the 1986 season. Everybody was happy, particularly Frank himself and Mansell.

1986: Blow out in Adelaide. The immediate aftermath.

1987: Mansell is stretchered away after crashing heavily in practice for the Japanese Grand Prix at Suzuka.

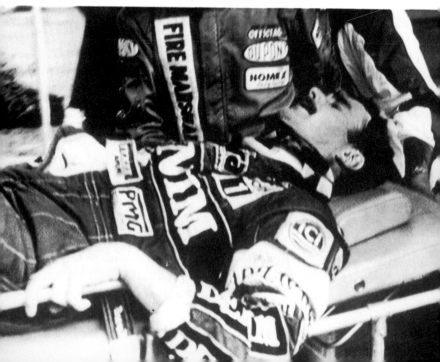

same flight and he did look content. Ominous, it was. Then he was gone into First Class.

On this day Frank Williams was already back home. He gave a most candid interview to an international Press Agency. 'When we took Nigel on it was as a good journeyman and a good team-man who would get points and win the odd race. I'm in wonderland now.'

Mansell himself gave a Press Conference at the track and said a great deal, charming the Mexicans with his earthy humour and his best relaxed manner. An earnest reporter asked how much he was paid. 'As is well known, I drive for pleasure not money.' This was offered with all the assurance of a millionaire in a sport of millionaires, and provoked hilarity.

Would breathing be difficult at this altitude in a cockpit? 'No,' he said, wrapping a hand round his throat, pretending to strangle himself and, at the same time, sinking towards the floor. More hilarity.

If you won't tell us how much you earn, please tell us how much you think the world championship would be worth? 'I've never been world champion. Nelson and Alain have. You'd better ask them.'

How much do you think it would be worth? 'Oh, about one peso.' Even more hilarity.

There were serious questions, too. What did Mansell think of Piquet? 'He is a fellow driver. I don't know much about his life and I don't know much about the man. It is a professional relationship.' And that was as candid as you can decently get.

Piquet, lean, equally relaxed, was down in the pits eyeing the engine of his own car. He had been doing altitude training. He said with his customary reluctance that he had come here to win the race, of course, but everybody understands how difficult the races are to win, and if 'Nigel and I have mechanical failures Prost will be waiting'. Ominous, it was.

Part of the track was a section of old-fashioned banking and this, too, was bumpy. Derek Warwick marched firmly away from his Brabham after going round and said: 'Haven't enjoyed myself so much for years.' He was almost alone in feeling this. You could see the cars bouncing on the banking, see the drivers' heads being battered. It was going to be a long race. 'Very bumpy,' Mansell said. Piquet ventured that cars could become airborne, as they had done at a notorious bump at Long Beach in 1983. You might be tempted to think that a few bumps wouldn't disturb any vehicle resting on those enormous tyres but you'd be wrong. And do you really want to take off at 180 miles an hour?

Then there was the problem of the tummy. Dire warnings had been given by journalists covering the World Cup. Don't touch the water, don't accept any drink with ice in it, don't eat the vegetables . . .

One Williams team-member was so alarmed by this that he decided to take the most drastic precautions, bring powdered porridge and mineral water from New York, mixing them together and eating the result cold twice a day. 'I am touching nothing else,' he said, 'until I get home.'

Two drivers at least would get the tummy. One would appear drawn and ill. He would win the race. The other would appear much fitter and happier. He would not win the race . . . .

And then there was still the altitude. How would turbo engines react at 7,500 feet? Whose turbo would react best? Nobody knew.

Mexico (on the outskirts of Mexico City). Extensively re-built since the last Grand Prix in 1970. Length: 2.748 miles. Race over 68 laps.

Stewart remembered that last race and now told *Autosport*: 'We should never have raced but everyone was frightened not to race because it would have resulted in a riot. People were lining the track and even sitting on it and despite repeated appeals from myself and Pedro Rodriguez it did little to help. The race was delayed and I remember very well the organisers finally coming to us and saying: "Everything is OK now, we have taken insurance and it doesn't matter if you kill anyone." '

This was not going to happen again. High fences had been put round the perimeter of the track to keep people firmly off it – in 1970 a child had actually run across during the race and almost been killed, never mind Stewart and the dog.

What was disturbing was at least one corner which had a concrete wall near it. 'I personally think it's very dangerous,' Peter Warr said. 'I don't know how the drivers will react when they see how fast the circuit is.' Apart from the bumps, the drivers reacted well. 'Same damned surface as 1970,' someone muttered, 'they haven't resurfaced it.'

In fact the track was fast and, even with two chicanes, would allow average speeds up to 124 miles an hour.

On that Thursday there were two exploratory sessions, morning and afternoon. In the first of them Mansell was quickest of all and said 'the track was getting faster all the time.' In the afternoon he was third quickest and although nobody was reading too much into any of this, it did at least serve as some sort of form guide. Prost had been fifteenth in the first session, although McLaren weren't saying

146

what the problem was. One of their directors, Creighton Brown – a most engaging and perceptive man – did say: 'Alain is tired. What he needs is a holiday, although I'm afraid there's no chance of that yet. We are trying to shield him as much as we can, we're keeping any social commitments to a minimum.'

We'd all seen Prost in 1983, how exhausted he had been in South Africa, how Renault had tried to shield him as he went for the championship then. But that had been wholly different. France demanded that Renault win the championship to justify all the taxpayers' money which had been spent. It put almost intolerable, unbearable strain on Prost. But this October day in Mexico Prost was another, more experienced, more hardened man. He had lost the championship to Lauda by half a point in 1984 – the cruellest result of modern times. Prost had won seven races, Lauda only five and because Monaco had been stopped before the end – a storm – only half points were awarded so Prost's win there was worth only four and a half, not nine. Nine would have given him the championship.

Prost had taken his defeat with considerable dignity, had returned in 1985 and won the championship with a magnificent 76 points – 73 counted – against Alboreto's 53. Only statistics mitigated against Prost now: no driver had successfully defended a championship since Jack Brabham in 1960. (Before that Fangio had won it four times in a row, 1954–1957, and Alberto Ascari in 1952 and 1953.)

Senna, of course, was quick and there were mutterings that Lotus were doing something illegal. They put out a strong statement:

There have been several stories that the John Player Special car used by Ayrton Senna during the 1986 qualifying sessions to obtain eight pole positions is in some way built or operating not within the Technical Regulations of the Formula One Championship or not within the spirit of those regulations. The car has at each event been certified both by the FISA Technical Delegate and the local ASN Scrutineers to comply completely with the Technical Regulations. While Colin Chapman would have been proud of, and enjoyed the controversy surrounding a car carrying the name Lotus, the defamatory and derogatory statements must now either

(1) Stop

or

(2) Be supported by an official protest as provided for in the Sporting Regulations

  (3) Be answered by the persons making them when Team Lotus will be forced to seek recompense for the damage to its reputation.

And that was that, really.

During qualifying Mansell would feel the effects of Montezuma's revenge. Where he got it is anybody's guess. One theory was that it might have been at Murray Walker's sixty-third birthday party in a pleasant restaurant in Mexico City's Zona Rosa shopping area. It seems unlikely. About twenty journalists and broadcasting people were there, too, and they didn't get it. Mansell, incidentally, sat very quietly – although clearly he was guest of honour – so that this would be Walker's night, not his. Walker, who wasn't expecting Mansell, was extremely moved when he came. 'Best present I could have had,' he said. What is certain is that Mansell did get it and 'my stomach problems certainly didn't help much.'

He didn't look too bad – certainly not as bad as young Berger, pale, wan, drawn and ravaged. Astonishingly this didn't affect Berger's driving and in the Friday session he was quickest – and the only man under one minute eighteen seconds. Piquet came after that, Mansell after that. This is how it looked:

  Berger 1:17.780
  Piquet 1:18.037
  Mansell 1:18.269
  Senna 1:18.367
  Fabi 1:18.971
  Prost 1:19.294

Already a theme was emerging: Berger and Fabi in the Benettons could be the spoilers to Mansell, Piquet and Prost if only their cars would go the distance. Prost had handling problems and the special turbos the team were using caused problems, too. But six was fine for him, par for his personal course.

After the first session the talk in the pit lane wasn't about Prost or the Benettons but Mansell and James Hunt and a feature article Hunt had written in *The Times*; and particularly one section which talked about 'the collective view of the insiders' in Formula One. 'The sad and bewildering fact is that by and large they do not want Mansell to win.' Hunt added that, 'Above all, the drivers want a worthy winner.'

148

This was patent nonsense, however much the rest of the feature – and it was a long one – was sympathetic to Mansell and truthful about him. Hunt's notion that Mansell was not right for a world champion begged a question which Hunt neither posed nor answered. It was: What is right? Certainly Mansell lacked charisma but of the whole crop of drivers, who had that, anyway?

What convulsed the British Press – who waited eagerly for photostats of the feature to be wired from London – was that Hunt, our last world champion, had picked this moment to say such things. It could scarcely help Mansell as the hours ticked by towards the race.

Hunt could certainly argue that as a commentator and now a temporary journalist it was not his job to help Mansell but to say what he thought and write what he thought. When I asked Hunt what his reaction would have been if he'd read such an article about *himself* just before his race in Fuji in 1976, he said typically and briskly: 'No time to read things like that, too busy driving.'

Mansell wouldn't be drawn on it and said, also typically, that he was treating this as just another race, not letting anything peripheral get to him. He was still obeying Stewart's dictum.

Nor, apart from Montezuma, was there any pressure he couldn't cope with. Rosanne had remained in the Isle of Man so that he could concentrate undisturbed. He stayed in his hotel in the Zona Rosa, and there was a helicopter service – a wonderful, almost miraculous release from the endless traffic jams which clogged and crippled the dual carriageway to the track and made the journey frustrating, dangerous (most cars bore the scars and indentations of accidents) of uncertain duration and deeply unpleasant because of the air you had to breathe all the way.

On this Friday, while we waited for the photostats of Hunt, Frank Williams was at home telling the *Daily Express*: 'I miss not being there a great deal, I miss the testing, the worrying, the talking long into the night. Could this go wrong, could that? Have we got it right here? What are the others doing? There are no individual triumphs in motor racing. It's a team effort. It's a great feeling.

'I live with the drivers in the cockpit. I really envy them. They are the car controllers, yet they are human. I've always hung over Nigel's cockpit when he is in, like a small boy.'

In the Saturday session – the final one for the grid, of course – Senna was quickest, though neither Piquet nor Mansell was far behind him or far apart themselves.

149

Senna 1:16.990
Piquet 1:17.279
Mansell 1:17.514
Berger 1:17.609
Patrese 1:18.285
Prost 1:18.421

For Mansell, the second row of the grid seemed good enough on a fast track with a wide straight.

Sunday, 12 October.
The cars came to that grid and rested there for the traditional half hour before the start with the traditional parasols held over the drivers to keep the sun off them. (Sun is a very rare sight in Mexico City because it has to penetrate hundreds of feet of pollution. Occasionally the pollution does clear for a few unexpected moments before it swallows the sun again.) Suddenly Mansell clambered urgently from the cockpit and set off cantering towards the pits where the mechanics had – cryptically – put up a Toilet sign with an arrow. Montezuma. With only minutes to go, and a hard, long, rough race in prospect, it wasn't good.

He was back comfortably before the start and the cars went off on their parade lap. They came like a snake round the banking to the grid, Senna leading them. At this moment Williams was saying on BBC television: 'There are no team orders. They are free to race as best they can but they mustn't crash the cars . . .'

At the green light Senna got away cleanly but Mansell, directly behind him, wasn't moving at all! The column of cars behind Mansell, all coming like an irresistible force, ducked round him . . . Patrese and Warwick to the left, Fabi to the right. Mansell was engulfed. And still the car didn't move!

'The start? I didn't do one. It's like a nightmare. You roll up onto the grid in first gear, you position yourself, you pull the gear lever back into neutral and you're waiting for the red light to come on. As soon as the red light does come you put the car into first and when you take your hand off if the gear knob doesn't jump back it obviously means that it's in gear. I didn't slip the clutch because I didn't want to burn the clutch. So I dropped the clutch and nothing happened. I got a bunch full of neutrals. My immediate thought was my gearbox was broken and I hadn't got any drive at all. I thought: *I can't believe it, I can't believe it.* Then I pulled back into second gear and managed to get that and I just chugged away from the line.'

150

Mansell had been so comprehensively engulfed that it was hard to know where he was. Around twenty-first.

'What I should have done is creep forward and make sure it was in gear but they'd made a big point at the drivers' meeting that any cars creeping would be penalised. That's the last thing I'd wanted, but in the end I penalised myself. It was a freak thing, it was very unusual. After that it was just a question of employing one's patience and skills and determination, and not panicking, and getting my head down, and getting on with the job. I thought it was possible to finish in the points.'

Senna was long gone, being harried along the straight to the first corner – a right-hander – by Piquet at his elbow. Senna locked up his brakes – wisps of smoke from the tyres told that – and Piquet got through. Mansell was now twenty-second. As they crossed the line to complete the first lap it was Piquet, Senna, Berger, Prost . . . Mansell eighteenth. He was charging as he would have to charge, but he couldn't afford to charge too hard. He'd have to try and conserve the tyres. On lap two, while Piquet was putting some distance between himself and Senna, Mansell overtook Palmer, then Boutsen, then Streiff.

Mansell: fifteenth.

At the front Berger was beginning to lose touch with Senna and falling back towards Prost, while on that third lap Mansell held fifteenth. On the next lap he overtook Fabi, then Warwick.

Mansell: thirteenth.

On lap six he overtook Arnoux and Patrese.

Mansell: eleventh.

He held it across the seventh lap but the crowd weren't bothered about that. Prost, timing everything with his usual perfection, moved past Berger to third place and Piquet was pulling further and further ahead of Senna. To millions of British televiewers it could hardly have been worse. As long as Mansell could keep going there would be attrition ahead, cars breaking down, the usual crises – but how much attrition?

Mansell held eleventh across the eighth and ninth laps, went past Dumfries immediately after.

Mansell: tenth.

On that eleventh lap Alboreto went out – turbo – and the attrition had begun.

Mansell: ninth.

But the charge was wearing his tyres and on lap twelve he had to come in, round the tortuous bend at the entrance to the pit lane, all the way along to where the mechanics waited. They did a 'fantastic' job but as Mansell came back out onto the long straight he had lost almost everything he had gained.

Mansell: fifteenth.

And on lap thirteen, as he warmed his tyres, he dropped another two places.

Mansell: seventeenth.

'I had a load of trouble in the race,' Mansell would say. Now he started charging again. He let the tyres warm then got safely past de Cesaris – and in a short, sharp burst overtook Danner while Dumfries' pit stop gave him another place. That was lap eighteen.

Mansell: thirteenth.

He ran evenly and sensibly there across laps eighteen, nineteen, twenty and twenty-one. The front runners, so far away, had settled, too: Piquet, Senna, Prost, Berger – Berger still there, Berger still dangerous, Berger still the spoiler.

On lap twenty-two Mansell overtook Palmer.

Mansell: twelfth.

Ahead now was Boutsen (again!) and Mansell had him on lap twenty-five.

Mansell: eleventh.

He took Alliot.

Martin Brundle made his pit stop for tyres on lap twenty-six and that was another place gained.

Mansell: ninth.

He ran evenly and sensibly there across laps twenty-six to thirty-two. By then Rosberg had had a disastrous pit stop, had started his rear wheels spinning before it was completed, had gone out with a damaged valve, accelerated hard along the straight and when 'I looked in the mirror I saw the rear tyre crooked.' He reasoned that the suspension of the car must have failed, and he returned to the pits, climbed out of the car and was astonished later to be told it was only a puncture. That did not alter the fact that he was out of the car and out of the race.

Mansell: eighth.

After three laps there he had to come in for a second pit stop – tyres again – but only lost one place to Danner (again!). Danner dropped spectacularly away, and would finish a lap behind the leaders. Meanwhile Warwick dropped out.

Mansell: eighth.

He ran evenly and sensibly there across laps thirty-eight to fifty-one. On that lap thirty-eight Berger was in the lead and he *was* the spoiler now.

Prost, Piquet and Senna, all on Goodyears, had made their pit stops but Berger, who was on Pirellis, was happy with his tyres and ran to the end with them. He had Montezuma and, all else aside, didn't want to break his concentration.

On lap fifty-two Mansell overtook Alliot (again!).

Mansell: seventh.

Just as significantly, Piquet had needed a third tyre stop and he was now just one place above Mansell. Lap fifty-two: Berger, Prost, Senna, Johansson, Patrese, Piquet, Mansell. Both Piquet and Mansell were a lap behind the others. On lap sixty Mansell set the fastest lap – 1 minute 19.788, an average speed of 123.947 miles an hour. On lap fifty-two while Piquet came in a third time, Mansell broke that – 1 minute 19.586, pushing the average speed up to 124.262. A lap later he broke it again – 1 minute 19.441, a speed of 124.489. It was breathtaking.

Now Mansell drew up to Piquet, who was being punished by that third stop and the time lost, but Piquet blocked and blocked. All at once Johansson's Ferrari was gone in a rolling ball of smoke. He pulled off, the rear of his car on fire, and scampered clear.

Patrese: fourth.

Piquet: fifth.

Mansell: sixth.

He had hauled himself into the points. It was lap sixty-five. Patrese, battling to overtake Boutsen, braked far too late and went off. He sat hunched and disconsolate in the cockpit for a moment then, like Johansson, walked away.

Piquet: fourth.

Mansell: fifth.

Could Mansell overtake Piquet and rob him of a point? No. In the end it was as simple as that. He didn't have the power or the time.

Mansell went back to his hotel, picked up his luggage and headed out towards the airport. On BBC Frank Williams was saying: 'I'm very, very disappointed but this is racing. If you have three stops for tyres (as Piquet did) there's no way you can win. Adelaide is a street circuit and Nigel truly excels on street circuits.'

How will the two men react to the pressure? 'Nelson? You wouldn't think he had a care in the world. He sleeps before a race, relaxes, he tells silly jokes all the time in shocking English. Nigel will play his golf. I don't think the pressure has got to him at all.' And team orders? 'If any orders were given, I'm sure the on-board phone wouldn't be working! The deal is they race to win.' A ghost of a smile flickered over Williams' face. He looked better. His face had filled out again. Whatever nationalistic feelings he might have, his team was an international team and Frank was enjoying himself.

Mansell arrived at the airport alone. You must see him: a wide check-in area, a few plastic seats grouped artistically in the middle of it and Mexicans who didn't recognise him at all sitting there, waiting as people wait at airports. He did seem relaxed as he stood checking in with Air France, hoisting his suitcase onto the platform, watching absently as a label was twisted and secured to its handle. His briefcase he kept in his hand.

Nearby other Mexicans milled, waiting too. There was that strange and subdued air of activity. Through plate glass doors ancient yellow Volkswagen beetles – they're taxis – came and left, dropping their cargoes.

A few Pressmen – four in fact, the *Daily Mail*, the *Daily Express*, the *Guardian* and the *Daily Telegraph* – surrounded Mansell. 'Let's go over to the plastic seats,' he said – evenly and sensibly – 'quieter to talk there.'

But he really wanted to eat so instead we all went up a narrow staircase to the restaurant and he ordered a steak, a fruit juice, sat, smiled his best benevolent, firm smile and said: 'You talk about luck. If the car had selected in first gear things might have been different. People must realise that our sport is totally on its own. There are so many things which are beyond our control. Instead of putting a lot of pressure on me people must leave me alone over the next week or so because in Australia, any one of Nelson, Alain or myself can win it. Really, in many ways, I am the underdog.'

The steak came and he began methodically cutting it. He sipped the juice politely, as a polite Englishman would do.

'I haven't won the world championship before. This week-end has been very difficult for me. All the well-wishers have been very nice but they've been calling me ''Champion'' and that's unkind because the last thing I'd do is accept I'm anything before I am.'

He ate slowly. The flight was two hours away. There was no hurry now.

'I think going to Australia with three different drivers able to win the title is tremendous for the sport, although perhaps not for my heartbeat. But the nice thing is, in Australia it will be finished and all over. For sure, I'm very disappointed here and if I'm honest, not just for myself but for the whole of England.' (As he pointed out, fifth place was worth two points but he'd have to drop those two points on the eleven-best-results rule so 'I did it all for nothing, but you have to accept that'.)

'Australia? If it will be, it will be. But it must be said it is almost out of my control. Elements of luck will come into play. Both Nelson and

154

Alain have held the world championship and it's odds-on that one of us is going to win the race, anyway. So people say that the odds are with me. Well, the odds are pretty much against, as well.'

He finished his meal, he made jokes in his slow, deliberate way – it is extremely difficult not to like Nigel Mansell, and if you are one of the few who don't, it is all but impossible not to respect him. That Sunday evening at Mexico Airport in October he was at peace with himself again, very nearly fatalistic. How else can you be when you've got the car in gear, you've got your foot on the accelerator, you're waiting for the green light and – not a damn thing happens?

Only after he'd gone – that firm handshake, those defensive eyes scanning you, that slightly awkward English way of not knowing quite how to leave (no kisses on the cheek, of course, no emotion, just 'OK, boys, see you') he was gone down the staircase to the departure lounge. He may have lingered among the souvenirs in the duty free – pottery dolls, a few dresses on hangers, the inescapable pocket calculators, a whole (equally inescapable) counter of French perfume, the bric-à-brac of conscience for the presents you didn't have time to buy, and none of it as interesting as the fare you can find in any English corner shop. He may not. I didn't follow him there. I suspect and expect that all he wanted to do was go home – we all did – and the Air France flight was the handiest. Not all airlines fly into Mexico City every hour of the day and you get out on what you can get. He'd go Air France, outbound, Paris Charles de Gaulle then London, then the Isle of Man.

It was time to sit on the plastic seats, once he'd gone, and remember that Berger had won the race, Prost second, Senna third, Piquet fourth, Mansell fifth, Alliot sixth.

Mansell: 70 points. Prost: 64. Piquet: 63.

That was the mathematics. But something else came back as a sort of subdued echo, and it was a phrase, and it was Mansell's own phrase. It was stilted, the words carefully selected. Elements of luck will come into play. Just that. A truth, of course, when you have thousands of parts on a car and any or all are capable of letting you down.

The eternal truth.

He could not know and did not know, as he waved and went towards the pottery dolls up there, beyond the passport control, that he would go to Adelaide with a world to win and the element of luck would move against him in a way so spectacular that the instant-by-instant images of that would astonish a whole nation – and make him the BBC's Sportsman of the Year against all comers. In Adelaide, everything would be proved, won and lost.

12   *What a Way to Go*

It is true that failure made Nigel Mansell famous and there can be only one other valid comparison – ironically at the same Aintree where he saw his first Grand Prix – when a horse called Devon Loch was 100 yards away from winning the 1956 Grand National and suddenly did the splits. That failure made the jockey, a certain Dick Francis, infinitely better known than if Devon Loch had simply gone on and won. The left rear tyre did that for Mansell particularly since – again as with Devon Loch – the cause was inexplicable.

Mansell had now entered the nation's consciousness, his face would be recognised wherever he went, he would never again have to explain to strangers what he did for a living. They would already know. But, as any sportsperson will tell you, don't look back. Between April and November you're in an entirely new 16-hurdle race and who wants to rake over the embers of last season?

Whatever he said and felt, he started as one of four favourites in 1987 and his curriculum vitae immediately before the first race – Brazil, of course – had filled out considerably: 90 races, four pole positions, seven wins, 141 points. I don't want to labour it, but the latter statistic placed him twenty-seventh in the all-time list, which is no bad place to be if you've had a slow start to your career. The boy was coming with a rush and by season's end would have hoisted himself past Rosberg, Hunt, Surtees, Moss . . .

This did not mean he was a better driver than they. Comparisons are deceptive when they take no account of different eras, but it did mean he had become thoroughly established. The crusade for credibility – at least – had been decisively won.

Brazil was humid, the way it usually is. You didn't need to be a prophet to see that little had changed since Adelaide. Mansell would have to beat Piquet, Senna and Prost for the championship. Others would have their moments but wouldn't have the packages to take them all through the hurdle race as front-runners. No matter that Goodyear were supplying every team. It was only a measure of equality because faster cars go faster on the same tyres as slow cars. The intriguing dimension was provided by Honda, now supplying Lotus as well as Williams. Honda had been extremely curious to see what Senna might do with one of their engines and so was the rest of the circus.

Brazil proved that little had changed. Piquet led, Senna led, Prost led and won, Mansell ran second at one point but drifted back to sixth with engine problems.

Then – Imola, and Imola was different, Imola had a moment of horror. In qualifying Piquet streamed past the pits into a lefthander and the car snapped out of control at 180 mph, maybe more, maybe as much as 200 mph. It plunged off backwards, smashed into the protective barrier and churned sideways, flinging shattered pieces off itself as it went. Piquet – mercifully, almost incredibly – was unhurt but out of the race. Concussion and racing cars, as Professor Watkins forcibly pointed out, don't go together. A technical matter passed almost unnoticed under the weight of Piquet's accident. Lotus had devised and were using an active suspension system and Senna put it on pole. Active suspension adjusts itself as the car moves, in theory, anyway . . .

Piquet had to sit, impotent as all the other spectators, and watch Mansell win the race. He tracked Senna from the green light, crowded him, pressured him, bored at him and as they moved together into lap two ducked out from behind and went clean through. Apart from a pit stop deep into the race, he would not lose this lead although the car shed a wheel balance weight early on which gave him unpleasant vibrations from the tyres. The pit stop put that right and as he left the circuit it must have been nice to contemplate the table. Mansell 10, Prost 9, Johansson 7, Piquet and Senna 6.

Any pretensions that this would be an ordinary season – or as ordinary as any Formula One season could be – ceased now, there in the pleasant gentility of Imola. It would become, starting at Spa in two weeks, a compound of incidents, suspicions, dark rumours, bitter private invective; it would call into question Mansell's honour and at a different level the honour of the Japanese; it would repay all this by giving Mansell an instant of self-fulfilment greater in intensity than any he had known at Brands Hatch in '85 or '86, an instant so overwhelming that he sank to his hands and knees and kissed a race track; it would be played out against a macabre rivalry with Piquet which would become more and more public – insiders

157

savoured every nuance, sniggered at every innuendo – and culminate in Piquet making other arrangements for 1988, namely signing for Lotus.

Of all places, Spa was the most inapt for the start of this. It puts you in mind of benevolent Belgians, those burgermeisters of the Common Market, picnicking in the rolling woodland as they watch the cars go by, puts you in mind of a pleasant place to be.

Mansell seized the lead but on lap two, far, far behind him the Tyrrell of Streiff crashed and was broadside on when Palmer in the *other* Tyrrell breasted a hillock and came upon it, plunging helplessly into part of the wreckage. Streiff's car had been bisected and the ragged, ravaged halves sent a shudder through those who wandered by them in the parc ferme* when they had been brought back. Neither man was hurt although Palmer – a doctor, remember – was visibly shaken. You can always tell. They're sweating more than usual, they're talking faster than usual, they've just returned from another *plane*. Streiff got into the only spare car for the re-start. (If you wonder how Piquet was excluded at Imola, Streiff included a second time around at Spa, I can't explain it any more than I can explain Devon Loch or Mansell's tyre-burst, except that all four happened.)

Green light again. From the second row of the grid Senna – cheeky, inspired, damn near incredibly quick on the draw – elbowed his way between the two Williams cars in front of him and grasped the lead all for himself, Mansell nosing directly in behind him. They flowed out into the woodland to where the picnickers could glimpse them, on and on, up and up, one shrieking engine shrieking against another in tumbling echoes amongst the trees. Mansell was fired up, as they say, and understandably so. He had been decisively ahead before Streiff's mauling and this had been taken from him through no fault of his own. As he and Senna approached a right-hander Mansell moved left and drew alongside. It is necessary to arrest it there: a right-hander, Senna tucked on the inside, Mansell describing a wide sweep outside him. Mansell was trying to overtake here and now. It was the wrong place, so wrong that for a fleeting instant Senna couldn't believe it was happening. But it was happening . . .

Mansell edged in front, squeezing Senna against the edge of the track and Senna had nowhere to go. The cars touched and spun together in complete rotations like partners in a dangerous dance,

*Guarded area for the inspection of cars, or what remains of them

spun until they were both completely off the track. Senna was out of the race and Mansell limped on until lap seventeen. The underbody of the car was too damaged for more.

He brought it back to the pits and an Italian journalist caught a glimpse of his eyes as he clambered out and thought: *I'll follow him.* Mansell strode to the Lotus pit. Senna was deep inside it. Mansell seized him around the throat and it needed three Lotus mechanics to get him off. Then Mansell went away. Senna recovered his composure enough to say, in answer to the question *Did you think he had come to apologise*? 'I do not think a man is apologising when he holds you round the throat.'

This incident provoked many, many people who knew Mansell only as a television figure – either a helmet in a car or giving those banal post-race words to Murray Walker – to wonder what manner of man he really was. He sensed this as the furore broke over him and confided to a friend: 'I'm only an ordinary bloke.'

The incident was so bizarre that when Walker heard of it he initially disbelieved it; so bizarre that few knew what to make of it at all. Motor racing is emotive, heightening all the senses, drawing a man to risk his life and this alone, perhaps, takes him beyond the point where sporting niceties have any meaning. The Williams team made a mess of damage limitation and Frank Williams himself took no action. Drivers are red-blooded males, he would imply, that's why they're racing drivers. (And later, when the friction between Mansell and Piquet had become intense, he would say: 'They're men, not pooftahs, you know,' pursuing the same theme.)

FISA took no action and the incident went away, leaving only a sour taste in the mouth and the question unanswered: what manner of man was Mansell? Mind you, in defending himself against accusations that he'd picked the wrong place to overtake, he said Senna had braked so early for the corner that he thought he could get through. Senna himself was bemused. It was only a question of time before he overtook me anyway, Senna would say, so why there?

Then Monaco, where Senna won, Piquet was second and neither Mansell nor Prost finished. Johansson, who had joined McLaren in the close season, was running with the Gang of Four at this stage. Prost 18, Senna 15, Johansson 13, Piquet 12, Mansell 10.

Monaco was the first victory for an active suspension car. Williams, who never seem to be far off the pace, were working hard on their own and would launch it soon but not yet, not quite yet.

Then Detroit and Mansell led until lap thirty-four when he got cramp in his right leg. 'Because of the pain I got tired very quickly,' he said. Senna won, Piquet second, Prost third, Mansell fifth. Prost, as ever, disliked Detroit and said: Now we get on with the real racing. Senna 24, Prost 22, Piquet 18, Johansson 13, Mansell 12.

Then France at Ricard and Mansell became imperious, leading the whole race except his tyre stop and resisting an inspired late attack from Piquet. Mansell showed that which is difficult to define. He made driving creative rather than mechanical, and this is a dimension above simply making a fast car go fast. Many do that every race. Few can express themselves distinctively through the constriction of a vehicle which, at a casual glance, is the same shape as the others, goes directly forward on four wheels like the others, assumes (more or less) the same line through the corners as the others, and all you really see of the driver is the tip of the helmet. The helmet markings are different colours so that you can tell one team's driver from the other. . .

From this constriction Mansell was portraying himself as he was, and in part it helped to answer that question: he was solid, he was strong and when he put his mind to it, never headstrong. He lacked Senna's inborn inspiration, Prost's canny cunning (softly softly catch the monkey), Piquet's strange ability to lunge all over a track, spin and set off again at vast speed. What Mansell had was a sureness of touch so that you might have been watching a passing train. This touch was *so* sure that it was easy to forget he was travelling faster than all the others in the race. In sum, it was the way an ordinary bloke would have driven the Williams, getting the most out of what he had.

A week later, this quality reached out to a hundred thousand people who isolated Silverstone from the rest of Great Britain by blocking all the roads to the circuit for many miles while they tried to reach the British Grand Prix on July 12. It was easy to see themselves in Mansell: he'd married the sort of girl they might have married, had the sort of family they might have had, spoke the way they spoke and, as I say, they'd have driven the car just like him – if they could.

It's the same in everything, I suppose. People worshipped the genius of Best but saw themselves more realistically as Nobby Stiles; worshipped Ali but saw themselves as Cooper; worshipped Botham but saw themselves as Gatting. . .

This is not a spurious diversion. Towards the end of the British Grand Prix, the communion between an ordinary Briton and an ordinary British audience was so strong as to be overwhelming.

The setting couldn't have been better. Senna 27, Prost 26, Piquet 24, Mansell 21. It was possible he could head the championship by nightfall. And there was the unknown: the famous chicane had gone, been replaced (on the grounds of safety) by a left-right from under the Daily Express Bridge. And there was the known: Mansell had been on pole in Brazil, the front row at Imola, on pole at Spa, Monaco, Detroit, Ricard, rat-a-tat. In making the fast car go fastest he stood quite alone and if his car was intrinsically faster than all the others except Piquet's, well, he'd decisively outdriven Piquet whenever both had been running unimpeded at full bore. Ultimately Piquet would complain that he wasn't getting equal treatment from the team but now, on the former aerodrome, Piquet took pole and revelled in that, Mansell alongside him.

The race was 65 laps.

The start was clean, Mansell getting on to the power fractionally before Piquet so that he bored ahead but by then Piquet was on the power, too, and they coursed along the pit-lane wall level. To their left Prost had out-gunned them both and as all three reached Copse Corner the Frenchman was in the lead.

But Piquet's Honda engine was delivering more than Prost's TAG and as the column of cars threaded through the left-right-left curve towards Hangar Straight Piquet moved effortlessly by. Mansell, surging, jinked out from behind Prost's slip-steam and moved into second place.

Sometimes whole races don't contain as much action as this and it had spanned only the first 42 seconds.

When they crossed the line to complete lap one Piquet was pulling clear. He shed the others, burnt them off, and his car was like some enormous spring uncoiling and uncoiling through the corners of the fastest Formula One circuit in the world. He shed the others bar one. Mansell clung to him and after seventeen laps the difference was only two seconds. This was a testing of will-power, man against man, not just machine against machine. You couldn't miss it: Piquet's car was positively twitching under the power and every time he wheeled and turned through a corner there, always within vision, was Mansell's car. The rest were nowhere and when they started to lap the back-markers Mansell was closer, not within lunging distance but closer. Behind the wooden staves which lined the track the thousands, shirt-sleeved, rose in tiers as the two cars passed – those anonymous, eager faces which melt into the blur of the moment but make the backdrop for theatre.

On lap thirty-five Mansell pulled off onto the pit-lane road like a sling-shot and stopped. Four tyres came off, four tyres went on, the pneumatic hammers driving them home in a shock of sudden, strident echoes, hands were raised – *our* tyre is on, *our* tyre is on, *our* tyre is on, *our* tyre is on. Exactly 9.54 seconds after Mansell had stopped the Williams he hit the accelerator and it went in a terrible rush along the pit lane back towards the track. An experienced observer thought: I've never seen anyone getting there quicker. . .

Mansell was 28 seconds behind Piquet but that meant nothing because Piquet still had to come in for tyres. Now Mansell exploded. On lap thirty-seven he set the fastest lap, one minute 11.968, average 148.516 mph. Piquet got that instantly – it's why you have in-board phones – and beat Mansell's time.

And now a great question was born, born of wondering and waiting and guessing: would Piquet risk going the distance without losing time changing tyres? Dare he? Piquet could afford to let Mansell nibble half a second a lap and still win on his old, worn tyres. As he moved along the pit-lane straight, a black and white board was held over the wall – held with the positioning of a matador's cape:

TYRES
OK
L 22

Of the hundred thousand, only those in the grandstand opposite the pits could see it, but they would all know what it was telling Piquet: twenty-two laps to go and we think your tyres really can go the distance. The gap was 23 seconds. Mansell had to find one second every 2.9695 miles to get to Piquet before the end.

Brands Hatch in '86 had been The Great Escape. This was The Great Chase. Mansell freely confessed that the crowd reached to him and: 'I drove the last twenty laps right on the limit.' On lap 46 he went down to 1:10.943, average 150.662 mph. That was nineteen laps to go and the gap was still twenty seconds. It was eighteen with eighteen to go. Piquet *lapped* Prost. On television screens around the world the Longines timing arranged and rearranged ghostly white numericals: *Lap fifty fastest lap Mansell 1:10.518, average 151.570 mph.* He was biting chunks out of Piquet's lead. He weaved between back-markers picking his position, forcing the engine, and they were gone from him as the impetus of the chase gathered and gathered. Twelve times he would better Piquet's fastest lap. Twelve times.

In the heat of it Prost pulled off, his McLaren rumbling gently over the grass until he had parked it in a convenient place. Electrics.

Lap fifty-five, ten to go, and the gap was 6.4. As Piquet reached the end of the pit-lane straight and angled the car into Copse the nose-cone of Mansell's Williams could be seen, sharp and predatory, just visible. As Mansell travelled urgently through Copse and Maggotts and Becketts the crowd were waving wildly, banners fluttered, flags flailed the air, creating the backdrop to the last act of the theatre.

The gap: 3.9 seconds.

And it came to this – Piquet out there on the wide, level track, then, quite by chance, the two Lotuses both on different laps but forming a wall between him and Mansell. At the end of any race random cars can't help getting in the way – because they're simply still going round – but they can alter everything. In one Lotus: Senna, not noted for giving anybody anything. In the other: Nakajima, alarmingly unaccustomed to being where it matters. Nakajima hugged the left of the track and saw the low-slung rear of Mansell's Williams stream past him and tuck in behind Senna.

They were on Hangar Straight and Stowe – a flat-out right-hand curve, hemmed by thousands in stands all its length – was rushing headlong at them. Mansell moved out and overtook Senna. The track is too broad to block the man behind if he has the power. Mansell had the power. Senna conceded this perfectly.

At this moment, Mansell positioning himself for Stowe, he and Piquet had lapped every other runner. Nobody cared. The race had not been won. Everybody cared about that. Lap sixty-two, three to go, and the gap had ceased to be a gap. It had become just a short physical distance between the rear of one Williams and the snout of the other.

In essence the cars were locked together.

But could Mansell overtake Piquet? He tracked him for a whole lap, and they were back at Club Corner, through Abbey Curve, under the Express Bridge, past the pits, into Copse, into Maggotts, through Becketts, through Chapel. Now the broad straight sweep down to Stowe, Mansell guzzling Piquet's slip-stream. He positioned himself exactly – and exquisitely – behind Piquet, and Piquet, vulnerable because of the breadth of the track, could not know – did not know – which way Mansell would attack him, to the left or to the right. Mansell feinted left, just a touch of the steering wheel. Piquet blocked that, moving across to cover where Mansell was – or Mansell should have been. By then Mansell had flung his car right, into that lovely empty breadth Piquet had just vacated. He was travelling as fast as the car would go. He was level with Piquet. Piquet cut to the right, searching even now for the racing line to get through Stowe. The cars veered together, might almost have touched – for a moment of anguish it did seem that Piquet's front wheel nibbled at Mansell's rear wheel.

Then Mansell was gone.

The thousands were lifted far, far up the scale towards emotional abandon.

It was one of the great moments of Grand Prix racing and in its context will stand comparison with any other.

Immediately Mansell pulled away, not far but away. He crossed the line and there were two laps to go and the thousands were clapping by raising their arms above their heads and it might have been a football match, generating *that* public passion. The roar was so deep that it could be heard above the noise of the engines.

That last, final, exultant lap the crowd rose in a rippling cadence as the car reached them. No-one wanted to miss their glimpse. Union Jacks were everywhere.

Mansell circled and Piquet circled and the distance between them remained constant and irrelevant. Piquet had nothing left to counter-attack with and he simply followed Mansell home. The actual distance between them was just under two seconds and posterity, without knowing its context, will imagine it a tight finish. It wasn't. From the moment Mansell overtook Piquet, Piquet was beaten. He had driven a great race, he had gambled – and he had lost.

Mansell crossed the line and his fist was out of the cockpit punching the air – it happens most races but not like this; this was no moment of shadow-boxing to punctuate a triumph, this went on as he slowed and drifted round Copse, this went on, the fist pumping and pumping, through Maggotts and through Becketts until he found himself on Hangar Straight. Now it softened to a wave being returned to those thousands waving to him, a driver speaking directly to a crowd and a crowd speaking directly to a driver.

At Stowe the constriction of the crowd behind the staves was too much to bear and they expressed themselves by swarming onto the track and engulfing Mansell's car. He slowed and was forced to stop. On the faces of those nearest the car: ecstasy, abandon, and tribal gestures of the triumph they felt and no longer wished to control. The crowd round the car grew and grew, people from distant places stampeding to join its ragged circular edge. In any other sport, you would have feared for Mansell's safety. That late English Sunday afternoon, surrounded by his own people, Nigel Mansell was in the safest place in the world.

A white official van marked Silverstone Circuit crawled up to rescue him but the ragged edge of the circle engulfed that too. Eventually he pressed a path through the crowd – the car abandoned – and clambered into the van, which did bring him back. He was sweating. His face kept adjusting to the sweat running down it, contorting gently to make the beads run away from his eyes. In the oddly formal way he has in public – it was a fleeting television interview, just a camera locked onto his face – he wouldn't raise that arm which had punched the air to smooth the sweat away. Improper, somehow, to do that. For the last fifteen laps, he would say, it was the will-power of the crowd which did it. In the blur, he had seen and sensed what the ordinary people wanted, and they all wanted him.

'It definitely put five seconds in my pocket,' he said, the sweat still running awkwardly. It was the kind of thing he had said all his life and he meant it, the way he always had.

He would do a second lap of honour as postilion on a police motor bike and ask the policeman to stop on Hangar Straight at exactly the point where he had overtaken Piquet. He was dressed in blood-red overalls, he wore a cap. He moved two or three places away from the motor bike – the policeman waiting in the exquisitely English way astride the bike, motionless, emotionless, doing what he did, another place, another job – and crouched, hands and knees, kissed the track, stood, punched the air again and those uncounted hands behind the staves were still waving. The communion was consummated.

It is tempting to search for an immortal phrase now, to conjure a sharp paragraph which penetrates great truths; but you lie if you do. The aftermath is a hundred thousand people blocking all the roads from Silverstone going the other way, and the memory had begun to recede already. I cannot speak for a hundred thousand people, nor will I, but it is probable that they had all seen something climactic spread over one hour nineteen minutes 11.780 seconds, and they must have all known as they stopped-started-stopped along the choked lanes that anything else but the championship would be anti-climactic.

The table suggested that everybody had everything to play for. Senna 31, Mansell and Piquet 30, Prost 26. But in the most basic matter of all – getting a car from the start to the finish quickest – it already looked like the Williams team. That Mansell and Piquet had lapped all the others – even Senna, who had a Honda engine himself – was significant and would become more so. It was unlikely they'd be beaten at any remaining race, provided of course they didn't break down. And in Germany Mansell did break down. . .

He'd taken the lead and was running second to Prost on lap twenty-five when his engine failed. Piquet won, and Piquet won the next, in Hungary where Mansell was crippled by the loss of a wheel nut (yes, these things happen, even in Formula One). The whole season had tilted towards Piquet, now with 48 points, Senna 41, Mansell and Prost 30. Mansell responded by winning in Austria but Piquet was second. You simply couldn't shake the man off. Piquet 54, Senna 43, Mansell 39, Prost 31.

But an undercurrent was surfacing, and the undercurrent was Honda itself or, more precisely, the conduct and motives of that company. Honda and Williams still had a year of their contract to run but the undercurrent suggested Honda were going to exit from it and supply Lotus and McLaren for 1988. Why? Penetrating the Honda logic was difficult but possible.

They had supplied Williams since 1983 and their investment was colossal. They had not made it because they thought motor racers were good chaps and they'd like to lend a hand. They wanted the name Honda to bestride the world and that meant ultimately one driver winning the championship with their engine. Since 1983 Williams had provided – going towards the Italian Grand Prix – nineteen victories, a superb achievement. But no world champion. It had seemed more than likely at Adelaide but Prost stole in and took it from Mansell and Piquet. Mr. Honda himself had journeyed there for the anticipated celebrations. What he thought of Prost winning is not recorded.

Why hadn't Williams told Mansell to back off long before the race so that Piquet, who was, after all, the number one driver could have the championship? Maybe the Japanese couldn't penetrate the logic behind Williams' policy: that you hire two good drivers and let them get on with it.

Why hadn't Williams told Mansell to back off at Silverstone only a few weeks ago and let Piquet have the nine points?

The problem may well have been compounded by the knowledge that the races were seen to be won by Williams assisted by Honda rather than Honda assisted by Williams. Would Honda dump

Williams? It was unthinkable but then nobody really knew what the Japanese thought anyway.

The undercurrent became immediately relevant to Mansell. How might Honda view a late-season charge by him which threatened Piquet's and *their* championship? The Brazilian was known to be one of Honda's favourite sons. Nor did it stop there. The car was controlled by a complex and utterly secret engine management system contained in a box and the box was in the hands of the Japanese. In fact, it was so secret that outsiders did not know whether – the box fed information to computers in the pits – it could be *controlled* from the pits. To put it starkly: the outsiders did not know if some totally anonymous man deep in the bowels of the pits could decide how fast the car went regardless of what the driver did, or – horror of all horrors – actually stop the car altogether at a chosen point on a circuit.

At Monza, Honda and Williams announced their parting. At a press conference, the first question aimed at Mr. Sakurai, managing director of Honda F1, was: will Mansell get the same equipment (namely, treatment) as Piquet? He said: Engine settings are exactly the same but because there are some differences in driving styles, Mansell, Piquet, and also Senna, we change a little bit the settings. But basically the performance/economy balance is the same.

In time Mansell would wonder aloud how his car was slower in a straight line than Piquet's – on one occasion ten miles an hour slower.

At Monza Piquet used the active suspension Williams and won the race. Mansell was third, which wasn't what he needed at all. Piquet 63, Senna 49, Mansell 43, Prost 31. In Portugal Mansell got his own active suspension but retired on lap thirteen. Electrics. Prost won and beat Jackie Stewart's all-time total of 27 wins, Piquet third. That wasn't what Mansell needed at all, either. Piquet 67, Senna 49, Mansell 43, Prost 40.

Spain was widely regarded as Mansell's last chance. The three races after it would be too late. This urgency produced another Mansell incident. In the Saturday qualifying Piquet set a storming one minute 22.4 seconds and with ten minutes of the session left, Mansell went out to try and beat it. Immediately down the pit lane he was directed over to have the car weighed. This is not sinister but it takes time. Mansell sprang out and ran back to get in his other car. For this he was fined 3,000 dollars. No matter. In that other car he did one minute 23.9 and left the circuit seething. He returned a couple of hours later, calmer now, and said: 'Today there was less grip and it was hot. I was busting a gut to get near my time from yesterday and suddenly in these conditions Piquet improves by a clear second.'

It might have been, of course, that Piquet's active car was just quicker while Mansell had spent most of the time in a non-active car.

The race belonged to Mansell. He overtook Piquet on the first lap and was not seen again. It was just like Ricard, just like watching the train. He finished twenty-two seconds ahead of Prost with Piquet fourth after a riotous time spinning and going off and charging and spinning and going off. . .

Piquet 70, Mansell 52, Senna 51, Prost 46.

And that was the end of the European season. The rest was long haul, Mexico, Japan, Adelaide but even before the drivers set off it was time for the pocket calculators again. At first glance Piquet's 18-point lead looked impregnable but, as with Mansell in 1986, he could be punished for consistency. He had already used up his quota of eleven races and would now have to start dropping points – three from Spain, then four from Portugal, then one of his six second places, worth six points. With only eight finishes, Mansell could count fully whatever he got from the last three. And Senna still lurked, a single point behind him.

There could be no doubt that of all the struggles in his career, Mansell now faced the hardest.

And the circus went back to unlovely, unloved Mexico City where they found – nobody was surprised – that the track had actually deteriorated and the bumps were bumpier. One observer described them as 'vicious'.

In the first qualifying session Mansell was trying to wrest pole from Berger and hit one. It sent the car *spinning* the length of the pit-lane straight at well over 150 mph. He was bruised. In the second session he did get pole and then something on the car broke. He struck a wall but – again – wasn't hurt. (In Formula One, mere bruising doesn't count.)

He kept pole and found himself starting from the front row of the grid for the fifteenth consecutive time, a record. But it had been tight. Less than a second separated the first six.

Berger was away like a hare followed by Boutsen, Piquet, Prost and Mansell, but going into a right-hander Piquet braked early and Prost ducked to one side to avoid him. Or rather try to avoid him. They collided and Prost ploughed off, not to return. His

Championship was gone.

Piquet, engine stalled, had a push start and set off last. It might have been the decisive moment of the season.

Boutsen overtook Berger and Mansell was running a long way behind them. On lap sixteen Boutsen pulled in to the pits with a misfire and on lap twenty-one Berger's turbo blew. Mansell was now in the lead and out of reach of Senna in second place. Piquet, charging as he had to charge, was up to sixth but an age away. Mansell was breaking the Championship wide open again.

On lap twenty-six Piquet was up to fourth but still an age away. At this moment Warwick's Arrows went off at 170 mph and the race had to be stopped while a crane hoisted it out of the way.

It meant this: the race would be rerun for another thirty-three laps, the combined times to count. Crucially Mansell had a 45-second lead over Piquet – fourth, remember – as they restarted. Piquet went for it and so did Mansell, who would say Piquet 'tried to push me off.' Piquet denied this and added cryptically that if he wanted to push anybody off he would have done.

The rest was anti-climax. Mansell let Piquet go and overall won comfortably. Somewhere back there, on lap fifty-four, Senna had spun off. *His* Championship was gone.

Mansell had his sixth victory of 1987, Piquet only three; but Piquet had been awesomely consistent with seven second places *and* a third *and* a fourth. In points, Piquet 76 but able to count only 73, Mansell 61. In reality, Mansell needed to win in Japan – badly.

The circuit was called Suzuka and although several Formula One drivers had some experience of it – not always in Formula One cars – it was, in practical terms, an entirely new circuit. Piquet, who had tested there, said tersely: 'It is very narrow, very bumpy, very quick and dangerous.' That word dangerous was chilling. It is not a word any driver uses carelessly.

Suzuka: a distant relative of Zandvoort (they had been designed by the same man), near the town of Nagoya and well south of Tokyo; 3.673 miles of curves and loops; and featuring a cross-over bridge and tunnel.

Because it was new to them, the cars went out on the Thursday to have a look. Mansell was quickest. In the untimed session on the Friday Mansell was quickest. Within five minutes of qualifying proper Mansell was quickest. Then he sat in the car in the pits and they put a small portable television in front of him, the times of the other drivers being constantly updated.

Piquet went quicker.

Mansell came out, but not to try and better that – yet. There would be ample time later in the session. What he wanted to do was have a feel of the track surface, gauge how much rubber the tyres of the others were leaving in a thin film, how much more grip that would give. He accelerated to the end of the pit-lane straight and travelled round the bend there. It contorted back behind the paddock and took him into an S-shaped curve. He was doing – he has estimated it himself – somewhere between 140 and 150 mph. He was into a sharp right-hander and seemed to be round it comfortably. It was an ordinary, forgettable moment and an ordinary, forgettable corner. But as the car emerged its tail had drifted wide, only fractionally wide, but wide . . .

The rear left wheel crossed the kerb and was instantly on dust. It was a foot over the kerb, maybe less, but there was no adhesion there. The wheel skimmed the dust, churning it. By then the car was being pitched sideways by its own impetus, was beginning to *rotate*. Mansell felt a fleeting sensation that the whole car had 'stepped away' from him. His foot was so hard on the brakes that all four wheels left black scars. He closed his eyes. He knew what was going to happen.

The car was moving across the track towards a short, grassy run-off with a tyre wall beyond and the rotation had turned it completely round. Its tail struck the wall, flinging the tyres crazily into the air in a violent cascade. The force lifted the Williams and *rotated* it completely round in the air. The churned dust *here* was so thick that the car could only be glimpsed like a spectre from another dimension.

For a dreadful instant – a milli-second, it just felt a lot longer – the car hung at an angle in the air and was going to flip before it landed. It didn't. It landed with its snout on the track but its belly straddling the kerb. That meant its tyres didn't absorb all the impact, the belly did. It hammered Mansell's spine.

And still the impetus was strong enough to take the car drifting lazily over to the other side of the track. It came to rest there. Once Mansell's helmet was off he threw his head back in the cockpit, his mouth held open in agony.

The Championship was gone.

They took him to hospital by helicopter. He had 'spinal concussion' and was detained overnight. 'All I heard in the night were screams. Someone in the ward died. At that point I didn't know if I had internal bleeding. When you are exposed to that kind of trauma, your thoughts are vulnerable.'

170

Piquet's celebrations were subdued. The race was still two days away. And in that – who would believe it? – his engine failed on lap forty-six. By then Mansell was back in the Isle of Man, watching it on television; but what if he'd been in the race and leading when Piquet's engine spewed oil all over the pit lane . . .

You can compound the irony. Over the years Mansell had survived so much physical damage and now he'd been beaten by a tyre wall designed entirely to soften impact. 'You can think about things too much after an accident,' he would say. 'For the first three days, my feelings were terribly inconsistent.'

Adelaide, '86.

Suzuka, '87.

More irony than most could bear.

His doctor firmly precluded any notion of him going to Adelaide for the final race. It would have been a long, long journey with Piquet already champion, but he wasn't fit, anyway. It did give him a little space to get his feelings sorted out, get his world back into its familiar focus. He concluded that his future was still driving racing cars.

He sat by the open fire in his lounge, the mantelpiece decorated by get-well cards, and he found the words which in every important sense echoed the whole of his life.

'I will not yield.'

13 Il Leone

A marquee at Silverstone: a press conference with several dozen journalists and photographers; a plain platform at the end which might in its context have represented a dais, an altar even; a thicket of microphones; a TV crew or two struggling under the weight of their hand-held equipment to get the best vantage point; murmurs of expectancy gathering everywhere into a low hum.

A hundred yards away lay the track and the chicane where almost a decade before plain Nigel Mansell had urged an uncompetitive car to its limit and Colin Chapman had watched with knowing, eager eyes, asking: Who is this fellow?

Now in July 1988 this fellow was authentically big news and, sitting there in the marquee craning his face to the microphones, he was about to announce in his very own soft, semi-whimsical voice news which would travel far beyond the confines of motor sport (itself normally a secular activity). He was joining Ferrari. It had long been rumoured and here all at once was the confirmation.

His son Leo was by his side, an instructive choice of companion for such a moment. 'I have,' he would say, 'a very, very nice family and when I look at my children it gives me strength.'

This press conference was inevitably something more because its very nature demanded that: Mansell at Silverstone where he put 20,000 or 30,000 on the gate just to watch him; Mansell at Silverstone where he had driven great races even measured in the historical terms of Moss, Hawthorn, Clark, Stewart and Hunt; now Mansell moving to the great emotive, all-enveloping blood-red cars whose badge, the Prancing Horse, was itself a kind of currency for wealth, a symbol of personal potency on a race track or off it and instantly recognisable anywhere in the world. This was the summit and authentically big news.

The press conference became at moments almost a confessional, an exploration of a man by himself. 'I've a bit of a philosophy about life that I have to implement at times. I have a home in the Isle of

172

Man which I adore. It's a lovely home, it's a lovely place to live and the people are extremely kind to us. No matter who you are or what you do you can socialize with them. They don't create the pressure that perhaps I would have if I was living in England. Give or take the World Championship I've got my own life and no one can take that away from me either. That's my safety-valve. At the end of the day you only have one life and, win or lose, nothing changes from that point of view. That's probably my strength.

'It would be fair to say that in the beginning I didn't have a regular job. I went professional in 1977 and I wasn't able to win enough to get support from sponsors. But my wife Rosanne worked the hours she worked . . .

'I feel I am cheating my children presently. It is very, very hurtful when you have a nineteen-month-old son who is only speaking a few words and crying and saying "Don't go, don't go." I think that is one of the hardest parts for me, because the children don't really understand the job of work I do.'

How many racing drivers, or indeed people in any walk of life, are this candid?

'I promise you one thing: I will not tell any lies. I might not tell you the complete truth but I won't tell any falseness. It took a lot of deciding to leave the Williams team after the last four years and the success I have had with them but in joining Ferrari I am very, very pleased. I went through the same situation two years ago and I chose to stay with Williams. Then I was blessed with the opportunity of going to Ferrari again – and that speaks for itself after the kind of results I have had this season and the problems the team has had. I think there is a time that comes with any relationship when it's probably best that you move on. That time is absolutely right for me now.'

But hadn't there been acrimony and threats of legal action that first time around when he didn't join Ferrari? In fact, 'we remained very good friends and we have kept a good relationship over the last two years. That piece of paper? Unfortunately there was a difference of view on what it meant. It was a catalogue of a meeting, it wasn't a contract. It was a misunderstanding, simple as that, but the misunderstanding was put right. I feel privileged to have become a Ferrari driver. I have come from a great team and I am going to a great team.'

Question: What about the legendary in-fighting at Maranello? 'I am a professional race-car driver not a politician so I shall just drive the car. I'll continue to live in the Isle of Man. If I have any problems I'll put my police uniform on.'

The phrase Mansell used about the problems Williams had had

was in the nature of an understatement, particularly after the heady years of 1985, '86 and '87 when he had done everything except be lucky. This year of 1988 Williams had Judd engines. They were simply no match for the Hondas now securely nestled in the back of the McLarens and driven by Prost and Senna. A glance at the race results will tell you all you need to know. Thus far in the season there had been seven Grands Prix.

Prost won Brazil, Senna disqualified; Senna won San Marino from Prost; Prost won Monaco after Senna led for 66 laps and crashed; Prost won Mexico from Senna, Senna won Canada from Prost; Senna won Detroit from Prost; Prost won Canada from Senna. Approaching Silverstone, Prost had 54 points, Senna 39 and Mansell not a single one; an electrical problem in Brazil, an electrical problem at San Marino, a crash at Monaco, an engine problem in Mexico, an engine problem in Canada, an electrical problem in Detroit, a suspension problem in France.

'It's been very difficult this year and I must pick my words carefully. People have said, ''You must be frustrated like crazy,'' but I would deny this very strongly. I am picking my words very carefully: I am very, very disappointed.''

Of course the questioning turned back to Ferrari, where he would be joining Gerhard Berger. 'I knew him before he came into Formula One and we were good friends then. I get on very well with him indeed. It will be a good, lively relationship because it will be an honest one. The most important thing besides the money is that the relationship is correct. Even for 510 million dollars I would not drive for anybody unless I was happy. Leo is 3½ and his happiness is more important than money. If I couldn't have got myself into a situation where I was happy I would have retired. I am in no position to make any statement technically about the team I am joining. All I can tell you is what I have seen with my own eyes and heard with my own ears.' And no, he said, he didn't speak Italian although he expected the mechanics to teach him the salty words the way mechanics in any team do.

(There is a nice tale about Berger–Mansell circa 1984, Berger had an horrendous road accident – two vertebrae in his neck badly injured – and he had a choice, either six months in hospital or a risky operation. He accepted the risk, and the operation, carried out in Innsbruck, was successful. It was Mansell who collected him from the hospital and that pleased Berger because the year before it was he who took Mansell to hospital after a skiing accident . . .)

At the press conference Mansell did offer a little more philosophy, and if it was couched in home-spun terminology – well, that's the way he is. I quote him exactly. 'My personal view with regard to Formula One is that it is a hill about one in six that you have to climb every time you get into the car. If you stand still you are going backwards. I'm talking about development, I'm talking about many things, and even in your own driving ability and standings you are only as good as your last race.'

Inevitably, too, he stirred a combative performance out of himself and the Williams Judd in the British Grand Prix at Silverstone a couple of days later. He was only on the sixth row of the grid, a position made easier because the race was run in a downpour, negating some of the advantage of the faster cars. He was seventh after the opening lap and deftly, safely moved up finishing a strong second to Senna although the gap was 23.344 seconds. There had been drama in the background, too. After the Friday qualifying session Patrick Head, Williams's technical director, decided to make a fundamental alteration to the car by building out its 'reactive' suspension – which had created problems – and making it a conventional car in time for the Saturday qualifying. It was achieved and Mansell was delighted.

He spun off in the next race, Germany, put the car on the front of the grid in Hungary but he'd had chicken pox and it left him too weak to complete the 76 laps. (He was replaced by Brundle for the Belgian Grand Prix, Jean-Louis Schlesser for the Italian.) Portugal ought to have suited the car and engine and it did. He locked himself into a cut-and-thrust duel with Senna and once, ducking inside, churned smoke from his wheels as Senna closed the door. This was not for the lead but third place. It was not diminished by that. Eventually he was momentarily baulked by Palmer in a Tyrrell – who was recovering after a spin – brushed the back of Senna's car and struck the guardrail. As he got out and walked away he still looked limp, almost lethargic. The virus clearly had ravaged his strength.

He was on the second row in Spain and speared the car past Senna at the start following Prost. He shed Senna and moved on Prost, calmly, prudently reeling him in, reeling him in; and this was Prost in the mighty Marlboro McLaren Honda, the one that won everything. After ten laps the gap was 0.742 seconds which is the scientific way of saying he's right behind you, Alain. Mansell set fastest lap of the race, an average of 104.972 mph on a twisty circuit. Think about that. Prost responded, squeezed something out of his car, and edged away, but Mansell closed again. By lap 32 (of 72) the gap was 1.233 seconds, which is the scientific way of saying he'll be right behind you again in an instant, Alain.

Mansell pitted for new tyres and was 29 seconds behind when he emerged. He cranked up fastest lap to 105.597 mph. The hunt was on. Prost pitted and was stationary for 8.35 seconds, Mansell devouring the circuit. The gap: 19.832. That was lap fifty and the race was essentially settled in the laps which immediately followed . . .

Lap	Prost	Mansell
51	1:29.481	1:29.346
52	1:29.211	1:30.352
53	1:29.584	1:29.534
54	1:30.542	1:29.145

These statistics show in their dispassionate way that Prost could match Mansell for speed, that Mansell could not close the gap and in the end that gap was 26.232 seconds. What Mansell had done was underline that he remained a powerful force at places where the normally aspirated Judd engine could not simply be blown away by Honda power – here and Estoril and the Hungaroring – and it's as well to remember that this was only his second finish of the whole season. In Japan he spun off, in Australia he spun off.

That was a quiet finish to four years at Williams, 59 races, 11 pole positions, 13 wins, 176 points (more wins, if you're curious, than James Hunt got in the whole of his career and only three points less, too). If he had mixed feelings about the leaving, small wonder. Williams did not make him: he made himself, but Williams gave him the vehicle. The team itself had ambivalent feelings, which in its own way emphasises that if Mansell was a real live hero he was also a dilemma for them. In a racing car he commanded respect and none could deny him that. Out of it he was somehow difficult to warm to. Frank Williams himself said the team would miss him, Frank would miss him as a driver but 'not as a bloke'. It was a chilling quotation in the context of the 59 races, the 13 wins and nearly the two World Championships. 'I can't honestly say I've any fond memories of him, but a brilliant driver.'

We shall explore the dilemma more fully in the next chapter. Suffice it to say here that during the years when he might have naturally outgrown it under the weight of his achievements Frank and Patrick felt it remained.

What would happen when the boy from Birmingham got to

Ferrari? If only life at Ferrari was buckling up your safety-harness and driving the car his future was already assured. In late 1988 Nigel Mansell had become one of the three best drivers in Formula One (Prost and Senna were the other two). The Italian crowd, which is actually the whole of Italy, would find a deep resonance in the way he drove, seeing themselves in him: strong, sure, aggressive, unafraid to risk everything. He could manipulate a car as if from your memory, as if you were watching an old black and white film – attack, attack, attack the way people did before the world got sophisticated and sanitised and sport had assumed a greater importance than, say, politics (about which large tracts of the population were ignorant, indifferent and suspicious) in the public consciousness. Mansell could actually be *thrilling* to watch and at Ferrari he would produce two instants which belonged entirely to him and which nobody except possibly Senna would have *dreamed* about. One of them, in a corner in Mexico, was so fast, so magnificent, so superficially impossible to do that I thought his Ferrari had broken and he was going helplessly straight on. He wasn't. He was overtaking Berger . . .

But, of course, in late 1988 everybody knew that driving for Ferrari was not just driving for Ferrari. Never had been. There was a sad irony too. In August Enzo Ferrari died. He had been a reclusive autocrat who had made road-going cars which were so sought after and so precious that someone said in a memorable phrase, 'He could pick his own customers.' In Formula One the man, his team, his cars and many of his drivers had to be seen in the domain of the mythological and even hardened observers felt that. The World Champions he had had were Alberto Ascari, Mike Hawthorn, Phil Hill, John Surtees, Niki Lauda, Jody Scheckter – and Gilles Villeneuve who wasn't but who was mythological all in his own right, quite possibly more than all the others except Lauda.

Mansell said quietly and diplomatically that he might be able to help the team recover because he had, after all, been through the same thing at Lotus when Colin Chapman died and the trauma and the void had been on a comparable level.

Ascari, Hawthorn, Phil Hill, Surtees, Lauda, Scheckter, Villeneuve.

The last driver that Enzo Ferrari signed was Nigel Mansell.

He first drove a Ferrari early in January at Fiorano. The car had a semi-automatic gearbox, a radical step first introduced to Ferrari by British designer John Barnard. It required a considerable adjustment by a driver who hadn't handled it before. On a bitter cold day Mansell had a spin on his third lap – only to be anticipated while he was in the process of making the adjustment – but completed 20 laps, enjoyed himself and pronounced himself satisfied. The Italian press, collectively a formidable force, pronounced themselves satisfied too.

The spin? 'It was very cold and I was excited driving the Ferrari for the first time. There are two levers, one on each side, the right-hand one controlling seven speeds up the box, the left hand for going back down. Anyway I went down the gearbox instead of up, locking the rear wheels, and it went straight off the circuit. A bit embarrassing considering that I was going down the straight at the time.' (*Autosport.*)

He journeyed to Ricard and tested for three days but this was a full-scale Formula One test with a great deal of experimenting going on. Naturally a driver wants to prove his speed even in the midst of all this and at the tail end of the second day he was beginning to go really fast when . . . darkness fell! He spun again incidentally at Ricard, said that Berger had longer fingers than he did which helped to reach the gear-change levers – Mansell had to move the palm of his hand to do it – but that special levers were being made to suit him.

In early February Ferrari unveiled their car for the season, the 640. (Thus far Mansell had been in an interim version.) Mansell and Berger dutifully posed in and around it, Berger did a few laps of Fiorano and they both tested at Jerez. Then they tested at Rio where Mansell achieved a time two seconds faster than that set by Senna for pole position the year before.

Throughout this rigorous period there had been problems with engines, electrics and the semi-automatic gearbox. As the Formula One world assembled for the first race, Brazil on 26 March, nobody thought the Ferrari could conceivably go the distance. It might do anything but certainly not the 190.686 miles of the race. Practice and qualifying almost proved that.

In the Friday untimed session the hydraulic pressure pump failed; in the afternoon session he was baulked by slower cars and almost spun; on the Saturday the pump failed twice. He did however get on to the third row of the grid. The Sunday morning untimed session, when the cars run in race trim, is often much more significant than qualifying but during it the pump failed again, bringing Mansell to a halt.

At the green light Berger made a bold move down the inside to try and wrest the lead from Senna, they collided – Berger out instantly – and that let Patrese through. Senna was cruising towards the pits hugging the edge of the track and that let through Boutsen, who'd replaced Mansell at Williams. Mansell tracked Boutsen.

Patrese looked immaculate, covering the first lap in one minute 38.742, then Boutsen at 1:40.969, Mansell at 1:41.487. On the third lap Mansell was through and a lap later Boutsen was gone altogether. Debris from the Berger-Senna crash had hit him on the helmet, shattered a mirror and most probably been sucked into the engine. Mansell went after Patrese, wheeling and turning, wheeling and turning round the twists of the circuit and obviously he was putting on a bit of a show the way he was fully entitled to do. Why not? He'd said himself before the start that he didn't expect the car to last five laps. Better to be in the lead when it failed than trying to nurse it round half-way down the field. And anyway Prost was third in the utterly reliable McLaren, lurking, biding his time. He'd be calculating that once Mansell was gone Patrese would become his prey, to be devoured somewhere up along the road. There were more than fifty laps left.

Mansell chased and hurried Patrese all the way to lap 16 and on the straight pressed the Ferrari into the air pocket behind Patrese, held it firm there for perhaps fifty fleeting metres and then, suddenly and gloriously, flung it out to the rim of the track. As he drew abreast he had two wheels fractionally off the track, grinding wisps of dust from the sandy-grassy strip which bordered the track.

The way he'd done at Suzuka, '87 when it had all gone wrong . . .

This time the car didn't deviate at all, kept coming straight on, Patrese left in its wake. You had all the essences of a driver in these moments – patience, positioning, precision at the crucial instant, power applied to a problem to solve it. Immediately he moved away from Patrese. Prost, in for tyres, was back in seventh.

Sure, the Ferrari would just plain fail any moment now but it had been good while it lasted, wonderfully good. As Mansell passed the pits he was seen to be gesticulating, which could only mean the end was near. Couldn't it?

On lap 20 Mansell pitted for tyres himself (hence the gesticulating to warn them); 10.07 seconds, which wasn't bad circa 1989. He rejoined third behind Patrese and Prost, now of course hustling along on his fresh rubber. It would be another Prost race, the canny little Frenchman drawing up metre by metre and Patrese hadn't stopped for tyres yet, anyway. That would fling him back a couple of places at least. On the straight Prost went the alternative way round Patrese – outside not inside – and headed off alone into the distance. Mansell meanwhile simply surged past Patrese and kept on surging. Whatever the Ferrari was or wasn't, it was fast. Just like the boy from Birmingham himself. The crucial laps were:

Lap	Prost	Mansell
23	1:36.356	1:34.423
24	1:35.582	1:34.613
25	1:36.451	1:34.369
26	1:36.076	1:34.386
27	1:36.735	1:36.400

The gap had become 0.493, so close in real terms that if Mansell had had fingers as long as Berger's he could probably have touched the McLaren. On the straight he went outside Prost, clean and clinical, and the Ferrari was a lot faster. Within three or four corners that was even more evident. Prost was drifting back. ('I lost my clutch shortly after my first tyre stop, which was extremely frustrating,' Prost would say. 'All I could do was make my second set last as best I could and run as quickly as necessary to retain second place. It was a big disappointment.')

This was lap 28 of 61. How much further would the Ferrari go now? Mansell was telling himself he'd missed the early aeroplane home which forgivably he'd anticipated catching. The Ferrari continued all the way to lap 45 when Mansell came into the pits, gesticulating again. He unhooked the steering wheel and cast it aside; another was fitted while all four tyres were changed. The lap before he'd felt the steering wheel working loose, enough to frighten the bravest in high-speed corners and not do your blood pressure much good elsewhere, either, when you're averaging 120 mph. The stop lasted 13.20 seconds and by then Prost had gone through into the lead. Not for long. Mansell surged again and within a couple of laps ducked inside on the straight.

All he had to do now was finish.

He did, 7.809 seconds ahead of Prost. He could barely believe it, barely express it. 'What can I say except it's the most laps the car has done ever in the history of its life.' A hard race, too, with bleeding blisters on his hands afterwards and on the podium the trophy was so large and heavy it became painful to hold and he had to set it down.

In Italy where it was late at night church bells rang (really), motorists sounded their horns (really), a priest at Mass blessed the car (really) and the priest in whose parish Maranello is received a telegram of congratulations from the Bishop of Modena. Yes, really. Imola and the second race of the season was almost a full month away. The rush for tickets began immediately and within days the grandstands were sold out. All forms of accommodation in the area and far beyond it braced themselves for the onslaught.

At Imola on race weekend the Ferrari banners were first sighted with a legend which seemed to growl as it echoed. Mansell, *Il Leone*. Mansell, the lion.

The San Marino Grand Prix carried within it other echoes. On the fourth lap Berger's Ferrari failed to follow the curve of a corner called Tamburello, thundered on and churned along the safety barrier, flames belching from it until it was a terrible bonfire. Berger survived but he was so concussed that he had absolutely no idea where he was. This is how it felt in his own words.

> *Where am I? I'm on holiday, no I'm not on holiday, somebody is trying to put something in my mouth, I don't want that, I'm afraid I'll suffocate, fight against it. Somebody says to me in English*: Don't move, you had an accident. *So I had an accident. But where?*

The race had long been stopped. Visual evidence suggested that something on the car had broken and when Berger turned it into Tamburello it did not respond. It had acquired a life of its own. In the Ferrari pit people were crying. Mansell made for the track's hospital where he was told that Berger was not going to die.

Nigel Mansell now had a decision to make and only he could make it. In ten, twenty, thirty minutes the race would be re-started. His Ferrari was the same as Berger's and there was no time, no time at all, to examine the wreckage of that, see what – if anything – had failed; but if it was a failure, what man on earth could guarantee Mansell that it wouldn't fail on his? Mansell needed time to reflect. He drifted inside the pit and voices were coming at him but he had no notion what they might be saying. It felt as if he were in a waking dream.

He made the decision to take the re-start for two reasons: he respected John Barnard so much and sensed with great clarity how important that might be to Barnard; and at least if his car failed he would already be on guard against it, prepared, thinking in those directions. Truly racing drivers are not like you and me. Nor did Mansell give the re-start anything less than his maximum, running a strong third until the gearbox let go on lap 23.

The gearbox let go again at Monte Carlo on lap 30 after he'd been as high as third, again in Mexico on lap 43 when he was second; and in Phoenix the alternator went on lap 31 when he'd been as high as third. This did not prevent him from re-signing for Ferrari for 1991 and from offering some publicity-speak of his own. 'I am happy to be staying with Ferrari and am very confident of the potential that the Ferrari has.' He *would* say that, wouldn't he? Actually the car did have enormous potential, as we have seen. His lowest high-point after five races (if you get my meaning) had been third.

Canada was bizarre. The surface of the track was wet, Berger stalled at the green light, the start was aborted and during the second parade lap to bring them all back to the grid Mansell (and Alessandro Nannini, Benetton) made a fundamental decision to peel off and pit for dry tyres. The reasoning was that there would soon be a 'dry line' on the circuit – a column of Formula One cars burn water off as they go round – and this would give them an advantage. When the dry line appeared all the other drivers would have to come in for dries. The risk was considerable because under the regulations Mansell and Nannini would have to start the race from the exit to the pit lane when the rest of the field had departed the grid and gone past.

But the risk carried an enormous potential gain. Within a couple of laps Mansell and Nannini ought to have been going faster than the rest and the true duration of a pitstop is, don't forget, much nearer 30 seconds, slowing as you come in, being stationary, accelerating away. With Mansell already flying, who could afford to give him 30 seconds? None of them.

Standard practice is quite clear for a car starting from the pit lane. The car proceeds to the end of the pit lane and, under the supervision of marshals, waits until the grid has been released and has gone past. The car is then free to join the race although by definition this is always at the back. This is governed by common-sense as much as anything else. A driver sits low to the ground and has a pit-lane wall between himself and the track. He cannot see what is happening on the other side; so he waits, the marshal gets the all-clear, he goes out and sets off.

Mansell arrived at the end of the pit and saw *no marshal at all* – nor even a red light, which again is standard and anyway a totally international signal meaning *stop!* to every human being on planet Earth, never mind racing drivers. What he did see was a flashing orange light which in the absence of a marshal you take to mean *proceed with caution*.

He did. So did Nannini. Once they were on the track they wondered where all the other cars were. They ought to have seen the tail end of the pack jostling away into the first corner. They saw nothing like that. All the cars were *behind* them, still on the grid and waiting for the green light. Television coverage, the conduit to the global audience, captured this entirely by chance. A camera faced the twin rows of the grid while at the bottom of the screen a red blur passed in a trice followed by a green blur also in a trice. This happened so quickly and the image was so insubstantial that commentators, their eyes locked on to the starting light – it had not yet moved to red never mind green – were utterly baffled. Murray Walker suddenly said: 'Mansell and Nannini have gone round to rejoin. This is an incredible situation. They will be starting a full lap back . . .'

Or a full lap ahead, Murray.

Hunt, partnering Walker, said when the race had started: 'To me it's very surprising that Mansell and Nannini went out of the pits at all. I'm sure they would have been better off to wait because they can't have been more than half way round the lap when the race was started. Why they didn't wait in the pits and take it from there I don't know. I'm also surprised that a lot more drivers didn't go straight in [for dry tyres]'.

Neither Walker nor Hunt, speaking live, had any chance to know that far from leading the race by half a lap Mansell and Nannini assumed they were half a lap behind and were no doubt asking themselves where all the others were. To those who savour farce this was another example of motor-racing officialdom at its worst and rendered more amazing because the sport had become much more professional, much more punctilious about getting these things right. You need only glance back to Berger's crash at Imola and the speed of reaction by the fire marshals – they were there in a matter of seconds and without question saved Berger's life.

Now in rainy Canada Mansell (and Nannini) were disqualified although Mansell's alternator failed anyway. A few days later Barnard left Ferrari after a lively and ultimately unsatisfactory relationship, to be replaced by an Argentinian, Enrique Scalabroni, from Williams. The long-term significance of it was largely unknown although, truth to tell, Ferrari always seemed to live from daily crisis to daily crisis anyway and who dares think of anything resembling long-term?

Surveying the very nature of Mansell's career and particularly this season, it was almost axiomatic that he would do something exceptional which would also, of course, be cloaked in good old drama. He did. Across the years the French Grand Prix at Paul Ricard has tended to be straightforward. After the death of de Angelis testing there in 1986 the circuit had been modified and the only point of contention, if one may express it like that, was the sharp right-hander immediately after the start where 26 cars would have to find a way through. Mansell was on the second row of the grid.

At the green Senna took the lead, then Prost, Nannini, Mansell, Berger, then the pack. In the midst of it Mauricio Gugelmin (Leyton House) braked hard, got smoke from all four wheels and the car veered sharp right, striking simultaneously the rears of Boutsen and Berger. It was launched sideways, a rear wheel already plucked off, shards of debris already cascading on to the track. The car landed on its side hammering into Mansell's rear before it scudded away – still on its side – down the escape road. It was like a bomb-burst. Mansell's Ferrari came to rest a little way further on, the whole rear wing gone. Eventually, the race stopped, it was towed back by a truck.

'I just couldn't take in what had happened,' he would say. 'There I was just turning into the first corner and something came out of the air and slammed into me. It gave me a hell of a belt. My helmet snapped back into the monocoque and for a while I couldn't really see very much. That cleared but it left me with a bad headache.'

Gugelmin trotted back to the pits to get the spare Leyton House while the track-clearing began. 'I saw a gap ahead of me,' Gugelmin would say, 'then the gap disappeared, so I put on the brakes hard and the car started to twitch. I couldn't tell who I touched but I launched into the air and there was nothing I could do to stop it.'

Mansell ran back to his pit and discovered that Berger, who thought he might have an oil leak, had taken the spare. There was no choice this time: Mansell had to take Berger's race car. 'The seat was half out, there were no seat-belts and I was angry.' The Ferrari mechanics now made a tactical error, which was certainly understandable in these circumstances. Instead of thrusting Mansell straight into it, letting him come all the way round slowly and cautiously back to grid where the cars would be stationary for a long time awaiting the re-start and they could work on it, they decided to do it in the pits. When they'd finished the pit lane was closed, just like it ought to have been in Canada. Mansell, already a prisoner of Berger's unfamiliar car – it was set up just the way Berger liked it and small differences can be important – was also a prisoner of the red light. Mansell really would start at the back of the field, when all the others had gone . . .

The re-start was clean, Prost away like a hare, Senna breaking down immediately – the differential failed – and Mansell twenty-first as they completed the first lap. This was his kind of situation and it could do nothing but draw the best out of him. Every lap until the ninth he overtook someone, Pierluigi Martini, Piquet, Cheever, Gabriele Tarquini, Satoru Nakajima, Stefano Modena, Eric Bernard, Arnoux. By lap 20 Mansell was ninth, he pitted for new tyres and that put him back to fifteenth. He would have to do it all again.

What followed was a very great charge, never letting what had gone before interfere with the thought-processes, and by lap 31 he was eighth. Palmer stopped for tyres and that was seventh. Nannini retired on lap 41 (suspension), and that was sixth. He overtook Boutsen and that was fifth. The order on ap 43: Prost, Ivan Capelli, Jean Alesi, Patrese, Mansell, Boutsen.

Capelli went on lap 44 (electrics), and that was fourth. Capelli clambered out – the car had stopped on the circuit – and began the walk back. Alesi, making his debut, was now signalled into the pits. 'I felt great in the car,' he would say, 'so good in fact that I was not really keen to come in for fresh tyres!'

And that was third . . .

Mansell chased Patrese for second place, caught him, pressured him and on lap 61 Patrese spun off. Patrese was in the spare car after Gugelmin's aerobatics had re-shaped his race car; the spare had been set up for Boutsen, it oversteered and Patrese simply lost it, as they say. 'Fortunately,' he would say, 'I didn't hit anything.' He rejoined but a long way behind Mansell.

And that was second . . .

There was of course no possibility of actually catching Prost unless something went wrong with Prost's car and they moved in stately procession to the end, Prost winning it by 44.017 seconds. Mansell found it was 'a little disappointing because if I had been in my race car who knows what would have happened? I'd have given Alain a good run, but it's got to be one of the best drives of my career, I think.' It was certainly that.

Prost chose this weekend to announce that he was leaving McLaren after what would be six rich seasons and three World Championships. He declined to say which team he intended to join for 1990.

Mansell qualified on the second row of the grid at Silverstone and before the race likened life at Ferrari to a marriage: both partners

185

have to work at it. He also felt he had proved to Ferrari that he was capable to working in 'many areas, not only driving the car'. He added that the marriage was based on mutual respect. Berger meanwhile signed for McLaren for 1990 to replace Prost while rumours – rife, naturally and uncheckable, naturally – suggested that half a dozen drivers were in hot pursuit of Berger's place at Ferrari. Prost was not one of them, if you listened to the rumours.

At the start of the race Prost made the better start but Senna outbraked him into Copse, with Mansell nicely into third. While Prost moved on Senna, Mansell set the fastest lap (144.870 mph) and was beginning to catch Prost. On lap 12 Senna spun clean off – and out. 'I had difficulty selecting third gear on the downchange almost from the start. Four or five laps before I finally spun off I almost went off at the same place. Eventually I couldn't get the gear and that was that. I could not take the corner in neutral.'

Prost: 'I was quite happy to run second behind Ayrton in the opening stages. I felt I was having an easier time and you cannot get too close to another car on such a fast circuit because of the aerodynamic turbulence. But I saw him have two or three "moments" before he eventually went off.'

Prost leading, Mansell pursuing – it was exactly what 100,000 British supporters, many standing ten-deep, adored: a real race to be run, a challenge to be overcome and here it was before their very eyes. Mansell liked that sort of thing, too, but the McLaren was simply quicker. Prost set fastest lap (comparison, 145.862 mph), Mansell pitted for tyres on lap 43, was stationary for 11.26 seconds – Mansell had a puncture on his front right – Prost came in for an ordinary stop on lap 47 and had a nightmare 24.27 seconds. There was a problem with the right-rear. And Mansell was coming, coming. As Prost eased back out of the pits and resumed, the gap was around 12 seconds but . . . the McLaren was simply quicker. Prost reeled off a couple of new fastest laps and won it by 19.369 seconds. 'The team made a slight mistake at my tyre stop but that's just one of those things. I am obviously delighted with the Championship points position,' Prost said as he contemplated the table. He had 47, Senna 27, Patrese 22, Mansell 21.

'I had a tyre deflate on me which caused a little bit of excitement on Hangar Straight [the flat-out section],' Mansell said. 'I pushed as hard as I could but he was a master again today, I think he won it very nicely' – and as he said that, Mansell winked at Prost sitting alongside him. A nice moment.

Mansell was third in Germany and in Hungary during the untimed Friday morning session he locked horns with young Alesi, who hit his brakes when Mansell, who was right behind him, wasn't expecting him to. Mansell, by now a very senior member of the Formula One world, took exception to this and marched down to Ken Tyrrell demanding that Alesi apologise.

Tyrrell said that he couldn't comment until he'd seen a video of the incident but that he'd have a word with Alesi. He did, explained that if you are young you ought to consider apologising if for no other reason than to maintain harmony.

Alesi weighed up the proposition and said: 'I don't think I want to do that.' It impressed Ken Tyrrell, it did. Mansell's opinion was trenchant. 'Some of the new drivers have no respect, no regard for anybody. Some of the antics they get up to are far less than professional. I decided that someone had to make a stand so I chose to report the incident to FISA.'

The race was typical Mansell, eighth after the opening lap, a long charge on a circuit where overtaking remained a perennial (and annual) problem and was often frankly impossible. Deep into the race Patrese, leading, saw his water temperature rising and Senna took a sling-shot past him on the start-finish straight. Mansell, running third, was not close enough to follow Senna and now they were in the hard-right at the end of the straight, curling round to another right, then a very, very short straight before a hard left. On that short straight Mansell jinked out on to the outside, marooning himself as it seemed towards the rim of the track while Patrese turned calmly into the corner. Patrese did take the corner calmly enough, the Williams being carried outwards from the exit of the corner by its own impetus.

Mansell twisted the Ferrari inside Patrese, accelerating hard, and was through. This was fingertip control and perfect balance, it was incisive and it was devastating. Mansell attacked Senna, swarming to one side and the other, probing, threatening but the deeply maddening problem wouldn't go away: the real overtaking place was on the long start-finish straight where, classically, you got a 'tow' from the car in front – using the hole his car cut in the air to suck you along – and as the first corner flooded towards you, you pulled out, drew up and out-braked him. But you had to be close enough to get the 'tow'. If you weren't you were flogging along in the aerodynamic turbulence which Prost had spoken of at Silverstone.

This straight was – as all other straights are – about top speed, about how much 'grunt' your engine could deliver to you when your foot was all the way down. Mansell might well be quicker through the corners – which constituted the rest of the circuit (and in fact was) – but that didn't help him. Senna held him on the straight and then all Senna had to do was follow the racing line, positioning the McLaren in the proper place to take each corner, and no room remained for Mansell to overtake. By simply staying on the racing line Senna covered the inside of each corner and the path around the outside of him was too far, the width of the track too narrow. And so on – indefinitely.

To put it succinctly: Mansell needed greater speed on that straight but Senna had the Honda engine, a powerful work-horse if one may characterise such a sophisticated piece of machinery thus. Impasse, maddening, continuing impasse lap by lap, through 53, 54, 55, 56, 57, each a loop of a newsreel you'd seen before, same cast, same motions, same backdrop of scenery, same action.

My own judgement, for what it's worth, was that by now Mansell had become the most creative driver in Grand Prix racing. A noted journalist, Maurice Hamilton, caught the relative merits of Senna, Mansell and Prost in a perceptive phrase which I wish I'd thought of myself: Senna is the quickest, Prost is the cleverest, Mansell is the bravest. That of course was a general overview and nothing specifically to do with the Hungaroring, near Budapest, on 13 August 1989 although as it happened on lap 57 they were running Senna, Mansell, Prost.

But creative? That's a hard word to apply and justify with cars controlled by computers as well as drivers, cars which stuck so rigidly to the ground that you couldn't outdrift anybody – and with many circuits essentially safe but also neutered. Overtaking places were clearly defined and nowhere better than on this snake of a circuit, coiling and uncoiling among the dried hillocks of the Hungarian countryside: you got the tow, you feinted here or there towards the first corner, ducked out, braked late, took the lead. It was like trains moving in sidings. Nothing remotely creative about that; more like the appliance of science, or the logistics of logic.

What Mansell could do, and had been able to do for several years, was either provoke the unexpected or capitalise on it when it happened, and in truth he was the only one doing these things.

Senna would blast past you or more likely already be ahead of you and staying there; lapping back-markers he would be fearless but straightforward: *here is a gap, even a small gap, I am going into it, you know that, I know that and, here I am in the gap, goodbye.* Prost would out-manoeuvre you as part of some weblike master plan constructed

188

to embrace a whole race; he'd be calculating on lap 20 where you would be on lap 40, and what he'd do when he got behind you, and how it would be done, and it was done so. Mansell might do anything. He had already in this race, pouncing when Patrese went wide and taking him on the inside immediately after one of the tight corners where such a move is implausible and usually impossible. But now – impasse. Senna circled, circled, Mansell waited, waited.

Another loop of the newsreel.

They came in tandem from the dried hillocks, came through the long right, the surge to another right, the surge to a loop-left, the surge to the horseshoe-right which fed them on to the straight. Going into the horseshoe Senna put the McLaren where he had every time before, tight, a foot away from the curved white kerbing on the inside, Mansell two cars' length behind. Another loop: Senna on the racing line, stoking the Honda to flee down the straight to begin another loop.

Stefan Johansson in a very uncompetitive Onyx had had an unhappy race, had long since been lapped and had now himself chugged through the loop and was just beginning his journey along the straight. If he had glanced in his mirrors he would have seen the red and white snout of Senna's McLaren boring at him, the red of Mansell's Ferrari being urged to try and get closer to Senna. There was a compression behind him but if you're driving an Onyx you've seen that before and you know what to do. Get the hell out of it.

Johansson was over to the left as the troika – him, Senna, Mansell – did start the long journey. Senna was within touching distance behind Johansson, Mansell within touching distance behind Senna. Compression. Senna instantly dived out from behind Johansson, but by now – the cars had travelled perhaps 20 metres, perhaps 30, perhaps 40 – Johansson was virtually full over to the left, vacating the breadth of the straight and that breadth permitted three abreast. This is the way it was: Johansson pointed directly ahead, Senna angled to move out and take him, Mansell angled more sharply to take both of them. Mansell had read everything in the milli-second, seized the shifting current, and had created his own gap.

He flung the Ferrari into it so hard it almost slithered and a milli-second later Johansson was still going straight ahead, hugging the kerbing; Senna had begun to emerge from behind him into open air in the centre of the track; Mansell was working the steering wheel to correct the slither and was still moving towards the other

189

side of the track. There was more open air there, a window of it. He flung the Ferrari so far that it grazed the white boundary line on the other side, twitched as he harnessed it, siphoning it forward. Now Johansson was spectating and behaving like the gentleman he is, Senna was in mid-track and not yet abreast, and Mansell was coming from the white boundary line and already half the length of a car in front of Senna. What he did then was outrageously wonderful. He flung the Ferrari again, this time fully across in another twitch-slither to the centre of the circuit. He was fully in front of Senna.

The result of the race was decided.

It was the move of the season and drew these humbled, circumspect, laconic words from Senna: 'It was obviously a good race and I lost the lead when I had to brake behind Johansson and Nigel managed to get by. He might well have passed me anyway perhaps, perhaps not. What matters is that he did and it was a good race. I eased up towards the end with a bad tyre vibration but that was after Nigel got ahead.' It was a way of saying he had been outdriven, and do not forget that the words came from a man widely regarded as the most awesome practitioner of inserting himself into gaps since . . . well, since the world began.

Mansell faced Murray Walker who craned deferentially with a microphone aimed firmly towards Mansell's mouth. Mansell said: 'I've got to say it for the first time in my life, that was my best race. I was very fortunate but I am very, very happy. I made my mind up that I had to make four, five cars up on the start and I got a beautiful start and I went outside on the first corner . . . and then it was just a question of being patient.'

The move of the season? This is authentic Mansell-speak again: 'Ayrton was pushing hard, I was pushing hard, it was just a question of who would get the little bit of benefit from the traffic and Ayrton was a little bit unlucky but I was there ready hopefully to take any opportunity because I knew I had to be right with him because he doesn't make any mistakes or very few. I had to be there just in case and I was very fortunate. An opening arose, I went for it and it was very close. But I am happy I managed to get past.'

I've quoted this BBC interview for a reason. If you watched the move of the season and heard the interview and the curiously stilted language you'd have thought that Nigel Mansell had had his early training as a special constable making reports on traffic offences rather than under the tutelage of Colin Chapman and Frank Williams and was now driving the most famous car in the world in

190

the wake (literally) of Enzo Ferrari. It was almost as if something had taught him to communicate this way, as if he were working from some unvarying script and the words chugged out of him as predictably as Johansson's Onyx was probably still chugging on somewhere out there . . .

The mystery remained: Senna expressive in Portuguese, Spanish, English and Italian; Prost fluent in French, delicious in English, comfy after his fashion in Italian; Mansell sometimes awkward in English. What does this matter? Not much if you've just won the Hungarian Grand Prix by 25.967 seconds from Senna, Prost fourth and a long way further back. But the public face leads to the private man and that was why the mystery remained, and remains still. Many pondered it, wanted him to find a way of celebrating himself which didn't sound like a grouping of phrases we could all have mouthed. We had heard them before. In the midst of the mega-million-dollar glamour-hype life-and-death state-of-the-art ultimate-exploration of man and machine he might almost have begun the press conference: I was proceeding in an easterly direction . . .

What compounded it was that in this most difficult human activity of driving a racing car – and given equal equipment – you'd think twice before backing anyone on earth to beat him. He had become as good as that.

Spa, no encore, a solid third behind Senna and Prost and afterwards Prost joined Ferrari. Since Mansell was number one he (graciously) made some concessions – Prost was a World Champion – although as Prost would subsequently confess, Mansell remained firmly number one, he number two. I wasn't present when Prost said that but I'm sure he was smiling.

Mansell said he welcomed Prost's coming, said he was one of the really few friends he had, respected him 'more than any other driver'. There is no reason to doubt this: if you cast your mind back to Adelaide '86 and the tyre blow-out, Prost said with obvious sincerity that he knew how Mansell felt; that he understood and sympathised, and added an echoing phrase about how genuinely sorry he felt for him. It was the right thing to say but it was the way he said it, the unconscious delivery, unprompted, the whole fibre of Prost vibrating as he spoke so softly, so deeply that it could never have been a platitude. After all, he could have said a lot of other things if he'd wanted and only mentioned Mansell *en passant*. That would have been proper and acceptable; but no, he'd chewed the word Nigel with undisguised affection, dwelt upon it, balanced his own happiness against it; and now, racing towards '90 and a new decade and the traditional new beginning which a new season brings (like a second marriage, hope versus experience) he was happy and Mansell was happy and everybody was happy and . . . they all live happily ever after. Don't they?

Portugal, 24 September 1989 and now it's really Senna (51 points) versus Prost (71 points) with Mansell on 38 and still capable of anything except winning the World Championship which, through no fault of his own, was beyond him. Four races left, he'd need to win them all and Senna and Prost finish nowhere. It wasn't even a calculation. It was the run-in to the end of another season.

Portugal was frankly controversial. Coming in for tyres Mansell overshot his pit and reversed to reach it, a clear infringement of the rules. When he went back out he was black-flagged for three consecutive laps but said – reasonably, surely – that following Senna, as he was, and with the sun in his eyes he simply did not see it. He said he would be prepared to swear on the Bible that he had not seen it.

Worse, Mansell and Senna disputed Turn One, Mansell went for the inside, Senna came across – and could say he was only taking the racing line – and they crashed. Senna, going so hard for the Championship, had had a crash with a man who was already black-flagged, already excluded . . .

Stormy weather. Senna gave a savage interview the following day saying that what Mansell did could have had 'disastrous consequences', Ron Dennis pitched in by questioning how Mansell hadn't been told by radio, Mansell countered that 'McLaren, although it had changed tyres on both cars, had tyres and equipment in the pit lane obscuring my view of the Ferrari pit.' FISA decided to exclude Mansell from the Spanish Grand Prix, which was next. Mansell and Ferrari were also fined $50,000 for reversing in the pit lane.

At Jerez Mansell called a press conference and said: 'My point is this. You can have a mass murderer with all the evidence you want but he is tried and found guilty beyond reasonable doubt before being hanged. I would suggest there is plenty of reasonable doubt as to whether I deliberately ignored the black flag. If they believe honestly that I saw it and ignored it I will have to consider retiring sooner rather than later from Formula One. I accept that I have broken whatever rule it was in the pit lane. I must also accept that I was black-flagged three times. Therefore the coming together that I had with Senna was for what? Nothing. I don't race to have accidents, I race to try and win. You can't win if you don't finish.

'It wasn't until I was getting changed that I found out that I had been black-flagged. To say I was amazed is an understatement. What I am questioning is the penalty for this infringement. A fine, yes, but $50,000 is very extreme. And a ban from this race? I cannot believe it is happening. This to me is a complete nonsense. I cannot believe my mistake in the pit lane and my failure to see the black flag warrants such severe punishment. To be made a scapegoat for ruining the Championship is ridiculous. I do not and will not accept this.'

There is a very basic question behind all this. If Mansell had seen the black flags, what point would there have been in ignoring them? Black flags – and the colour black is not chosen randomly, it denotes finality – are not negotiable and you can't plough on to the end of the race and have them retrospectively withdrawn under appeal. Mansell knew that. Everybody knew that. In the simplest terms to continue after being black-flagged was pointless (no pun intended) and itself a very serious offence.

The whole thing sank mercifully into the background when at Suzuka Prost and Senna crashed amid much more acrimony with the title itself at stake. (Mansell, running fifth at one stage, dropped out with engine problems.) Australia was run in a storm, an extremely controversial decision, and Mansell spun twice, the first time doing a complete high-speed rotation and catching it, the second time striking a wall. He found a telling word to describe his feelings about Grand Prix drivers having to compete in such conditions.

'Diabolical.'

Pit Stop

Life with Alain Prost across 1990 was not necessarily easy. Prost spoke Italian as I've said and that obviously helped while Mansell, who still didn't, had a sequence of wretched races: engine problems at Phoenix, a distant fourth in Brazil, engine problems at San Marino, electrics at Monaco. He was third in the wet in Canada. Then Mexico. At this stage Prost had 14 points, Mansell 7; not that that mattered. Senna already had 31 and now dominated most of the race, until he had a puncture; Prost led, Mansell second, Berger coming hard third. Mansell spun on to the grass, stopped the Ferrari before it hit the barrier, reversed (quite legal on the circuit, please note) and set off again.

Berger drew up, went for the inside at a right-hand corner, locked his brakes as Mansell assumed the racing line – which brought Mansell across him – there was a billow of smoke from Berger's tyres and the cars rubbed together as they went through the corner. Berger emerged ahead.

Nigel Mansell did not care for that.

Two laps to go. Down the straight Mansell got a tow, tried to power past Berger on the outside; he couldn't, but tried again in a left-short surge-right, the Ferrari dancing at his touch. Berger held him, held him through the twisty section – no chance there – Mansell danced again, probing right – or was it a feint? – going left so that he was lost on the outside as they moved into a left-hand corner.

Mansell took him on the outside.

Mansell took him on worn tyres further worn by his spin. Mansell took him not just on power but a beautiful balance and if it was born of anger it was an anger ruthlessly and ferociously controlled. Mansell took him on feel: he felt the limit of the car and felt that it was further than Berger's limit. It was an extraordinary move and (again) only he would have done it; arguably only he, Prost and Senna could have done it. That's a hard judgement on a

194

lot of other Grand Prix drivers but a fair judgement. He was 25.351 seconds behind Prost when the chequered flag fell; not that that mattered either after what we had just witnessed.

In France the engine went; at Silverstone the gearbox went and the crowded pressroom might have anticipated something because Mansell gave a clue. 'One car works perfectly. I just don't understand why mine keeps breaking down.' Alain Prost won the British Grand Prix.

Mansell called a mini-press conference and announced his retirement from Formula One. This hadn't been prompted by breaking down at Silverstone – he'd been thinking about it for a long time, he'd talked it over with Rosanne and, in a phrase which might come to haunt him, 'I'm looking forward to putting my family first for the first time in my life.'

The British, who had never been quite sure of what to make of Nigel Mansell, were almost unanimous. Don't do it. There were phone-ins: should he? shouldn't he? register your vote. Even among those who didn't warm to him there was a rare unanimity: he will leave a void and it might take a decade for another Briton to fill it. Mansell had taken a decade to create it and, remember, only one other Briton in the 1980s had won races – John Watson, the last of them Long Beach, 1983. As of this moment on a dying Silverstone race day, 15 July 1990, Mansell had won fifteen races and only one Englishman, Stirling Moss, had ever won more – sixteen. Odd. Moss hadn't been World Champion either.

While the stampede to the telephones in the press room was growing in intensity and the gabble of voices was rising and front pages were being cleared to accommodate it, those journalists who didn't have to file immediately started thinking and thinking hard. Where did Mansell's void leave them? Which newspapers would send them round the world at considerable expense to report races without Mansell? This emphasised the stature to which Mansell had grown. He was air tickets to a lot of people and surely worth 20,000 on the gate at Silverstone, too. Nobody had time to go find out what the Silverstone people thought, though if you use the yardstick that once each of the 20,000 had paid to get in, fed and watered themselves they'd each be spending a minimum of £50, it was a million pounds. Or putting it more prosaically, two years of Mansell plus the 20,000 equalled the £2 million Silverstone would spend creating an extensively revised circuit in 1991.

When the supporters heard they began to wonder too. Where was the successor? In this British Grand Prix there were only two other British drivers (compared to ten Italians). Derek Warwick, liked by all, was nearer the end than the beginning and anyway marooned with Lotus, no lifeboat in sight, and Martin Donnelly was just beginning, no sign yet that he would ever be called *Il Leone*. He seemed more like Watson, Ulster, homely. Martin Brundle, a contemporary of Senna's, was driving Jaguars in the World Sportscar Championship and won Le Mans having made a calculated retreat from Formula One. Winning Le Mans is a fine and wonderful thing demanding organisation, stamina, team-work, long hours of concentration and the ability to be repetitive at big, big average speeds. To win a single Formula One race was a different matter and this is a very sharp contrast: between 1980 and 1990 eight drivers with Grand Prix experience would find them-selves winning Le Mans (along with twelve who had not tasted Formula One at all) and of the eight only two, Jacky Ickx and Jochen Mass, had actually won a Grand Prix. Brundle was good, had always been good but the years and the opportunities might be starting to move against him.

And that was the void when the afternoon at Silverstone died and night fell and the immense crowd were blocking every lane from Silverstone bumper to tail, bumper to tail, talking about it. They had seen him for the last time.

Mansell would certainly give nothing less than his utmost (and never, ever had) as the season worked to a close . . . he didn't finish in Germany, crashed in Hungary (or rather was involved in a crash with Berger), didn't finish in Belgium, fourth at Monza, then he won Portugal superbly, was second in Spain, didn't finish in Japan, was second in Australia. A strong finale to a career which was also an epoch, an exact decade which had been many things and had occupied him most days of it one way or another for more than a quarter of his life.

He was 37. He was rich however you cared to measure it; he could spend time with his family; he had businesses to keep himself occupied; he could make a grand tour of the golf courses of the world if he so chose; and all this he had earned.

One private day long before the end of 1990 Frank Williams flew to the Isle of Man, journeyed to Port Erin and sat with Nigel Mansell. They talked. It did not matter that Frank had proffered that phrase, about 'not having any fond memories of him, but a brilliant driver' when he'd left the team that time before. Motor racing was no longer about affection, if it ever had been, but about our old friend the package and the string and who ties it and what the package contains. So they talked. Senna was bound to McLaren and Prost to Ferrari. Mansell was the only other driver who could win races on a regular basis, Mansell was free and Williams needed him and Williams had the bait. Frank Williams made the most profound offer you can receive: we will make you World Champion on whatever terms (within reason) that you lay down and we can make you World Champion.

For Mansell the haunting of 'putting my family first' would begin. If he joined Williams he would be negating that, a delicate matter and one which could not be avoided. Mere money could not compel him to go on because he had enough; the joy of manipulating an expensive machine he had drunk to the full, 149 times on all five continents. But the Championship . . . wouldn't you, dear reader, roll the big dice one more time? Maybe, maybe not. That's why the dilemma about him wouldn't go away, just as he was coming back.

14 The Charger

On the evening of 12 May 1991 the World Championship seemed over. There had only been four races, Phoenix, Sao Paulo, Imola and now Monaco. Ayrton Senna had won all of them to construct a Championship table which looked like this: Senna 40, Prost 11, Berger 10, Patrese and Mansell 6. Twelve races remained and superficially Senna was a clear favourite to win all of them.

Mansell's Canon Williams was a beautiful car to behold, tight and crisp, with economical lines. The chassis handled tracks well and the Renault V10 engine was delivering a lot of power but the semi-automatic gearbox lacked reliability. It had failed in Phoenix when Mansell was running third, failed in Brazil when he was running second and at Imola he couldn't find a gear at the very start, was hit from behind and didn't cover a single lap. At that stage Senna led him 30 points to nil.

Round the tortuous streets of Monaco he went the distance, including an electrifying surge past Prost at the chicane down from the tunnel. In the tunnel he wound himself up and on the slope beyond it slotted the car inside Prost as they surged to the 90-degree left. There was smoke from the tyres when he braked into it, Prost obediently turning in behind him. It was a distillation of everything Mansell was about, courage, judgement, the unexpected and all of this harmonised by a very profound mastery of car control. Many another driver could have dug into the Renault engine for its power and gone inside Prost but how many, reaching the chicane on the wrong line and braking so hard that smoke was churned, could have got through it?

Mansell ran in second place to the end and promptly said that 'to be honest the Championship is already over'. This was not a judgement with which Ayrton Senna agreed, and for several reasons. When he had first tested the McLaren Honda at Estoril before the season he complained publicly that it lacked power, not enough progress had been made and he knew that winning the first four races had camouflaged that. In fact it made convincing people more difficult.

Meanwhile Patrese was regularly out-driving Mansell, itself an amazing thing. He had made his Grand Prix debut in 1977 virtually two generations distant (it was at Monaco) and here is the front of the grid:

John Watson

    Jody Scheckter

Carlos Reutemann

    Ronnie Peterson

Hans Stuck

    Niki Lauda . . .

Patrese's career had been one of those which never quite fulfilled itself. He'd driven for a lot of teams – Shadow, Arrows, Brabham, Alfa Romeo, Brabham again – and was now in his fourth season at Williams. On this evening of 12 May 1991 he had taken part in 212 races, an absolute record although he'd only won three of them. That was the unfulfilment.

Frank Williams ordinarily did not favour team orders as we saw with such clarity when Piquet and Mansell were together, and although Patrese was firmly number two, that meant nothing – as Patrese would subsequently point out – the very moment the cars left the pits. They were very equal then. Whatever lingering thoughts Mansell nursed about the Championship even if he had conceded it, Patrese had become a factor. At the age of 37 Patrese was getting better and better. Put Prost into the equation, assume that Gerhard Berger's long sequence of ill luck would come to an end at McLaren on the law of averages if nothing else, and Mansell was hemmed in every way he looked.

Worse (in truth much worse) was the revised points system which now bestowed ten for a win rather than nine and allowed all sixteen results to be counted instead of the best eleven. Senna would not be punished for consistency as he had been in the past, would not have to calculate that other drivers could make a late run at him when he was having to drop his worst results. Senna was liberated to build a mountain nobody could climb, high as he liked.

That May evening, as the exodus to Nice Airport gathered strength and the transporters were being loaded, the invincibility of the package Ron Dennis had tied together with such acumen – an expert, motivated workforce of nearly 200, Marlboro money,

Honda power – was surely beyond all question. Since 1988, when Dennis acquired this Honda power, McLaren had taken 46 pole positions out of a possible 52, had won 35 of the races out of a possible 52 and won the World Championship each year. The history of Grand Prix racing offered no parallels. Williams conversely had taken two pole positions in this period and had won four races (all with Renault). That was the background as the teams arrived for the Canadian Grand Prix, Montreal on 2 June:

McLaren   46,35,3
Williams   2, 4,0

There had been a moment before all this (I forget which race) when Senna had noticed something alarming. It was in a sense almost a private moment, a driver drawing a conclusion within the seclusion of the cockpit. He'd had Patrese directly behind him and was fighting hard to hold him off, Patrese had been baulked by a back-marker and drifted a long way back and Senna thought: *well, that's taken the pressure off me for a while*. Patrese was up behind him again very, very quickly, so quickly that Senna knew this Williams Renault had the beating of him.

Round the Isle Notre Dame at Montreal confirmation was not long in coming. Mansell was fastest in the first session of the grid, Patrese and then Mansell in the second. Senna had started no race lower than the front row of the grid since Portugal the previous September. The confirmation continued in the race, Mansell under challenge briefly from Patrese as they moved away from the green light towards the left–right corners and then both pulling decisively away from Senna, third. All across the early laps they pulled further away and Senna, as he confessed, was impotent in the face of it. Senna covered only 25 laps when the electrics failed.

Patrese had a puncture which dropped him a lap behind, leaving Mansell 51 seconds ahead of Piquet. He was so far ahead on the last lap that he began to wave to the crowd, or rather return their applause of him. You're tempting the fates when you do that and the fates lurked. At the hairpin, a trifle of a distance from the line itself, Mansell slowed and stopped. He'd been changing down from fifth when the semi-automatic gearbox put the car into neutral and the engine died on him. He beat the steering wheel with his left hand in purest frustration and when he'd parked the car on the side of the track he held both arms outstretched in a universal gesture which means, and only means: what can you do? That was five races gone, still only six points.

Senna came to Mexico with ten stitches in his head from a jet-ski accident, was pronounced fit by Professor Watkins, wore a modified crash helmet and promptly landed on his head. In the first qualifying session in the fearsome long-right corner called Peraltada he was in the act of changing gear – which meant only one hand on the wheel – when the McLaren hit a bump (the circuit Hermanos Rodrigues is infested with them) twitched, slithered, rotated across the run-off area into the tyre wall and flipped. Senna crawled out from underneath and headed towards Professor Watkins' mobile clinic again . . .

Patrese pole, then Mansell, Senna, then Jean Alesi trying so hard, perhaps too hard, to prove himself at Ferrari. The front of that grid was combative. From the grid there is a long, long run down to the first corner, long enough to permit a race within a race to unfold. Patrese was away fast, Mansell was away fast, Senna trying to nose between them. As the two Williams shifted towards one side of the track, Berger – from the third row – was trying to nose between them now. Alesi headed towards the other side of the track, Senna flirted with going there too and had to flick the McLaren away from Alesi. At the mouth of the corner all this produced an unexpected order: Mansell clearly ahead and turning in, Alesi behind and tight to the kerbing on the inside, Senna turning in behind Alesi, Patrese – now stranded in his position over to the left – having to turn in behind Senna. Nor was that all. Berger, seeing a gap, pressed the McLaren inside Patrese to try and get through. He didn't make it.

As they settled on that first lap Mansell was already pulling away from Alesi but behind him, down the straight to complete lap one and begin lap two, Senna and Alesi suddenly began to slug it out and as Senna darted across and in front they almost collided. Alesi weaved behind Senna searching for a way back through but by then they were already at the first corner again. Order: Mansell, Senna, Alesi, Patrese, Berger. Could Mansell shed Senna? The whole season might turn on it because if Senna won he'd have 50 points. Patrese took Alesi so that Senna found himself in a sandwich, Patrese harrying him and on the eleventh lap taking him on a power-play down the straight. Patrese moved up behind Mansell, there were no team orders and Patrese made his intentions clear by trying to get past here and there. Alesi nipped past Senna and moved up towards the two Williams but you could be forgiven for

201

not noticing that. Down the straight Patrese went to the outside trying another power-play, but didn't have enough to be able to turn in ahead of Mansell. Both drivers hit the brakes hard.

After the first corner – a hard-right, remember – there's a twist into a hard-left and a twist into another hard-right. Patrese kept to the outside and reaching the hard-left that became the inside; Patrese took it and took the corner and took Mansell. Alesi spun and it settled again, Patrese, Mansell, Senna; it remained like that all the way to the end, although Mansell mounted a late charge and almost caught Patrese.

A few days later they were tyre-testing at Silverstone, which traditionally is also the start of the build-up to the British Grand Prix. Riccardo Patrese is sitting in the Williams motorhome at peace with himself and the world beyond, his day's work over. He's already done the usual chores, signed a few photographs, shaken a few hands. After Mexico moreover the points table had significantly altered to Senna 44, Patrese 20, Piquet 16, Mansell 13. Patrese was emerging as the challenger, not Mansell.

Patrese is good company, a handsome and matured man who smiles a lot (sometimes ironically) and is invariably chirpy at such relaxed moments. So, Riccardo, tell me about Patrese versus Mansell.

'Number one and number two – what does that mean? It doesn't worry me. When people talked about it I wasn't bothered at all. Mansell may have what he has (a golden contract bestowing several benefits), but the moment the cars come out of the pit entrance – at exactly that moment – we are equal, we have the same cars prepared to the same high standard, the best man will win. I regard Nigel just as I regard Ayrton Senna and Alain Prost, as someone to be beaten. I like, you see, the taste of winning.

'I am getting better because the car is so good and it gives me the opportunity to be that. And after so many years I have everything under control. There are no team orders from Frank Williams and if people tell me there are I laugh about this. If Nigel was in a position to win the Championship I would help him, as I did with Piquet in 1983 when we were at Brabham, but the Championship is open. I won't discuss my own chances until we have done ten races but to beat Nigel, Prost and Senna is not easy. You must go into the races with the attitude that you are going to fight. I have to fight very strong.'

Yes, it had been a long road to this, spanning fourteen seasons, changing teams seven times, now embracing 214 Grands Prix races. 'I am getting a little bit back now from what the past didn't give me.'

He was 37, which is a long way down the road from the first flush of youth. He swivels his eyes to look directly at you, his face opens into a lovely, warming grin and he says: 'You tell me a young man who wins Grand Prix races.' It is manifestly true. The last driver under 30 to do it was (inevitably) Senna himself, Spain, October 1989.

Patrese also said: 'I don't care if Nigel gets more money than me. I negotiate for what I think I'm worth and when I get that I am satisfied. I have a value of myself.' And: 'Our relationship is fine, it really is, no problem at all, but we both understand that we both want to win.'

France, a few days after the Silverstone testing, changed everything. Magny Cours had replaced Paul Ricard and where on earth was Magny Cours? Near Nevers. Where on earth was Nevers? Somewhere in France, approximately in the middle. At least you could find that on the maps but Magny Cours, no. Must be in a field. When the switch from Ricard had been announced in 1990 horror stories began to be circulated immediately. You couldn't find an hotel room for several hundred kilometres in any direction and even if you did you'd never get to and from the track. The approach was country roads which hadn't coped with minor meetings already held there and pessimists (of which there were a goodly number, and with reason) spoke of the journey in days rather than hours. And as it happened the mechanics of some teams abandoned this altogether and slept in the transporters behind the pits . . .

Nevers itself was charming, a solid, stone-clad old French town which had never known such excitement before – and quite possibly no excitement at all before. The excitement was twofold: the hustle and bustle which inevitably a Grand Prix meeting brings in its train and that Alain Prost, who'd been flogging the Ferrari 642 round the circuits of the world for a mere 11 points, would now have the new 643. What could Prost make it do? Could Prost revive his season, salvage Ferrari? It's the sort of question which French people like to see answered for themselves; it puts a lot of behinds on a lot of seats, and how would those country roads cope?

Magny Cours was full very early on race day and local radio stations were pleading with people en route to turn back. There were ugly scenes with the police when people who'd waited it out in twelve-kilometre queues were refused admission, gates were wrenched open, special stands for photographers were bodily taken over and in the heat people were fainting all over the place. The pre-race atmosphere crackled.

Patrese sat on pole but Prost was alongside him on the front row, then Senna and Mansell. Magny Cours was constructed to be a very daunting circuit if you had overtaking in mind and Mansell himself described overtaking as a 'nightmare'. That put a premium on getting a good start. Patrese didn't. At the green light he was changing from first to second but the semi-automatic gearbox put it into neutral and he was engulfed by the pack, Prost long gone into the lead, Mansell long gone after him, Senna third.

Prost flew. Mansell pursued him and began, slowly, carefully to catch him, Senna far behind and being harried by Alesi. Prost was baulked by traffic when he came up to lap them for the first time and Mansell was on him, right on him. De Cesaris stayed stubbornly in front but, emerging from a right-hander on to a very short straight before a left-hander, de Cesaris moved full over to the left. Prost took centre track, Mansell flung the Williams full over to the right and was fractionally ahead when they reached the right-hander. Prost, seeing this, twitched the Ferrari out of the way and conceded the corner.

It was lap 22, a third of the way through the race. The pit stops for tyres reversed the order, Prost first and stationary for a fraction under seven seconds, Mansell next and stationary for 10.51. Prost was back in the lead. When they completed the next lap the gap was 5.3 seconds. That didn't matter. The nature of the circuit produced bunching. That did matter. Prost had four back-markers in front of him and each moment he was behind them Mansell drew closer and closer. Prost took the first of them, three to go. Mansell himself was behind three back-markers so that it looked like a rolling cavalcade rather than a race. Prost took another of his back-markers and Mansell in a swoop of a surge took two of his. Prost tiptoed past his last two and a wonderfully inviting clear track opened up in front of him.

Mansell was not long in following and Prost was not long in coming up on Thierry Boutsen, he and Mansell danced through and now at last it was a straight two-way fight. That lasted only half a lap. Two more back-markers loomed, were dealt with and Prost was 2.2 seconds ahead. But Mansell was in the mood. He set fastest lap of the race, caught Prost and positioned himself behind him. Down to a right-hander Mansell moved to the outside with the power on and darted in front of Prost who had to brake very hard indeed. This was consummate, this was like Monaco again, a compound of skill, bravery and judgement which ultimately was capable of execution only through the medium of complete car control.

Mansell won the race by five seconds, Senna a distant third and almost swamped by Alesi at the very end. This was Mansell's seventeenth victory, taking him beyond the total of Stirling Moss which had stood since 1961. 'To go past sixteen is history for an Englishman and I have made history for my country and myself today,' Mansell said. He was clearly emotional. (Some hapless radio announcer at home, who clearly knew nothing about Formula One and very little about geography, caused a minor storm when he said Mansell had become the most successful British driver of all time and soon enough the phone lines were humming with Scottish voices pointing out that Jackie Stewart had twenty-seven and Jim Clark twenty-five. I don't mention this to diminish Mansell in any way, only to keep the record straight.) As the country roads around Magny Cours refilled with 100,000 people now trying to leave, the leaderboard had tightened. Senna 48, Mansell 23, Patrese 22, Prost 17. Seven races gone but nine left, 90 possible points left. The Championship wasn't over at all. No. The charge was on.

Silverstone, ah Silverstone. They gave him a cake shaped into the numerals 17, Moss himself held up a pit board with 'Nigel 17 wins' on it in green day-glo colours, put an arm round Mansell's shoulder and was clearly delighted. It was a very civilised moment and symbolised perhaps the manners of a bygone era when drivers enjoyed racing for itself, didn't expect to earn – nor did they earn – fortunes, and sport was seen in its only true perspective: as sport. The fate of nations did not hang on it.

Off the track Mansell seemed particularly relaxed, flitting round on a moped. On the track he was triumphant and no other word will do. He was fastest in every pre-race session – Friday morning and afternoon, Saturday morning and afternoon, the Sunday warm-up. The only session he didn't dominate was the pre-qualifying and that, of course, because he wasn't in it. (I am not being entirely flippant. JJ Lehto in a BMS Dallara was fastest there but four seconds slower than the time Mansell would set to get pole, thus demonstrating the time-warp between the front runners in Formula One and the others.)

Silverstone, as we have seen, had been extensively revised with a new 'complex' from where the cars came under the bridge to entering the start-finish straight: an array of tight corners. The revision at Becketts was even more dramatic, right–left–right–left but taken at much, much bigger speeds than the complex.

David Owen, who works for Williams, puts it very pertinently indeed. 'You are talking about a Formula One car accelerating from 0 to 200 mph and braking to a stop in fourteen seconds. One of the major advances is the carbon fibre brakes we have. Let's say you're going down a straight at 180 mph and you have to go round a hairpin at 55 mph. You'll start braking at about 150 yards, you'll dab the brakes for a second and three-quarters and you'll be down to 55 and you'll be going round that corner.

'That's where the drivers take some of the major G-loading. One of the most daunting sets of corners is at Becketts. You are going in to that at about 160 mph and at each of the corners you are experiencing up to 4.5G. Nigel described it. "You go into the left and you have 4.5 lateral G and then within a second you're snapping over to 4.5G the other way." We call that a 9G snapover. Nigel said the main problem is trying to get your eyeballs to focus on the next apex because physically you can't drag your eyeballs round – and the next apex is coming up within one second. What people don't understand is the physical stress the drivers are going through. I remember seeing Nigel's elbows after the final qualifying session at Silverstone and they were black and blue.'

Mansell himself said 'the new layout is the best in the world. It's hairy all the way round. You have to commit yourself in the corners and hang on. It's very demanding.' Yes.

In the race Senna got away quicker and what followed was astonishing. By the time he and Mansell were through Becketts, which is not even half way round the first lap, they were more than a hundred metres ahead of Roberto Moreno, third. At Stowe Mansell jinked inside Senna and was clean through. He was not to be remotely threatened from this moment on and only really saw Senna again when it was all over and Senna had run out of fuel. Mansell obligingly slowed on his slowing-down lap which had now also become a lap of honour and gave him a lift back, Senna comfy enough nestled behind him and holding on. It was the picture of the season – thus far.

'The crowd were cheering me on every single lap and I was doing my best to ignore them and concentrate,' Mansell would say. 'The last thing I wanted was get distracted and miss a corner. But they are just unbelievable. I salute them and I dedicate this race to all of them. I was very worried over the last ten laps because I was in major gearbox problems and I am just happy to have finished the race. For the last couple of laps I was changing up to fifth at the start-finish line and staying there all the way to Club Corner (which is much more than half a lap) because I was frightened I wouldn't get another gear. I was going to try and go the whole race on one set of tyres and I was pacing it pretty well but then I lost one or two wheel-weights and I had a huge vibration. Through this the tyres blistered so I had to pit and change them for insurance.'

Bernard Dudot, Renault's engine man, showed a nice sense of history. That evening he said: 'The 14th of July 1977 Renault started in Formula One here at Silverstone with the famous "yellow teapot" car. The 14th of July 1983 Alain Prost gave Renault their first Silverstone Grand Prix victory. Today the 14th of July 1991 Williams Renault and Nigel Mansell have won the British Grand Prix together. With three consecutive victories [Patrese in Mexico, Mansell in France and here] we are now in a good position for the World Championship. For us it has been a quiet race, Nigel driving with intelligence and not being too hard on the car or the engine.'

This was perhaps the most complete drive of Mansell's career and one which only maturity allows. You can always tell. It looks easy, it acquires an air of inevitability, it gathers a pace of its own which ultimately is nothing to do with the race itself but only the car and the driver exploring themselves on a circuit, alone. It is not exciting if you like cut and thrust for your money because it becomes clinical, safe and secure, repetitive although there was a human moment, and a cheeky one – Mansell tempting the fates as he emerged from the complex a last time by waving briefly to the crowd. Canada couldn't happen again anyway. He was close enough to the line to free-wheel to it.

There was a glow around the Williams motorhome that evening. Peter Windsor offered this race as proof that Mansell was a better driver than Senna and did so with conviction. Windsor has maintained a constant position that Mansell is the best thing since Jim Clark and doesn't care who knows it. Sheridan Thynne, a long-time member of the team, was gushing. Frank Williams himself was applauded as he was wheeled back and smiled in that slightly defensive way he was, happy enough but seeing it all in context. Another race, another place.

Only Patrese couldn't share the mood. He and Berger had collided at the very first corner and now Patrese said cryptically: 'I have really no comment to make because I think you should watch the re-play on television. I am out of the race and I think it wasn't my fault.' Senna, classified fourth, had 51 points, Mansell 33, Patrese 22, Prost 21.

Between Silverstone and the next race, Hockenheim, tragedy stalked motor sport, Paul Warwick, 22-year-old brother of Derek, was killed when his Formula 3000 car left the track at Oulton Park. He was driving for the Mansell Madgwick team of which Nigel Mansell was chairman. Paul Warwick was a gifted young man, already leading the Championship. Like his brother he earned respect and affection in equal measure, unspoilt, down-to-earth, approachable; or to use a more pertinent and particularly English phrase, nice with it. Despite its history motor sport does not cope with this at all easily and the closer you are the harder it is. Mansell was distraught. For many hours he could bring himself to say nothing and when he did make a statement it was brief, dignified and came from deep inside him. 'No words can adequately express my feelings.'

Hockenheim fitted uncomfortably with this. After Mansell had taken pole from Senna he complained that Erik Comas (Ligier) had baulked him and went to have words. The background was that in the morning's untimed session Comas had crashed heavily and was taken to hospital. He returned to the track for the final qualifying session in the afternoon and despite doctor's advice took part in it. Towards the very end of that session he managed a lap which was twenty-sixth fastest and just squeezed him into the race. He was not aware of that – drivers aren't always given precise information at precisely the time they need it – and continued without going in to the pits, trying for a faster lap still. During the lap Mansell was out on the circuit in a final effort to find a faster lap for himself. He reached Comas as they both moved towards the chicane before the Stadium complex and, being fair to Mansell, the disparity between the Ligier and the Williams was so great that at first glance you couldn't say whether Comas was on a 'hot' one or simply going round.

Comas stayed on line through the chicane which effectively wrecked Mansell's lap and got the Frenchman a shaken fist when they did reach the Stadium. Comas was neither overawed nor repentant when Mansell arrived on foot to explore the topic. Comas cryptically apologised for 'being on the same track as Mr Mansell'. When Mansell understood that Comas had been on a 'hot' one he wrote a magnanimous note which said: *To my friend Erik as a souvenir of our first encounter, Nigel, Hockenheim, 27 July '91*.

(It's a sensitive business, this baulking, and an eternal sore. In theory every driver no matter how slow his machinery is fully entitled to follow the racing line all the way round on his qualifying lap and it's up to the others to overtake him or time their own run so that they don't meet him. But . . . at any given moment there may be a lot of cars out there and essentially you have to take your chance, hoping you'll meet them on nice long straights not chicanes. You can understand the thought-processes of the fast men: they might need pole, the merest fractions gained or lost are crucial. The slow men are slogging towards a distant place on the grid and what can it matter whether they start twenty-first or twenty-third? Of course it matters a lot to the slow men, it's their whole being, their reputation and as a rule of thumb a Formula One driver always make the car go as fast as it can be made to go. Otherwise what the hell is he doing here? Further, hoisting a slow car from twenty-third on the grid to twenty-first can be a notable achievement. The desires of those at the front of the grid and those at the back can never be reconciled and Formula One will have to live with it, just as it has been living with it.)

The race? Mansell stormed it all the way from the green light, crisp through the chicanes, stretching the whole field behind him all the way from lap one. He constructed a gigantic gap and towards the end only Patrese, who'd made another disappointing start, could stay with him. Mansell won it by just under fourteen seconds, Senna ran out of fuel and that was Senna 51, Mansell 43, Patrese 28, Prost 21.

At this point in the season Mansell announced he was leaving the Isle of Man to go and live in Florida and that heightened the dilemma which many people felt about him, as if they could never quite get him into focus. A letter to *Autosport* encapsulated it by posing and answering several pertinent questions:

Why does the media assume that all 54 million of us Brits love Nigel Mansell [the writer began]? Is it because he is English? But I thought he lives on the Isle of Man (to avoid English tax) and is planning to move to Florida (to avoid the English weather). Perhaps it's because he's a family man and announced he was putting his family first after Silverstone last year. Perhaps it's because he's a good team man in the English spirit. Remember how well he worked with Piquet and Prost? Perhaps it's because he encourages young drivers – like Erik Comas at Hockenheim

Hard sentiments, and hewn from a hard sport, this Formula One, where love itself is not a word you hear from one decade to the next. A driver's domicile doesn't seem to affect his patriotism (to me) – wherever you go in the world you find ex-pats – but the other points do make you think and do make you wonder.

The media itself had an ambivalent relationship with him: some journalists instinctively stayed close to him because he was the big story, the meal ticket and anyway they may just have plain liked him, other journalists stayed away altogether and let the thing unfold all by itself, whatever it was. My own relations moved from calm to storm and ended one year at Spa in the pits where, across the carcass of a car being prepared for action, he vented extreme anger over my writing the first edition of this book; and what I said in the *Daily Express* after he seized Senna by the collar at Spa didn't, I suppose, help. I had some trenchant things to say about Mansell's behaviour and I added: 'These are not comfortable words to write since I was once an admirer and, perhaps a friend. I am neither now.'

Relations were then placed in a deep-freeze or more properly deep in a deep-freeze. Even as late as summer 1991 he was proffering harsh words whenever anyone asked him to autograph this book and it was some four years after its appearance. Two aspects need to be cleared up once and for all. I remain an admirer of everything he has done in racing cars and I haven't met anyone, even among those who don't go near him, who offers any other sentiment. At the end of Hockenheim, July 1991 and his third win in a row he had touched authentic greatness, however you care to measure it and, begging Peter Windsor's pardon, if he wasn't a Jim Clark, which of them were anyway? He actually made races come alive by doing what historically all the great ones had done: *race*. Oh, and Jim Clark lived in Paris, which if you'll allow me to be flippant again, is not in Britain . . .

Any journalist is uncomfortably aware of the maxim that we build them up to knock them down; many journalists are not aware of the cumulative effect of what they write, and understandably so. TV and radio interviewers are the same. We're all living for the moment and the moment is now.

The media has grown in numbers, scope and appetite and the leading sportsman has become a hunted species with the demands on him increasing proportionately. A sprained ankle is likely to appear on news bulletins along with famine, warfare and the other items of the daily diet of disasters. A single misplaced word is likely to be dissected and enlarged on and raked over, judged. Once upon a time this mattered not at all because it didn't happen.

A book *Mon Ami Mate* by Chris Nixon appeared in mid-season

'91 and it told the truth about Mike Hawthorn and I assume most people reading it were either completely unaware or only vaguely aware of what manner of man Hawthorn really was. Some of it did not make pleasant reading. Hawthorn of course had never known daily grillings by journalists, hadn't given TV interviews after each pole position and each finish on the podium (and be fined if he didn't), the camera up tight to lay bare every drop of sweat, every roll of the eyes, every mannerism; hadn't heard his own words echo round the world time after time after time; hadn't opened newspapers to discover that a domestic incident with a step-mother was considered fair game for publication. Hawthorn lived his life as publicly and privately as he wished.

Mansell had known nothing but the microphones, tape recorders, notebooks. Moreover as sport became more democratic – in the sense that anybody could play, not just the born-rich – people came forward with a talent and prospered on that talent while remaining what inescapably they were: ordinary people. Why not? But the extent of their exposure in the media showed, the great talent aside, how ordinary they were. Some (particularly footballers and jockeys) frankly found difficulty speaking even simple coherent sentences with the verbs in the right tense. So what? So nothing, except that no generations before had been subjected to this and it was always going to be hard to emerge from it undiminished. Many, many sportsmen trawled up in the media net were just being themselves because they had no idea how else to handle it even if they'd wanted to; and it could be agonising listening to them grapple with their emotions and vocabulary to describe their feats – as endlessly they were obliged to try and do. This gives an answer to the question so many people keep asking me: why does Mansell seem to be whingeing the whole time? I reply that he isn't. He's just being himself. Whenever you judge him remember that.

Before the Hungarian Grand Prix, which could have been a pivotal race, I went along to see a certain Niki Lauda in Vienna to pose the question which was now intriguing Formula One more and more. How does Mansell go about winning the World Championship? Here is the dialogue, repetitions and all, so that you get the full flavour.

CH: You have been through this three times, the pressure of a country expecting someone to win in a leading team. Now Mansell's got exactly the same thing.
NL: The problem with Mansell is very simple. He is a balls-out

flat-out racing driver. In the past he was not able to use his head to slow down at the right time, save the car and drive an intelligent race. Prost is the ideal racing driver. Mansell says to himself 'you go for it' and he goes for it until everything blows up or he wins. There's nothing in between. Maybe you can win the Championship that way but there are other ways too. This year he's surprised me in a way that suddenly he realises that he has to be safe, use the speed at the right time and not do these crazy things. In the last three races he's won in a perfect style using his head, being quick enough at the time he needs to be – but his car is good enough that he can go slow if he needs, too.

If you have a crappy car and you have to do everything with your balls OK, but if you don't have a crappy car the most important thing is to go slow and not use the potential of the car. A hundred laps? Use it only twenty, make sure it stays together. This year to me he is the biggest surprise because he is able to control himself. He understands now – and I hope it stays like this because it's going to be more important, he has to attack hard to try to make up the points which doesn't help – that he has to use his head even more. Towards the end of the season that is the critical thing.

At the moment he is on the right track. I hope he continues because then he will win the Championship. If he makes stupid mistakes just because he wants to win a race and falls off, that's wrong. It's better to be second, third. You know I've been through this many times. He needs more and more brains the more the season progresses. So it's not finished yet that he got clever, he needs to get more clever and more clever and more clever. He has all the potential. He should not worry about anything because he has the best car. Therefore he can use all of his power in his head to work out how to use this huge jewel of a car to make this thing happen.

CH: You were famous for the way you could think. I've seen you isolate things from your mind, you don't think about them. Is that what you have to do in the run-in to a Championship?

NL: Sure. I mean, emotions and countries and crap and British and flags, nobody wins the Championship with that. You can't win it with a British flag, you can only win it with your throttle and your head. So the most important thing, as I said – and I think he is intelligent enough to understand it – is to keep his feet on the ground, work hard and get more clever every bloody lap.

CH: Who is the biggest danger to him now?

NL: Senna. Senna, but it looks like they are not getting their act together.

CH: What about Patrese? How should he handle Patrese, because Patrese is very quick?

NL: Ah, Patrese, yes he is quick. Frank has to handle him. This is another push for making a Champion. Frank should go and say, 'Come on chaps, you Nigel have the better chance, you are number two Patrese, you're not allowed to attack.' This gives another boost to Nigel because it gives him more protection. It's important psychologically for the team to give Nigel support. There's no support at all when you read in all these newspapers that Senna has been offered thirty million bucks by Frank and all this bullshit [there were public rumours that Williams wanted Senna] because really Mansell will think: 'Is it me who's going to be changed? Is it Patrese? What the hell is going on here?' – and at a time when you're fighting for the Championship, when you're riding so much on the edge, you need every little support from the team. It's logical now that Mansell's got a better chance and Patrese not, so you have to tell him: 'Sorry, we have to win the Championship, you support Nigel,' and that will give Nigel another boost in a positive way to use his head even better to win the Championship.

CH: But Frank in the past has not done that.

NL: Yeah, but maybe that's why he lost so many Championships. From my point of view when I look into the potential of Mansell's car and the team, and now hopefully Patrese gets under control and Senna and McLaren are getting worse and worse – they can't even get the right amount of fuel in the car, and . . . and . . . and – Mansell is in a fantastic situation but again the most important thing is not to make stupid mistakes. He can retire because his engine blows up or he has a puncture, those things happen, but if he adds on his own mistakes he might lose it. He will stop (for mechanical problems) in a couple of races anyway, but he has to make sure he doesn't stop because of his own fault. This is the extra you don't need when you need points.

Immediately before Hungary Mansell and Patrese re-signed for 1992 and that removed the Senna pressure from the equation. In Hungary Senna took pole, then Patrese, then Mansell and that was the race order, too, until lap 45 when Mansell went past Patrese and followed Senna home. Both the Williams cars had brake trouble.

Patrese said: 'It was certainly a tough start. Ayrton is going for the Championship and the first corner is very important so this was racing. The brake problem started when I was very close to Ayrton. At that time I had decided to charge because I didn't want to spend all the race just sitting behind him. I saw Nigel coming very quickly and I said to myself that it was very difficult for me to stay at the same speed as Ayrton and maybe Nigel didn't have any problems. I then tried to save my brakes to the end of the race and I managed to learn how to drive the car in that situation.'

Mansell said: 'I would like to thank Riccardo for letting me past – because he called me by. He had a great fight with Ayrton for about the first forty laps and I had a good view of this. I had the same problem as Riccardo with the brakes from about half distance and I wasn't able to push as hard as I would have liked. I then decided to back off and settle for second place, but it was a great race and Ayrton was a worthy winner.' Mansell had done exactly what Lauda had recommended and done it as well as Lauda himself could ever have done: take a safe second place. Senna 61, Mansell 49, Patrese 32, Berger 22.

Spa seemed to have settled it. Mansell pressed Senna for the lead early on, was briefly in the lead himself but was halted after 22 laps when the electrics went. Senna won despite a gearbox nightmare – he couldn't get the low gears at all – and because Jean Alesi ahead of him dropped out with engine trouble. The luck which always appeared to ride with Senna was running very, very hard against Mansell now. Senna 71, Mansell 49, Patrese 34, Berger 28, only five races left.

Between Spa and the next race, Monza, Mansell took part in an interesting golf competition to open a new course in Essex. I use the word interesting for three reasons. First, he formed a team with Ian Botham from cricket and decathlete Daley Thompson to play Nick Faldo in what they call a Texas Scramble, three against one. Mansell, Botham and Thompson all drove off and then all played their second shot from where the best of the first had reached and so on while Faldo of course only had one shot each time. It made the competition equitable.

Second, here were four leading British sportsmen who were not from privileged backgrounds and had all known the media net. Botham and Thompson avoided the press almost completely while Faldo had had his problems (and was not averse to ringing up journalists and telling them what he thought, if you get my meaning – a fascinating role-reversal but not one designed to encourage harmony).

More than 2,000 came to watch and the really interesting aspect was how they responded to these four. Here was a representative sample of the Great British Public surveying sportsmen who had made a lot of headlines and not always for the right reasons. The public adored them, adored the informality of it, savoured the delicious and sometimes genuinely witty banter begun by Thompson and then carried on by the other three, appreciated that Mansell could actually play golf, Botham could actually hit a golf ball prodigious distances in a variety of directions and that Thompson's forte was as a raconteur not a player, saw that really these were ordinary people enjoying themselves and communicating the pleasure unashamedly. This public did not have to deal with them on a daily basis, of course, in pressured moments – or indeed deal with them at all; only watch and savour and then go home. But you could not mistake the respect in which the four were held irrespective of whatever, rightly or wrongly, the media had previously done to them. Yes, interesting. Incidentally somebody asked Mansell to autograph my book and drew the usual tirade from him.

Mansell needed Monza. Senna got away at the green, then Mansell, Berger, Patrese. For eighteen laps Mansell attacked but this was inevitably a race steeped in tactics. Mansell's car was moving around in the turbulence behind Senna and that was scrubbing the tyres, which he didn't like. Patrese was moving fast and soon enough was behind Mansell who let him go through. Mansell's reasoning: Patrese is Italian, this is Monza, he's bound to have a go at it and maybe he can lay pressure on Senna; maybe he'll scrub his tyres more than he likes . . .

Patrese attacked Senna, attacked him hard and took him on the inside at the approach to the Ascari chicane. Patrese's lead lasted a lap. He spun off at this same Ascari chicane when the gear box fumbled all by itself and locked the wheels. Senna leading, Mansell attacking again, jinking, probing. Senna resisted for seven long laps. It was done at Ascari, done as Patrese had done it, a thrust down the inside and Senna nowhere to go but back off and follow Mansell through. Senna immediately pitted for fresh tyres and launched a long sustained charge to maximise the advantage of them. Mansell responded by setting fastest lap of the race and if he could do that on his worn tyres all he had to do was run to the finish. He did, sixteen seconds ahead and that was Senna 77, Mansell 59, Patrese 34, Berger 31, only four races left. 'It was hard,' Mansell would say typically, 'because I'd blistered all my tyres by the end.'

Team orders were established for Portugal, Patrese promising to help Mansell. Patrese you see was on pole from Berger, Senna and Mansell on the second row and Estoril is very much like the Hungaroring, the first to Turn One potentially able to dictate the whole afternoon from exactly there.

Mansell made an extreme start.

At the green light and under the power they were all laying down the leaders were drawn across the track: Patrese over to the left, Berger in the middle. Mansell simply flung the Williams in front of Senna, who was following Patrese, and did it so violently that Senna had to twitch out of the way. Senna responded by diving towards the middle and lining up behind Berger. This was the order going through Turn One: Patrese well clear, Berger, then Mansell and Senna side by side. After Turn One there is a short straight to a right-hander and halfway along that straight Mansell now flung the Williams inside Berger so violently that Berger had to twitch out of the way.

What you make of this depends on a great many things, not least your definition of what a racer is, balanced against what justifiable risks are. Senna thought Mansell's behaviour unacceptable (which wrung wry smiles out of one and all). Was Mansell being too robust? Was it not legitimate to go hard for it? The moves were certainly the essence of Mansell and you had to gaze in awe at his speed of reaction in being physically able to do it and Senna's speed of reaction in avoiding him, not to mention Berger's own speed of reaction . . .

Patrese, as he had promised, let Mansell through and the two Williams cars were visibly superior. Mansell was going to win the race and with Senna only fourth that broke the whole Championship open again. On lap 30 Mansell came in to the pits for what he could afford to be a leisurely tyre stop. His lead was extensive enough to permit that.

It is very, very easy to write such words, detaching yourself from the atmosphere which generates itself all down the pit lane all through a Grand Prix race and seeing a tyre change only as a clinical, technical exercise; and the World Championship was in play now, too. That's pressure upon pressure. The gut instinct among every mechanic is to get their man back out on the track as fast as they can – this is a race. The simplest way is for each mechanic, who has an allotted and much-practised role, to do it at maximum revs knowing that all the other mechanics will be doing their bit at maximum revs too and they'll all be finished within a second of each other. Then – exit Mansell.

Superficially that is what happened, that and nothing more.

Arms were hoisted from each wheel to signal work complete and Mansell moved away. He had travelled barely twenty or thirty yards when the right-rear wheel detached itself and bounded into the Tyrrell pit playing skittles with a couple of their mechanics. Mansell was beached on the remaining three wheels in the pit road, beating his hands against the monocoque in a very powerful frustration. The mechanics arrived at full tilt to refit the errant wheel. It was illegal to work on the car there but they could have done nothing else. You simply don't push cars on three wheels around the pit road (Peter Windsor used the word 'suicidal' in contemplation of doing that). Other cars will be coming in – or going out – at high speed and not expecting to meet stationary objects along the way. Williams did not contest that they had broken the rules, simply explaining that they did what they had to do in the only place they could do it: where the car had come to rest.

So what did happen? You need to dissect a tyre stop, any tyre stop, to understand it. Four squads of three men are positioned so that the instant the car halts there is a squad grouped around each wheel ready to work on it. Each squad has a man crouching with a pneumatic gun poised to unscrew the nut on the wheel facing him. Beside him a second man stoops ready to take this wheel off and get it out of the way. The third man stands already holding the new wheel. He fits it and holds it steady while the gunman replaces the nut and screws it tight. Normally the crucial signal is given by the gunman. Only he knows whether the nut is tight or not.

Patrick Head explained during a subsequent television interview: 'In the sequence that occurs when the nuts are undone, the wheels come off and the new ones go on and there is a position where the chaps on the guns stand up holding the guns above their heads. That is a signal to the jackman (who has the car up on the jack) that their job is complete. The person controlling the pitstop can step away and let the car out. In that process there was a breakdown. The right-rear wheel was not complete and the guys had not given the signal that they had completed their job but the process that allowed the car to leave the pits was allowed to occur.'

The tyre blow-out at Adelaide had been a freak, the crash in qualifying at Suzuka the following year had been no more than getting the car a fraction off line but this was total irony. The nut had cross-threaded on the right-rear wheel as the gunman put it back on and he had to remove it again, which meant withdrawing it in the gun. This withdrawal motion was inescapably the same as if the job had been completed. As the gunman turned to get a fresh nut a wheel man raised an arm – assuming completion – and that was taken to be the signal.

These are men not machines, they're held within the pressure upon pressure and there is a certain exultation in handling that pressure, beating it by being able to work fast and precisely within it. There is also – understandably – an element of competition, a desire not to let the side down, not to be the slow one; and that is why at a pit stop you see mechanics leaping into the air. They're saying: *we've done our bit . . . we've done our bit . . .*

To blame any person in the chain would be extremely unfair. Each reacted as he thought for the best, each tried to make the stop as swift as possible and at each stage each person reacted logically, through the gunman to the tyreman to the jackman to Windsor, controlling it, who saw the raised hands, to Mansell who hit the throttle hard the moment the jack deposited the car back on terra firma and the signal was given to go.

Once the wheel had been re-fitted in the pit road Mansell did get back out and was up to sixth with third place a distinct possibility when he was black-flagged for the work done in the road. He returned, clambered out stunned and suddenly so sad it was bowing him down. Some say there were tears later and if there were you can forgive him those.

No World Championship had been decided like this.

Patrese held Senna to second place which was meagre consolation but at least some and that was Senna 83, Mansell 59, Patrese 44, Berger 31, only three races left. The pocket calculators were out again just like '86 and '87. If Senna won Spain at Barcelona, a new track, he was Champion whatever Mansell did. If Senna finished anywhere in front of Mansell he was Champion. If Mansell did not score four more points than Senna the Championship was gone and the only way Mansell could be sure of a four-point gap was to win. Even that left him long odds against. If Mansell won Spain and Senna was second Mansell had to win the last two, Japan and Australia, with Senna getting no points at all and even that, itself dramatically unlikely, only gave him the title on a tie-break at 89 points all, Mansell taking it on the most number of wins – 7 to 6.

Senna increased the tempo, whether he meant to or not, before Barcelona by saying that he thought that what Mansell had done at the start in Portugal was 'crazy'. The tempo would be increased a great deal more when they did reach Barcelona. Berger took pole, then Mansell, Senna, Patrese but not before Mansell played in a football match against The Press and sprained his ankle. (He scored twice in a 2–2 draw if you're curious.)

The traditional drivers' briefing before the race was reportedly far from a love-in. The briefing, to sort out good behaviour, was taken by the august presence of Jean-Marie Balestre himself and though of necessity the description which follows is a reconstruction (journalists don't attend briefings) I have no reason to doubt the accuracy of it. The briefing began badly with, evidently, Berger giving Mansell's ankle a playful tap, to which Mansell grasped Berger and perhaps a blow was thrown before they were separated.

Monsieur Balestre then made a speech which said, much as a boxing referee does, come out fighting cleanly and no holding in the clinches. (He was not of course alluding to the contest just witnessed and anyway I am paraphrasing Balestre's words.) Balestre said he didn't want any more of what had come to pass before, during and after Turn One at Estoril, which Mansell took as a reference to himself.

Mansell asked plaintively and pointedly why he was singled out every time he was involved in something but Senna wasn't. (This itself was an extraordinary statement bearing in mind Senna's running battle with FISA and Balestre from his crash with Prost at Suzuka in 1989 onwards, embracing acrimony, charge and counter-charge, a fine, a possible suspension, possible legal action and the rest; Senna waited until Balestre was voted out of office before having a final, enormous verbal blast at him.)

To Mansell's words at the briefing Senna took great exception, using his command of Anglo-Saxon to the full; and all this before Piquet weighed in with an attack of his own, the gist of which was that for a long time he'd heard all this talk of safety but what was ever done about it? With that the drivers' briefing ended.

In the race Mansell was superb, irresistible, running a current, taking every pressure-point the race produced and taming it: holding his nerve (while the world held its breath) down the straight wheel to wheel with Senna to pass him and after the pit stops having to pass him again. Actually it didn't come to that. Senna spun, thundered back across the track and Mansell, following, had a moment of horror not knowing which way Senna would go. As Mansell said: 'Fortunately I guessed right.'

Berger led and on the 21st lap Mansell dived inside him at Turn One *here*, the cars were perilously close for a second, Mansell was away, the race settled. Senna, oddly tentative, drifted home fifth and that was Senna 85, Mansell 69, Patrese 48, Berger and Prost 31. The pocket calculators told it the way it was and it was simple now. If Senna was first or second at Suzuka he was Champion. If Mansell won Suzuka and Senna was no higher than third it went to Australia, where Mansell had to win and Senna get no points – that would be the 89-point tie-break.

But the way Mansell had driven round Barcelona – and the way Senna hadn't driven round Barcelona, for that matter – suggested that it was possible. In a subtle sense the load had shifted on to Senna. Mansell had nothing to lose and his strategy scarcely needed to be a strategy at all. Win or bust. Senna had to assume that Mansell would win both the remaining races and that he, Senna, still needed points. He couldn't afford mechanical breakdowns, couldn't afford crashes (assuming they weren't with Mansell). Senna said he would be *quote* quite a lot less timid *unquote* in Japan, which was a hell of a way of putting it after the crashes with Prost in '89 and '90. Mansell was relaxed.

It did cross my mind that Mansell was the first driver that Senna had not been able to psyche out. He'd done it with all his team-mates, Johnny Cecotto and Stefan Johansson at Toleman, Elio de Angelis and Johnny Dumfries at Lotus, Alain Prost and now (without my being rude to a good man and a good driver) Gerhard Berger at McLaren; but Mansell – no, and you only had to glance at Mansell's career to understand that he was mentally as tough as Senna, physically as brave and on the track he'd respond like a hungry fighter. You pressured him, he'd pressure you right back, you dodged and wove, he'd stick with it, you challenged him in a corner nerve for nerve he'd still be there, you shook your fist at him he'd shake his fist right back. The drivers' briefing may well have been quite unconsciously a significant psychological moment: don't push me around, any of you.

In a Formula One car Nigel Mansell was unafraid to measure himself against any man on earth, including Ayrton Senna, and clearly out of a Formula One car, too. Turn One in Japan, where Senna had encountered Prost a year before, might not be for the squeamish. The grid:

Berger

Senna

Mansell

Prost

Patrese

220

The immense crowd was a mere fraction of those who wanted to be witness to it. Some 4.4 million – repeat 4.4 million – had applied for tickets and a system of lottery had been needed to prune them. Among them were the Brits, some of them ex-pats no doubt, with their Union Jacks and their Go Nigel Go banners.

The cars came so carefully and so slowly all the way round the parade lap past this long-left Turn One with a run-off area wide as a beach outside it, through the left–right–left curves which at speed are almost a kink, through the Degner Curve named after the East German motor-bike rider who defected years before, under the unique cross-over where the return leg to the track passes above, round the horseshoe hairpin, on to the corner shaped like a spoon, full on down a long slope with tall trees to the right, up the slope again and over the top of the cross-over, through the chicane which had been moved and remodelled so that it was absurdly tight and, stately, stately they came to form the symmetry of the grid.

Turn One turned out to be fine, just fine, Berger a car's length from Senna a car's length from Mansell and the McLaren ploy was revealed: Berger would move like the wind into the distance while Senna ran at an even pace keeping Mansell behind him. Difficult, that. Mansell needed to get past Senna – it wasn't easy because it couldn't be done anywhere but the start-finish straight and Senna had the Honda V12 taking him down that, lots of grunt as they say – and moment by moment Berger fled on, making his lead into a monument.

They circled and they circled and it became one of those situations where something was going to happen because something had to happen. Thus far it had been a settling, an establishing of relative positions, a basis for negotiations although the gap Berger-to-Senna had gone out to 7.954 seconds and Berger fled on, increasing it. Mansell might have been held in the web of a conspiracy; and was. But 53 laps is a long way to go and eleven years into his Grand Prix career Mansell was perfectly aware of that.

NL: The most important thing for Nigel is not make stupid mistakes . . .

Patrese drew up in fourth position riding shotgun, himself biding his time, waiting. Patrese, wise in the ways of it, would do what was necessary, unscramble the permutations, go past Mansell and attack Senna if that was what was wanted, keep riding shotgun if that was what was wanted – but Patrese was also held in the web.

He circled and circled, searching for his appointed role, which certainly wasn't going to be staying fourth.

Senna and Mansell moved equidistant down the straight, moved equidistant into this Turn One. Berger's flight had taken him to nearly ten full seconds up ahead and far out of sight. Patrese was thirty metres behind Mansell, steady and safe and strong there: a friend.

Senna moved into Turn One very normally as he had done nine times before and fully intended to do another 43 times which would bring him to the end of the race and the Championship: you go out to the left and describe a bow-shaped curve which brings you nicely across to the centre, you hold it there and go through. The car is constructed to do this easily. The centre of the track? That was a strategic and protective position. The man following can't go inside because there is insufficient space and can't go outside because there's no space there either. Senna was covering his rear as he fully intended to do for those next 43 times. At precisely the turn-in Mansell was classically placed also, the same line as Senna and not too close to him. Another corner along the way, nothing more.

Without warning Mansell went inexplicably wide, crossed the kerb and found himself on the beach. This lasted less than half of one second. At the entry to the corner the car had seemed to skip a fraction and was simply gone. Mansell had had no warning himself. The brake pedal had gone soft. His on-board camera showed what he saw in the immediate aftermath: the car angling back towards the track as the wheels rode the kerbing and this might, just might, have given the wheels grip and bite, could have dragged him back on to the track. The outward impetus was too strong. The car skimmed on full across the kerbing and vanished into a dust storm, burying itself deeper and deeper on to and into the beach, slewing sideways then backwards, bump-bump-bumping over the sandy-shale which had been raked into rows of shallow rilles.

The car settled as the dust storm settled all around it, settled into a final resting place. There is a line, by T.S. Eliot, about the way the world ends – 'Not with a bang but a whimper'.

Mansell got himself out of the car and skipped across the track, the sprained ankle clearly still painful. He walked from it all. As he walked he seemed suspended from animation. It was nothing but a man walking as he might have done if he had been taking a stroll any Sunday afternoon, that easy pace, that lack of needing to be somewhere but it was as if he had been released.

He waited until the Japanese Grand Prix at Suzuka, 20 October

1991, was over, waited so that he could hoist Senna's hand in the pits and it was a touching moment, a genuine moment of sport worthy of the good old days themselves. Nor did he make a fanfare of it, didn't overplay the gesture at all, he did the decent thing and vacated centre stage.

But I kept thinking about that long walk back. I'd seen him do it often enough in the bad old days themselves, particularly at Lotus, the same pace, the same look on his face drawn into great resignation. There was a symbolic element to it because somehow he had walked alone the whole decade. He saw himself that way, on an often lonely journey only he would truly understand, the ordinary man strong enough to withstand whatever the world threw against him and frequently reacting like that. And ultimately it was so. He withstood. Along the way he made a virtue of being himself, made his millions, excited many millions of spectators and what else did people want of him? If some did not care for his company he'd live with that. Celebrities, I suppose, have to. They can't like everybody and everybody can't like them.

Maybe the ones who stayed away were tired of the posture of withstanding when the depth and scope of his career, the very success of his career, had lifted him far beyond it years before. The world had not conspired against him, the world had given him the chance to exploit himself and he'd taken it; he was happily married with a smashing family, had enough money in the bank to keep his children, grandchildren and great-grandchildren in luxury; he was healthy and fit and famous and to some genuinely heroic. He could (literally) afford to be gracious for ever and ever and ever.

As he walked back at Suzuka he felt, I am sure, many familiar feelings: resignation, the consolation that he had done his best, the self-protection that nothing else could have been done, the acceptance that it's all happened again and it wasn't his fault. Very British: the hero in adversity. Me? I wrote after the Hungarian Grand Prix that he'd win the World Championship. With a fair wind behind him he would have done and Senna wouldn't have got near him.

The contradictions remain and to demonstrate the point I give you two strange moments. At the British Grand Prix I'm walking with Andrea de Cesaris towards the cluster of motorhomes chatting about this and that. Nigel Mansell is in the act of accelerating by on a moped. As he passes me he calls out 'Hi, how are you?' and before I can turn to reply he's gone. Since we have passed each other many, many times like blind people and spoken no single

223

word for four years this seemed – well, unexpected, to say the least. It concerned me because I appeared ungracious – he was accelerating on the moped too fast for me to reciprocate. So I waited until Hungary and I chose my moment there. He was walking along the paddock area with Windsor. 'Hi, how are you?' He didn't lift his head, he grunted something incomprehensible and walked on by.

Trivial as well as strange moments, no doubt, but emphasising something. This was the man the Italians called, and rightly called, The Lion; this was the man who took his place, and rightly took it, among the Bothams and Thompsons and Faldos as a Briton who had far outgrown the confines of his own sport and become a national – nay, an international – presence; a man of genuine achievement dug out of the perpetual and very real danger of racing a car.

Those contradictions.

Adelaide, the final race of 1991, was run in lashing rain on a soaked track and was mercifully called off as it entered lap 17, although points (half points actually) were awarded on cars' positions at lap 14 which placed Mansell second. Out there in the walls of water he had challenged Senna as best he could, both cars slipping and sliding, Mansell with no visibility whenever he was directly behind Senna and yet somehow mounting this challenge, nipping out to have a look when he could, tucking back when he had to. These brave gestures ended when he spun and clouted a wall, suffering minor concussion and a leg injury. He was helped into an ambulance. So, because lap 14 was the cut-off point, he had the second place and the meagre three points. It was scant consolation, if any consolation at all. It was in the end a tiny piece of luck but at a meaningless time. If he'd had luck when he needed it . . .

He headed immediately for the airport. It was the only place to go now.

Statistics

P = pole position; R = retired; DNQ = did not qualify; DNS = did not start; FL = fastest lap; NC = not classified; DIS = disqualified.

1976   7 races in Formula Ford 1600, 5 wins
1977   27 race meetings in Formula Ford 1600 largely run over heats, a total of 20 wins including heats
1978   5 races in Formula Three, no wins
1979   19 races in Formula Three, 1 win
1980   9 races in Formula Three, no wins; 4 races in Formula Two, no wins. This was the year he also entered Formula One.

17 Aug	Austria	Osterreichring	Lotus Cosworth DFV	R
31 Aug	Holland	Zandvoort	Lotus Cosworth DFV	R
14 Sep	Italy	Imola	Lotus Cosworth DFV	DNQ

1981

7 Mar	South Africa	Kyalami	Lotus Cosworth DFV	10
15 Mar	USA West	Long Beach	Lotus Cosworth DFV	R
29 Mar	Brazil	Rio	Lotus Cosworth DFV	11
12 Apr	Argentina	Buenos Aires	Lotus Cosworth DFV	R
17 May	Belgium	Zolder	Lotus Cosworth DFV	3

225

31 May	Monaco	Monte Carlo	Lotus Cosworth DFV	R
21 Jun	Spain	Jarama	Lotus Cosworth DFV	6
5 Jul	France	Dijon	Lotus Cosworth DFV	7
18 Jul	Britain	Silverstone	Lotus Cosworth DFV	DNQ
2 Aug	Germany	Hockenheim	Lotus Cosworth DFV	R
16 Aug	Austria	Osterreichring	Lotus Cosworth DFV	R
30 Aug	Holland	Zandvoort	Lotus Cosworth DFV	R
13 Sep	Italy	Monza	Lotus Cosworth DFV	R
27 Sep	Canada	Montreal	Lotus Cosworth DFV	R
17 Oct	USA	Las Vegas	Lotus Cosworth DFV	4

1982

23 Jan	South Africa	Kyalami	Lotus Cosworth DFV	R
21 Mar	Brazil	Rio	Lotus Cosworth DFV	3
4 Apr	USA West	Long Beach	Lotus Cosworth DFV	7
9 May	Belgium	Zolder	Lotus Cosworth DFV	R
23 May	Monaco	Monte Carlo	Lotus Cosworth DFV	4
6 Jun	USA West	Detroit	Lotus Cosworth DFV	R
13 Jun	Canada	Montreal	Lotus Cosworth DFV	R
18 Jul	Britain	Brands Hatch	Lotus Cosworth DFV	R
8 Aug	Germany	Hockenheim	Lotus Cosworth DFV	9
15 Aug	Austria	Osterreichring	Lotus Cosworth DFV	R

29 Aug	France	Dijon	Lotus Cosworth DFV	8
12 Sep	Italy	Monza	Lotus Cosworth DFV	7
25 Sep	USA	Las Vegas	Lotus Cosworth DFV	R

1983

13 Mar	Brazil	Rio	Lotus Cosworth DFV	12
27 Mar	USA West	Long Beach	Lotus Cosworth DFV	12
10 Apr	Race of Champs*	Brands Hatch	Lotus Renault EF1	R
17 Apr	France	Paul Ricard	Lotus Cosworth DFV	R
1 May	San Marino	Imola	Lotus Cosworth DFV	R
15 May	Monaco	Monte Carlo	Lotus Cosworth DFV	R
22 May	Belgium	Spa	Lotus Cosworth DFV	R
5 Jun	USA	Detroit	Lotus Cosworth DFV	6
12 Jun	Canada	Montreal	Lotus Cosworth DFV	R
16 Jul	Britain	Silverstone	Lotus Renault EF1	4
7 Aug	Germany	Hockenheim	Lotus Renault EF1	R
14 Aug	Austria	Osterreichring	Lotus Renault EF1	5
28 Aug	Holland	Zandvoort	Lotus Renault EF1	R
11 Sep	Italy	Monza	Lotus Renault EF1	8
25 Sep	Europe	Brands Hatch	Lotus Renault EF1	3 FL
15 Oct	South Africa	Kyalami	Lotus Renault EF1	NC

1984

25 Mar	Brazil	Rio	Lotus Renault EF4	R
7 Apr	South Africa	Kyalami	Lotus Renault EF4	R
29 Apr	Belgium	Zolder	Lotus Renault EF4	R
6 May	San Marino	Imola	Lotus Renault EF4	R
20 May	France	Paul Ricard	Lotus Renault EF4	3

* non-Championship

3 Jun	Monaco	Monte Carlo	Lotus Renault EF4	R
17 Jun	Canada	Montreal	Lotus Renault EF4	6
24 Jun	USA East	Detroit	Lotus Renault EF4	R
8 Jul	USA	Dallas	Lotus Renault EF4	6
22 Jul	Britain	Brands Hatch	Lotus Renault EF4	R
5 Aug	Germany	Hockenheim	Lotus Renault EF4	4
19 Aug	Austria	Osterreichring	Lotus Renault EF4	R
26 Aug	Holland	Zandvoort	Lotus Renault EF4	3
9 Sep	Italy	Monza	Lotus Renault EF4	R
7 Oct	Europe	Nurburgring	Lotus Renault EF4	R
21 Oct	Portugal	Estoril	Lotus Renault EF4	R

1985

7 Apr	Brazil	Rio	Williams FW10-Honda	R
21 Apr	Portugal	Estoril	Williams FW10-Honda	5
5 May	San Marino	Imola	Williams FW10-Honda	5
19 May	Monaco	Monte Carlo	Williams FW10-Honda	7
16 Jun	Canada	Montreal	Williams FW10-Honda	6
23 Jun	USA East	Detroit	Williams FW10-Honda	R
8 Jul	France	Paul Ricard	Williams FW10-Honda	DNS
21 Jul	Britain	Silverstone	Williams FW10-Honda	R
4 Aug	Germany	Nurburgring	Williams FW10-Honda	6
18 Aug	Austria	Osterreichring	Williams FW10-Honda	R
25 Aug	Holland	Zandvoort	Williams FW10-Honda	6
8 Sep	Italy	Monza	Williams FW10-Honda	11 FL
15 Sep	Belgium	Spa	Williams FW10-Honda	2
6 Oct	Europe	Brands Hatch	Williams FW10-Honda	1

19 Oct	South Africa	Kyalami	Williams FW10-Honda	1 P
3 Nov	Australia	Adelaide	Williams FW10-Honda	R

1986

23 Mar	Brazil	Rio	Williams FW11-Honda	R
13 Apr	Spain	Jerez	Williams FW11-Honda	2 FL
27 Apr	San Marino	Imola	Williams FW11-Honda	R
11 May	Monaco	Monte Carlo	Williams FW11-Honda	4
25 May	Belgium	Spa	Williams FW11-Honda	1
15 Jun	Canada	Montreal	Williams FW11-Honda	1 P
22 Jun	USA East	Detroit	Williams FW11-Honda	5
6 Jul	France	Paul Ricard	Williams FW11-Honda	1 FL
13 Jul	Britain	Brands Hatch	Williams FW11-Honda	1 FL
27 Jul	Germany	Hockenheim	Williams FW11-Honda	3
10 Aug	Hungary	Hungaroring	Williams FW11-Honda	3
17 Aug	Austria	Osterreichring	Williams FW11-Honda	R
7 Sep	Italy	Monza	Williams FW11-Honda	2
21 Sep	Portugal	Estoril	Williams FW11-Honda	1 FL
12 Oct	Mexico	Mexico City	Williams FW11-Honda	5
26 Oct	Australia	Adelaide	Williams FW11-Honda	R P

1987

12 Apr	Brazil	Rio	Williams FW11B-Honda	6 P

3 May	San Marino	Imola	Williams FW11B-Honda	1
17 May	Belgium	Spa	Williams FW11B-Honda	R P
31 May	Monaco	Monte Carlo	Williams FW11B-Honda	R P
21 Jun	USA East	Detroit	Williams FW11B-Honda	5 P
6 Jul	France	Paul Ricard	Williams FW11B-Honda	1 P
12 Jul	Britain	Silverstone	Williams FW11B-Honda	1 FL
26 Jul	Germany	Hockenheim	Williams FW11B-Honda	R P FL
9 Aug	Hungary	Hungaroring	Williams FW11B-Honda	R P
16 Aug	Austria	Osterreichring	Williams FW11B-Honda	1 FL
6 Sep	Italy	Monza	Williams FW11B-Honda	3
21 Sep	Portugal	Estoril	Williams FW11B-Honda	R
27 Sep	Spain	Jerez	Williams FW11B-Honda	1
18 Oct	Mexico	Mexico City	Williams FW11B-Honda	1 P
1 Nov	Japan	Suzuka	Williams FW11B-Honda	DNS

1988

3 Apr	Brazil	Rio	Williams FW12-Judd	R
1 May	San Marino	Imola	Williams FW12-Judd	R
15 May	Monaco	Monte Carlo	Williams FW12-Judd	R
29 May	Mexico	Mexico City	Williams FW12-Judd	R
12 Jun	Canada	Montreal	Williams FW12-Judd	R
19 Jun	USA East	Detroit	Williams FW12-Judd	R
3 Jul	France	Paul Ricard	Williams FW12-Judd	R
10 Jul	Britain	Silverstone	Williams FW12-Judd	2 FL
24 Jul	Germany	Hockenheim	Williams FW12-Judd	R
7 Aug	Hungary	Hungaroring	Williams FW12-Judd	R
25 Sep	Portugal	Estoril	Williams FW12-Judd	R

2 Oct	Spain	Jerez	Williams FW12-Judd	2
30 Oct	Japan	Suzuka	Williams FW12-Judd	R
13 Nov	Australia	Adelaide	Williams FW12-Judd	R

1989

26 Mar	Brazil	Rio	Ferrari 640	1
23 Apr	San Marino	Imola	Ferrari 640	R
7 May	Monaco	Monte Carlo	Ferrari 640	R
28 May	Mexico	Mexico City	Ferrari 640	R FL
4 Jun	USA	Phoenix	Ferrari 640	R
18 Jun	Canada	Montreal	Ferrari 640	DSQ
9 Jul	France	Paul Ricard	Ferrari 640	2
16 Jul	Britain	Silverstone	Ferrari 640	2 FL
30 Jul	Germany	Hockenheim	Ferrari 640	3
13 Aug	Hungary	Hungaroring	Ferrari 640	1 FL
27 Aug	Belgium	Spa	Ferrari 640	3
10 Sep	Italy	Monza	Ferrari 640	R
24 Sep	Portugal	Estoril	Ferrari 640	R
22 Oct	Japan	Suzuka	Ferrari 640	R
5 Nov	Australia	Adelaide	Ferrari 640	R

1990

11 Mar	USA	Phoenix	Ferrari 641	R
25 Mar	Brazil	Sao Paulo	Ferrari 641	4
13 May	San Marino	Imola	Ferrari 641	R
27 May	Monaco	Monte Carlo	Ferrari 641	R
10 Jun	Canada	Montreal	Ferrari 641	3
24 Jun	Mexico	Mexico City	Ferrari 641	2
8 Jul	France	Paul Ricard	Ferrari 641	R P FL
15 Jul	Britain	Silverstone	Ferrari 641	R P FL
29 Jul	Germany	Hockenheim	Ferrari 641	R
12 Aug	Hungary	Hungaroring	Ferrari 641	R
25 Aug	Belgium	Spa	Ferrari 641	R
9 Sep	Italy	Monza	Ferrari 641	4
23 Sep	Portugal	Estoril	Ferrari 641	1 P
30 Sep	Spain	Jerez	Ferrari 641	2
21 Oct	Japan	Suzuka	Ferrari 641	R
4 Nov	Australia	Adelaide	Ferrari 641	2 FL

1991

10 Mar	USA	Phoenix	Williams FW 14/2	R
24 Mar	Brazil	Sao Paulo	Williams FW 14/2	R
28 Apr	San Marino	Imola	Williams FW 14/2	R
12 May	Monaco	Monte Carlo	Williams FW 14/2	2
2 Jun	Canada	Montreal	Williams FW 14/2	6
16 Jun	Mexico	Mexico City	Williams FW 14/2	2
7 Jul	France	Magny Cours	Williams FW 14/5	1
14 Jul	Britain	Silverstone	Williams FW 14/5	1
28 Jul	Germany	Hockenheim	Williams FW 14/5	1
11 Aug	Hungary	Hungaroring	Williams FW 14/5	2
25 Aug	Belgium	Spa	Williams FW 14/5	R
8 Sep	Italy	Monza	Williams FW 14/5	1
22 Sep	Portugal	Estoril	Williams FW 14/5	DIS
29 Sep	Spain	Barcelona	Williams FW 14/5	1
20 Oct	Japan	Suzuka	Williams FW 14/5	R
3 Nov	Australia	Adelaide	Williams FW 14/5	2

Index

236

AYRTON SENNA
The Hard Edge of Genius

BY CHRISTOPHER HILTON

The revealing biography of the world's number one racing driver

From his World Championship victories in 1988 and 1990, to the stormy disputes which closed both the 1989 and the 1990 seasons, Ayrton Senna is rarely out of the headlines. Yet many consider him mysterious, shy and introverted.

Now Christopher Hilton's revealing biography gives us the first complete portrait of the man widely recognized as the most talented racing driver since Jim Clark.

Here is Senna through his own eyes and those of the people he has been close to along the way. Here is the kid from Sao Paolo who taught himself to drive in a farm jeep. Here is the youngster who astounded spectators at the Le Mans World Kart Racing Championships, and who stormed his way through the Formula Ford 1600 scene to earn his place in Formula One. And here is the Senna few people know – his philosophy, his religious beliefs, his feelings about his achievements and his setbacks, and his fascinating explanation of the idea that drives him on to greater goals.

Ayrton Senna: The Hard Edge of Genius is a unique portrait of a unique man.

'This is a book you can rely on'
Ayrton Senna

A CORGI PAPERBACK
0 552 13754 5

ALAIN PROST

BY CHRISTOPHER HILTON

A compelling biography of the most successful Formula One driver of all time

No man has won more Grand Prix races than Alain Prost. Few have known such veneration or, as in his feud with Ayrton Senna, such venom.

In his revealing biography, Christopher Hilton builds up a detailed picture of Alain Prost, starting when he was a teenager destined to join the family carpentry business in a small, obscure French town. At that time, he nursed dreams of football and had no interest in being a racing driver at all until one day he tried his hand at driving a go-kart. What followed was a career which moved swiftly up from karting, through Formula Renault and on to Formula One. It was a career which Prost pursued from the beginning with single-minded determination and unwavering ambition and which resulted in three Formula One World Championship titles.

Yet Prost's achievements and personality have also led to conflicts and tensions with some of those he has encountered during his career. His notorious relationship with Ayrton Senna, his sometimes troubled association with Ferrari are explored in detail and provide new insights into the workings of a Formula One racing team.

Christopher Hilton's biography is provocative and controversial – a book for all those who are fascinated by the most dangerous sport in the world.

A Partridge Press Hardcover
0 185225 1506

A SELECTION OF SPORTS BOOKS
FROM TRANSWORLD PUBLISHERS

☐	0 552 13343 4	**Nigel Mansell**	*Christopher Hilton*	£5.99
☐	0 552 13754 5	**Ayrton Senna:** **The Hard Edge of Genius**	*Christopher Hilton*	£5.99
☐	1 852 25150 6	**Alain Prost (Hardcover)**	*Christopher Hilton*	£14.99
☐	0 385 40354 0	**A Different Kind of Life**	*Virginia Williams*	£4.99
☐	0 385 40116 5	**Enzo Ferrari**	*Brock Yates*	£6.99
☐	0 552 99448 0	**Boycott on Cricket**	*Geoffrey Boycott*	£4.99
☐	0 552 99318 2	**Boycott: The Autobiography**	*Geoffrey Boycott*	£4.95

All Corgi/Bantam Books are available at your bookshop or newsagent, or can be
ordered from the following address:
Corgi/Bantam Books,
Cash Sales Department,
P.O. Box 11, Falmouth, Cornwall TR10 9EN

UK and B.F.P.O. customers please send a cheque or postal order (no currency) and
allow £1.00 for postage and packing for the first book plus 50p for the second book and
30p for each additional book to a maximum charge of £3.00 (7 books plus).

Overseas customers, including Eire, please allow £2.00 for postage and packing for the
first book plus £1.00 for the second book and 50p for each subsequent title ordered.

NAME (Block Letters) ....

ADDRESS ....

....